THE OPEN BOUNDARY OF
HISTORY AND FICTION

THE OPEN BOUNDARY OF HISTORY AND FICTION

A Critical Approach to the French Enlightenment

Suzanne Gearhart

Princeton University Press
Princeton, New Jersey

Library of Congress Cataloging in Publication Data will be
found on the last printed page of this book

ISBN 0-691-06608-6

This book has been composed in Linotron Galliard

Clothbound editions of Princeton University Press books
are printed on acid-free paper, and binding materials are
chosen for strength and durability

Printed in the United States of America by Princeton University Press
Princeton, New Jersey

The boundaries between fiction and nonfiction, between literature and nonliterature and so forth are not laid up in heaven. Every specific situation is historical. And the growth of literature is not merely development and change within the fixed boundaries of any given definition; the boundaries themselves are constantly changing.

—M. M. Bakhtin

CONTENTS

CONTENTS

ACKNOWLEDGMENTS

PARTS of this book have previously appeared in print: Chapter One was published in a slightly shorter form under the title "Rationality and the Text: A Study of Voltaire's Historiography" in *Studies on Voltaire*, vol. 140 (1975); a version of Chapter Three, entitled "The Place and Sense of the Outsider: Structuralism and the *Lettres persanes*," appeared in *Modern Language Notes*, vol. 92, no. 4 (May 1977), and a version of Chapter Four, in *Yale French Studies*, no. 59 (1980), under the title "Reading *De l'Esprit des Lois*: Montesquieu and the Principles of History."

With the exception of references to *De l'esprit des lois* in Chapter Four, the English translations of eighteenth-century works cited in this study are my own. I have used English editions of all other texts cited whenever possible, but where the reference is to a French edition, the translation is also my own.

THE OPEN BOUNDARY OF
HISTORY AND FICTION

The Open Boundary of History/Fiction

BOUNDARIES are established to separate and distinguish entities one from the other, but by the very same process, they link the delimited entities together. As a boundary is traced, it defines the integrity of each entity in terms of and in opposition to the others; it establishes where each begins and ends. A boundary therefore should be clearly marked or posted with visible signs in order to function as a boundary. When one crosses it, one should know immediately that one is in a different place where a different language is spoken, and different laws, rules, and procedures are followed. Because boundaries mark areas and limits, they assure us that we are where we think we are, and that wherever we are, we are on safe, familiar ground—for each area has been charted and defined, made recognizable and mastered before our arrival there. To be at home when we cross over boundaries, all that is necessary is to conform to the practices established on the other side by those inhabiting the area, by those who respect its boundary and remain within it.

The problem with the boundary separating history and fiction is that it does not function this way. It is more open than closed, more often displaced than fixed, as much within each field as at the limits of each. It is in play throughout history, whenever and wherever the question of history or fiction is raised, but nowhere does it function in an unproblematic, unequivocal manner. It is not just open, then, in the sense that it permits passage over it—all boundaries do this. It is open in a more radical sense, for the very domains it is supposed to separate and delimit continually cross over it also. This creates an unstable situation with which all theories of literature and all theories of history seem uneasy and which they have tried to remedy. They have consistently sought to fix the boundary between them and to establish once and for all the specificity of the fields in one of two ways: democratically, in that each accepts a mutually agreed upon boundary which grants to each its own identity and integrity; or, just as often, imperialistically, in that each tries to extend its own boundary and to invade, engulf, or encompass the other. In the first case, history and fiction exist side by side as uncommunicating opposites; in the second, one dominates the other—as when history makes fiction into its subject and treats it as just another historical document, or when fiction makes history into one form of fictional narrative among many possible forms. In the first case, the other is kept "outside," under surveillance, at a safe distance. In the second, it is overcome, cannibalized, incorporated into the sameness of the imperializing field, and frequently the incorporation or invasion may even be facilitated by the existence within the invaded area of elements already cooperating actively with the invaders. In either case, the location of the boundary, the assumptions that permit it to be traced, and the strategies elaborated for its defense or destruction are the crucial problems.

Contemporary criticism abounds with theories of history and fiction; some are concerned with the integrity of these objects or domains, others stress their overlapping. The interdependence of theories of history and fiction has been increasingly apparent in the work of a broad range of contemporary theorists, but, I would argue, the question of this relationship on its most fundamental level—that of the open boundary—has not been directly addressed by the great majority of theorists, historiographers, and literary critics. Or rather, when the question of the boundary between history and fiction has been the object of critical scrutiny, a prior assumption concerning the nature of the relationship between the two permits that relationship to be fixed or closed in one of the two ways already outlined. As a result, the potentially critical aspect of the analysis is undercut from the start.

The contradictory situation the French structuralist anthropologist Claude Lévi-Strauss finds himself in is perhaps the best example of what occurs when the question of the open boundary is pursued in all its complexity. Much of his work challenges the certitudes upon which the distinction between history and fiction (or myth) is based. In particular, in *The Savage Mind*, Lévi-Strauss criticizes Jean-Paul Sartre's conception of history and argues that it is itself a myth that places Western consciousness and Western culture at the center of the world, just as the myths of so-called primitive peoples invariably designate their own tribes as uniquely human and all others as inhuman.[1] And yet, although he thus erases the boundary between history and myth, Lévi-Strauss nevertheless continues to an important extent to accredit the rigid distinction between them, inasmuch as he posits them as a pair in which each term defines the other through a process of mutual exclusion. Thus in criticizing Sartre, Lévi-Strauss champions analytical thought as opposed to dialectical thought and compares this opposition to one between myth and history. Lévi-Strauss's approach to the problem is typical of the most complex theories of history and fiction in that he sometimes defends the integrity of the boundary between them and at other times allows this boundary to be overrun, erased, or simply ignored. But Lévi-Strauss does not directly confront the contradictions in his position, nor do most other contemporary theorists. In the context of contemporary theory, the boundary between fiction and history thus remains largely unquestioned; as an open boundary it works, as it always has,

[1] Claude Lévi-Strauss, "History and Dialectic," *The Savage Mind* (Chicago: University of Chicago Press, 1966).

to separate history and fiction, but at the same time it inevitably indicates the way they overlap and are inextricably and internally implicated in each other. The most fundamental problem posed by this relationship, then, is not that of determining which term has priority over the other, nor of determining the identity or integrity of either term. It is rather that of understanding the significance of this open boundary as it defines from the outset and in a contradictory way both history and fiction.

The work of Lévi-Strauss exemplifies the difficulties involved in addressing the question of the relationship between history and fiction in a definitive fashion, and, equally important, indicates that the importance of the question goes beyond one or two disciplines to affect our understanding of the broader context of contemporary theory as a whole. The question of this particular boundary is most often a background issue in debates concerning the status of language, perception, memory, culture, reason, and the subject, as well as in the definition and practice of the various disciplines that take these terms as objects of inquiry. But at crucial moments in contemporary theoretical debates, the problem has emerged as an explicit and fundamental issue. If Claude Lévi-Strauss's critique of Sartre represents one such moment, another is Michel Foucault's critique of traditional history in the name of a madness for which, he argues, history has been radically unable to account. Foucault's opposition of "madness" to "civilization" also relates to the opposition between history and fiction, for there is a profound affinity between Foucault's concept of madness and his concept of fictive or poetic language. It is not just madness that lies in some sense outside history, but also the fiction of Cervantes, Bataille, Sade, Roussel, and others. The "new history" or archaeology proposed by Foucault models itself after this type of "superhistorical" fiction as it captures the silence of "cosmic" or "tragic" madness, and not after any traditional, dialectical, or evolutionary historical theory. One could argue that Foucault, unlike Lévi-Strauss, thus postulates a boundary even more absolute and closed than that presupposed by traditional rationalist history, but closed now in order to protect the integrity of madness (and a certain form of fiction). In this way, no matter how important and powerful his critique of history is, he limits his critical enterprise by directing it at history alone and by not questioning the boundary that makes such a critique possible.

Roland Barthes represents still another position on this question when, in "Historical Discourse," he discusses the relationship of history to (fictional) narrative and makes explicit a critique of history implicit in all structuralist theory of narrative.[2] History, he argues, is essentially a form of narrative, constituted, like other narrative, by a set of relationships internal to it. Only its own denial of its determination by these internal relationships distinguishes history from other forms of narrative, and this distinction itself is only relative, inasmuch as "realist" fiction implies the same sort of denial. Here Barthes forcefully questions the traditional opposition between history and fiction, but at the same time he continues to accredit it in a somewhat different form, as an opposition between different categories of narrative: the "realist" narrative and narrative that in some way acknowledges its fictional status. In a similar vein, Hayden White, though accepting to some degree the distinction between history and (fictional) literature, nonetheless posits history as ultimately determined by formal and rhetorical structures and argues that the "impasse" history now faces can be overcome only through an ironic consciousness of the formal nature of history—in other words, by accepting its similarity to fiction.[3] White's position could thus in a sense be considered even more radical than that of Foucault or Barthes, and yet it too depends on a delimitation or boundary closing off fiction and making it a dis-

[2] Roland Barthes, "Historical Discourse," *Introduction to Structuralism*, edited by Michael Lane (New York: Basic Books, 1970). The essay was originally published in *Social Science Information* (International Social Science Council), vol. 6, no. 4 (August 1967).

[3] See, in particular, his *Metahistory: The Historical Imagination in Nineteenth-Century Europe* (Baltimore: Johns Hopkins University Press, 1973).

crete object that can be represented in a formal system that is itself given as clearly distinct from fiction. In a different context—that of the Anglo-American philosophy of history— W. B. Gallie, like White, stresses the similarity of history and fiction when he argues that history should be understood as offering the same type of explanation of events as the story.[4] Despite the radical implications of his analysis, however, Gallie never seriously questions the distinction between history and fiction, preferring instead to view his work as complementing the research of others who have sought simply to establish rather than to question the specificity of history.

All of the above, then, could be seen as resolving the complex issues raised in their critical analysis of the boundary between history and fiction by falling back on another form of that boundary, one they argue or imply can be more surely defended. And yet each in a different way attests to the central, strategic importance of this problematic relationship for contemporary theory. Because of its general ramifications and because of the difficulties it poses—difficulties that, as in the case of Lévi-Strauss, often put the theorist who seeks to address them at odds with himself, on both sides of the boundary at the same time—the relationship between history and fiction merits attention as one of the most important questions facing contemporary theory. Ultimately, I shall argue that, analyzed from the perspective of their open boundary, history and fiction each represents a radical critique of the other. And yet, because of their interdependence, there can be no unique perspective from which to formulate this critique and no simple, direct way to analyze its implications for the various disciplines directly involved or for theory in general. In order to come to terms with the openness of the boundary between history and fiction it does not suffice to note that history has formal, narrative aspects or that fiction attains its ends through the formal organization of what are essentially historical materials. Instead, it is necessary to understand how,

[4] See his *Philosophy and the Historical Understanding* (New York: Schocken Books, 1964).

before either history or fiction is constituted as such, a theory of what the other is has already defined the space, the scope, and the limitations of each.

Though more or less explicit theories of the relationship between fiction and history are at the center of contemporary theoretical debates, the pervasiveness of such theories should not be interpreted as a reflection of the self-evident, universal, or empirical nature of the terms of this relationship. Both have complicated histories, and their existence is tied to that of specific institutions. Any debate concerning their status is thus also a debate about that history and those institutions. Indeed, modern history and modern institutions—academies of science, learned societies, and, above all, the university—have for some time determined that most of the explicit discussion of the relationship between history and fiction shall take place within the context of two disciplines: history and literature. Even if in the modern period at least, the boundary between history and fiction is commonly identified with a boundary between these two disciplines, the concepts and the institutions of history and literature are in an important sense relatively recent. It was in the course of the nineteenth century that the gradual specification and specialization occurred that give history and literature their modern aspect and accentuate so radically the difference between them. As Lionel Gossman has argued:

> In the final phase of neo-classicism . . . the term "literature" gradually became more closely associated with poetry, or at least with poetic and figurative writing, and, especially among the Romantics and their successors, took on the meaning of a corpus of privileged or sacred texts, a treasury in which value, truth and beauty had been piously stored, and which could be opposed to the empirical world of historical reality and even, to some extent, to historiography as the faithful record of that reality. Indeed, it was at this point that historians began to look in the history of historiography itself for the origins

9

of a divorce—which they felt their own time was about to consummate—between historical writing and poetic writing.[5]

To understand the sense of contemporary debates over the boundary between history and fiction, it seems necessary, then, to look at a very particular moment in the history of such debates, the eighteenth century, when "literature" does not yet have the specificity it will acquire later on and which, in many ways, it still possesses even in the eyes of those modern critics who see it as one use of language among others. In its more broadly defined, eighteenth-century form, literature may include philosophy, political philosophy, and history, as well as those domains covered by the contemporary use of the term. What was for the eighteenth century a distinction between history as a category of literature on the one hand and fable, fiction, or the irrational on the other has been transformed into a modern opposition between history and literature. The difference between the eighteenth century and the modern era is not the sign, however, of a cataclysm or an absolute discontinuity separating the Enlightenment concept of fiction from the modern concept of literature. Nor does it mean that dogmatism concerning the status of history or fiction is confined to one period or the other. But if the two sets of terms— fiction/history and literature/history—are not unrelated, neither can the difference between them be ignored. An analysis of the relationship between history and literature is necessary in order to confront the "modern" significance of the relationship of history to fiction. Conversely, an analysis of the relationship between history and fiction in the premodern period is necessary in order to confront both terms with their own historicity, that is, to question the "self-evidence" of the relationship between history and literature as it has been institutionalized in the modern university.

---

[5] Lionel Gossman, "History and Literature," *The Writing of History: Literary Form and Historical Understanding*, edited by Robert H. Canary and Henry Kozicki (Madison: University of Wisconsin Press, 1978), p. 5.

The boundary between history and fiction thus has a history, but that history is not continuous and uniform.[6] Its nineteenth-century phase opens with an intense reaction to the historical and literary practices of the Enlightenment, and its form and development follow from the character of this initial reaction. Moreover, the effects of the conflict or difference between the *philosophes* and their successors are as significant for historical as for literary institutions. The historiographical conflict between the Romantics and their predecessors is described by Ernst Cassirer in *The Philosophy of the Enlightenment*, where he roots historicism and, more broadly, modern historical thinking in a rejection of what the nineteenth century saw as the inadequate historical sense of the classical age. According to Cassirer, the Romantics' negative assessment of the Enlightenment involved them in a contradiction: "This movement, which devotes itself so wholeheartedly to the past in order to grasp its pristine reality, fails to live up to its ideal when it encounters that past with which it is still in direct contact. . . . Romanticism never attempted to judge the Enlightenment by its own standards, and it was unable to view without polemical bias the conception of the historical

---

[6] In "The Logical Status of Fictional Discourse," *New Literary History*, vol. 6 (1975), John R. Searle takes the position that literature and fiction are overlapping but ultimately distinct categories. He asserts that while fiction can be logically and rigorously defined, literature cannot. I would argue, however, that the definition of fiction is not purely logical and thus that fiction and literature cannot be distinguished in the way Searle says they can. The fictional status of a discourse is determined, Searle asserts, by the author, not the reader. Moreover, he claims that unlike fiction, literature is continuous with the nonliterary. In contrast to Searle, the historiographers of the Enlightenment were concerned precisely with those forms of discourse that had once functioned as science or history both for their authors and for previous cultures, but that had come to be seen as myths or fictions by later civilizations. For the Enlightenment, then, there is a troubling continuity between the fictional and the nonfictional, and even a suspicion that their own "science" might be a "myth." This continuity cannot, moreover, be interrupted by an author or his intentions, for no author can completely control the context in which his discourse will be interpreted by succeeding generations— or his own.

world which the eighteenth century had formulated."[7] In Cassirer's view, the contradiction in the position of the Romantics stems from their failure to practice in the case of the eighteenth century what they preached as historians and philosophers of history. But the contradiction goes even deeper than this assessment would lead one to believe. The conception of the historical world that the eighteenth century had formulated was, according to Cassirer, one whose "condition of possibility" was that it could be understood by a universal reason (*The Philosophy of the Enlightenment*, pp. 197, 199). However, from the perspective of the Romantics, reason was not universal, but rather a metahistorical value which the Enlightenment had erected as a supreme standard for the judgment of other historical cultures as well as for the transformation of its own. The contradiction in which the Romantics found themselves was thus not the result of a practical failure to apply their principles in a particular and especially difficult case. Rather it was a contradiction inherent in historicism, and so much so that the Romantics could not choose between being faithful or unfaithful to the Enlightenment, but only between two ways of being unfaithful. They could seek to treat the Enlightenment in "its pristine reality." But in that case their method itself would constitute a betrayal of and a negative judgment passed on the Enlightenment and on the Enlightenment's use of history in the defense of its own political rallying cry— "reason." Or they could treat the Enlightenment in the way Cassirer claims they did: they could reject it out of hand. Either way, the Romantics' respect for the "pristine reality" of the historical subject would be revealed for what it is: a historicism as polemical and arbitrary in substance as the "rationalism" of the Enlightenment. The very existence of a competing historiography could only reveal that nineteenth-century historicism was not as neutral as it claimed to be, and to undermine this claim to neutrality was to undermine the very basis

[7] Ernst Cassirer, *The Philosophy of the Enlightenment* (Boston: Beacon Press, 1965), p. 198.

of historicism. In this sense, it was inevitable that the historical thinking of the Enlightenment should be ignored in one way or another by the Romantics and their successors.

It follows, then, that it is always too late to ask why we must turn to the Enlightenment in order to understand the relationship between fiction (or literature) and history. For we *do* return, either negatively, by dogmatically asserting that the relationship is purely logical, or positively, by recognizing that it has a history. But if we continue to frame our investigation of this relationship solely within the context of the contemporary university and the disciplines as they are presently defined, we prejudge the question of that relationship and claim, at least implicitly, that fiction (or literature) and history are uncommunicating opposites as the Romantics argued they were or should be and that our own concepts of history and reason are neutral, at last purged of all ideology and myth.

Such a stance would not be neutral, it would imply that we were taking a position in the conflict between the Romantics and the Enlightenment, and thus, whatever its subtleties, our own position would be more or less dogmatically historicist. The present work returns to the French Enlightenment in order to pose the question of the contradictory nature of the relationship between history and fiction, and in the light of the history of the institutions that serve as the modern context for this question, this appears to be the only possible course. For we must either ignore this conflict and the way it has shaped our institutions and our knowledge, in which case it will continue to determine theoretical discussion in an "unconscious" way, or make of it an explicit problem.

The present work, then, seeks to understand the implications for theories of literature and history of a critical analysis of the philosophy of the Enlightenment. It argues that the relation between history and fiction is not peripheral but rather the central question in the philosophy of history of that age; and, moreover, that, in this form, the problem of history itself was not peripheral to the French Enlightenment but was instead a major, if not the major problem it faced. Several practical aspects of the present work follow directly from these two general theses. The texts whose interpretation serves as the basis for my argument include works that today would be more likely to be treated as representative of differing disciplines; notably, of history, literature, philosophy, and political theory. If the relationship between fiction and history is a key to understanding the philosophy of history of the Enlightenment, then it follows that the "literary" work has as much to say about history as the more properly "historical" or "philosophical" work, and vice versa. The parceling out of individual works to specialists of various disciplines seems the most artificial and gratuitous when one is confronted, as one often is in eighteenth-century studies, with texts that, despite their range, comprise the work of a single writer. A second tendency when dealing with writers whose work encompasses as many fields as that of the writers treated here is to subordinate one aspect of a writer's work to another or to consider certain works more central than others. Jean Starobinski, for example, considers Rousseau's political works to be "failures" whose ultimate function is to pave the way for a later, more successful group of literary works reflecting a private world of imagination, and this interpretation typifies the arguments of many less important scholarly works.[8] By focusing on the relationship between two spheres touched on by each of these writers, and by not seeking to privilege one aspect of their work over the other, I have sought to open the boundaries closed by the specialization and departmentalization of literary criticism and historical interpretation.

Because this study seeks to demonstrate the crucial nature of the relationship between fiction and history to a general understanding of the French Enlightenment, it is based on the interpretation of the works of four figures generally acknowledged to be the principals of the age—Voltaire, Montesquieu,

[8] Jean Starobinski, *Jean-Jacques Rousseau, la transparence et l'obstacle* (Paris: Gallimard, 1971), pp. 49-63.

14

Diderot, and Rousseau.[9] For in the French Enlightenment, history is not only the concern of a relatively anonymous group of scholars and philosophers; it is also a central issue for precisely those figures who have received the most attention from subsequent scholars and critics, but without the question of their role as historical thinkers having been vigorously pursued, except from a standpoint that, like the Romantics', tends to subordinate it to their "rationalism."

The question of the significance of these figures in the history of the philosophy of history has been explored through an interpretation of several of their major works. I have sought to avoid merely applying the labels—such as "determinist," "sensationalist," "relativist"—most frequently used to characterize these works, for, more often than not, their use naively presupposes a universal agreement as to their meaning. The labeling of texts and of thinkers is to some extent inevitable and necessary, for one could argue that in many cases it begins with the texts and thinkers themselves. Moreover, the label is clearly unavoidable in the sense that it belongs to our historical and philosophical language and thus provides a currency without which intellectual exchange would be impossible. But

[9] This is one of the most significant respects in which the present work contrasts with Lionel Gossman's *Medievalism and the Ideologies of the Enlightenment* (Baltimore: Johns Hopkins University Press, 1968). The latter focuses on a large network of scholars and philosophers whose writings both shaped and reflected Enlightenment attitudes toward history. Major figures such as Voltaire and Montesquieu are treated, but they do not dominate; rather they serve as background figures for La Curne de Sainte-Palaye, whom Gossman selects as his central figure in part because of the intrinsic interest of his work but, more important, as a representative of this larger network. In individual essays, Gossman has focused more closely on the historical thinking of the "major" figures: see, in particular, "Voltaire's *Charles XII*: History into Art," *Studies on Voltaire*, vol. 25 (1963). Other essays by Gossman that treat the problem of the relationship between history and fiction are the already cited "History and Literature," and *Augustin Thierry and Liberal Historiography* (Middleton, Conn.: Wesleyan University Press, 1976). Readers interested in the relationship between historiography and the novel in the Enlightenment will also want to consult Leo Braudy's *Narrative Form in History and Fiction: Hume, Fielding, and Gibbon* (Princeton, N.J.: Princeton University Press, 1970).

it can never be a substitute for the process of reading and interpretation from which it derives its legitimacy. Labeling is just one version of a tendency, built into all interpretation, to postulate the unity of the work in an a priori way and then to produce an interpretation that conforms to that postulate. While there is no reason to prefer the complex and the contradictory to the simple, there is no reason to privilege the simple either. Each of the texts analyzed here exhibits a basic complexity which I have not sought to reduce, a complexity that gives these texts their fundamental historicity. In other words, it is only insomuch as they remain open to new interpretations and are not fixed within the narrow boundaries of their own age that these texts "live on" in history. A text whose sense would only be that determined by the explicit context of its "own" era (as in a historicist reading) would be a text without a history, a text produced, read, and interpreted in a single instant without duration. This concept of the text is the ideal of critics who look to the consciousness of the author, or to his or her biography for evidence of an authorial intention, or to the social context or "history" for a meaning with which the work would coincide perfectly. It is a reductive and ultimately ahistorical version of the text, one that simplifies its historical no less than its literary complexity.

Just as it is arbitrary to posit in advance the unity of a given work, so it is arbitrary to posit in advance the unity of history or of a historical period. "The Enlightenment" is itself also clearly a kind of label, and as such its use often presupposes such a unity. The problem, however, is not so much how to do away with this label as how to analyze critically the unity it implies, a unity based on the concept of "lumières" or reason. The view that the eighteenth century is above all an age of reason is shared by a broad and heterogeneous group of philosophers, historians, and literary critics that includes traditional eighteenth-century scholars and such radical critical thinkers as Michel Foucault. A critical analysis of Voltaire, the most militant "rationalist" of the eighteenth century, indicates, however, that what historians from Cassirer to Foucault have called "reason" in the eighteenth century signifies not one but many contradictory things. In Voltaire's histories, reason is shaped and defined by its struggle with the forces "external" to it, just as those forces are shaped and defined by reason itself, and thus reason is determined by an open, "dialectical" process that is in principle infinite, that arrives at no ultimate synthesis, and that, as a result, can never be said to vindicate reason. A reason "defined" through such a conflictual process cannot be assumed to be at one with itself, and thus, even if it continues to play a central role in the interpretation of the Enlightenment, it cannot be simply posited as the basis of the homogeneity of the Enlightenment as an age.

The conflict within history as it is portrayed, for example, in Voltaire's *Essai sur les moeurs* is both "substantial" (for Voltaire, it involves conflict between what he considers to be reactionary cultures or groups such as Egypt, the Jews, the Greeks, medieval civilization, and the "noblesse de robe," and the forces of Enlightenment, such as the Chinese philosopher–civil servant, the enlightened despots, and eighteenth-century *philosophes*—or at least some of them!) and "formal" or generic. In its formal aspect, the struggle is one between different kinds of historiography: a true historiography or history and a false one which Voltaire calls fiction or fable. Theorists of history have frequently pointed out the semantic "confusion" inherent in the term "history"—between history as a substance or process and history as the totality of historical writing (or as a description of a type of writing). Voltaire implies that this is not confusion at all, for the political triumph of philosophy is one and the same with the formal triumph of history over fiction. In this sense, the substantial questions of history are, for Voltaire, formal questions as well.

The significance of the form of history is a topic that has been largely ignored, not only by contemporary scholars who have looked at the historiography of the Enlightenment, but by modern historians and philosophers of history as well. The Enlightenment is particularly well suited for an investigation of this issue, for it is a period when such modern concerns as

17

the authentification of documents and textual criticism exist side by side with the view that history is a form of literature. That history can be subjected to the same kind of formal analysis as literature is a relatively novel thesis in our own century, and to date it has been extensively treated and forcefully argued by only one historiographer, Hayden White. Although the present study parallels White's insofar as it seeks to emphasize the formal nature of history, it is not formalist in the way his is. Though White uses his tropology to describe and differentiate between historical periods, he openly asserts that formal categories are metahistorical. For him, a history of historiography is possible, but it would always be subject in the last instance to formal analysis, that is, classifiable within the categories of a transhistorical, formal system. Like White's *Metahistory*, this study is designed to show that the form of history is never inconsequential, that is, that history is never "metaformal." Unlike White, however, I am equally concerned with demonstrating that form (as a system of tropes) cannot be considered metahistorical. The interdependence of history and form and the limitations they mutually impose on each other become evident when one considers Voltaire's historiography. There the concept of a metahistorical form or genre is shown to be entirely compatible with a naively mimetic, "metaformalist" concept of history, because both depend on the assumption that the literal meaning of language preexists and thus can be distinguished from its figurative or rhetorical meanings. My point is to show that in Voltaire as in White, the premises that make possible both metaformalist and metahistorical systems limit the scope and complexity of the concepts of history and form being defended or opposed.

The present study emphasizes the problem of form in eighteenth-century historiography and literature while remaining cognizant of the limitations of formalist approaches. It attempts, moreover, to take a critical perspective not just on form, but on history as well, to confront one with the other. One could say that this study practices a kind of historical criticism, but that, at the same time, it rejects the metahistorical concepts of history that in most cases provide the basis for such criticism. In the chapters that follow, different critical strategies are used to frame questions of interpretation of special thematic, formal, or historical relevance to the work in question. Though the focus is on methodologies and theorists whose work has figured prominently in recent debates in "critical theory," the aim of this study is not simply to "apply" these "new" theories to a group of "old" texts, but rather, to create genuine dialogues between them. In each chapter the theories of literature or history in question have provided a point of departure for the reading of the eighteenth-century work, but the consideration of those works has invariably revealed the contradictions as well as the coherence of the modern theories themselves and their place in a complicated historical series that extends at least as far as the eighteenth century. Historical criticism in this sense does not merely demand that one consider the absolute historical specificity of any given "event"; it is not historicist in form. It requires rather that one question the degree of specificity of the "event," the way in which it continues, repeats, and transforms other "events." In many respects, the eighteenth century and our theoretical modernity are part of a single age, and it is as frequently the case that an eighteenth-century work represents a critique of a modern work as the reverse. The present study thus does not privilege the "contemporary" approaches to the theoretical problems that are evoked. To do so would be to practice a historicism different in style but not in substance from that of the scholar who strives to treat texts in their "own" context, in their "pristine reality." To privilege "contemporary" categories and "contemporary" methods (or to deny that they could possibly be relevant to "past" writings) is to assume that their meaning is transparent to "us" and not implicated in and limited by the contradictory history they carry on and transform. The same critical method must thus apply to these modern texts as to those of the past.

History is not always concerned with contradictions. It may be more concerned with discovering totalities or with locating a cause or a complex of causes thought to explain a historical event or set of events in a way that is "consistent" or "logically satisfying." History, moreover, is not always concerned with the historical nature and historical specificity of its own methods. Whereas it may serve to debunk myths of progress in other domains, it is not necessarily interested in doing so with respect to historiography. Most liberal historians decry teleological views of history from Aristotle to Marx and would no doubt argue that history progresses and becomes more scientific as it leaves such teleologies behind. Yet it is only fairly recently that a number of historians, principally the group known as the *Annales* School, have sought to analyze the role of "hidden" teleologies, based on concepts of the "event," in liberal historiography itself. Anglo-American philosophers of history have frequently distinguished sharply between teleological history and a history that would conform to general laws as in the natural sciences.[10] The difference between teleological views of history, scientific views, and those of a philosopher of history such as Collingwood, who rejects both teleology and science as models for history, are ultimately not as substantial as might first appear, however. For all of them assume the existence of "one historical world" that serves as the ultimate basis of the criteria of unity and of noncontradiction in each particular form of historical explanation.[11] Assumptions such as this very frequently form the basis for historical inquiry without ever becoming the object of historical inquiry. When viewed in a critical light, history can be said to be determined by a more or less explicit decision to treat only

[10] Carl G. Hempel, "The Function of General Laws in History," *Theories of History* (Glencoe, Ill.: Free Press, 1962). In his essay, Hempel considers attempts "to account for features of organic behaviour by reference to an entelechy" to be "pseudo-explanations" based on "metaphors rather than laws" (p. 347), and contrasts them with genuine historical explanations based on general hypotheses identical in kind to those of science.

[11] A notable exception is W. B. Gallie, who criticizes the notion of the "one historical world" in his *Philosophy and the Historical Understanding*, pp. 56-64.

certain concepts, *certain* events, and *certain* methods as having a history, and to treat all others as though they do not. Clearly, however, historical criticism by right extends to all "concepts," "events," and "methods," including those of history itself and those that philosophers of history have ascribed to "extrahistorical" disciplines such as science.

If the term "history" is such an unreliable one, if there is always a danger, in seeking to use it in a critical way, that it will be interpreted in keeping with previous definitions, why use the term at all and why place it at the center of an investigation? One answer is that "history" is no different in this respect from many other terms that might also have served as a focal point for this work. To make "language," "text," "form," or "representation" the center of an inquiry entails the same sort of risks and the same necessity of redefinition and reworking. This answer, however, still leaves the question open, for if history is one "unreliable," contradictory term among others, the decision to make it a center of attention still must be explained. In response, it is important to state first of all that this work does not have a single center. History is *a* center; fiction is also a center. Second, if history is, nonetheless, one of the centers, it is because in the context of the theoretical developments that constitute a point of departure for the methodological reflections in this work—developments that, for better or for worse, are known as "structuralism" and "poststructuralism"—history is the discipline that has been the most heavily criticized, both implicitly and explicitly. Although there exist a structural linguistics, anthropology, and psychoanalysis, it is still unclear whether or not such a thing as a structural history is possible, and inasmuch as structuralism is now generally spoken of only in the past tense, it is doubtful that the question will be taken up in the future.[12]

---

[12] Michel Foucault has consistently denied that his own work can be considered a structuralist historiography, arguing instead, in *The Archaeology of Knowledge* (New York: Harper and Row, 1972) and elsewhere, that it represents a continuation and refinement of autonomous developments in economic and intellectual history. In many respects, however, Foucault's work

In this way the conflict subsists between the methods of structuralism and the methods of history, or, more broadly, between certain methods that treat language as a closed system producing signification through the differentiation of elements internal to it and other methods that make "empirical" data (documents, records, monuments, etc.) the ultimate criteria for determining the sense and validity of language. It could be argued that the nature of the relationship between structuralism and history is such that each survives and prospers by either ignoring or attacking the other, and by insisting, in both cases, on the closed nature of the boundary separating them. More recently, the problems implied in the relationship of structuralism to history have been relatively neglected in an era that calls itself "poststructuralist." If these problems are no longer being considered, however, it is not because they have been resolved, but only because they are being ignored. In the context of a poststructuralism where the problems of structuralism persist without being acknowledged, a consideration of history still has a strategically important, critical role to play.

The debate between structuralism and history is an essential part of the context of this work as a whole. But, as I argue in Chapter Four, that debate is ultimately one over the priority given to one *set* of terms as opposed to the other (structure or language vs. history, synchrony vs. diachrony, the ideal vs. the historical), while underneath the conflict, there exists a basic agreement as to the ways in which the two sets of terms are opposed and defined. A critical approach to history and form cannot come about then, through a simple reversal of the hierarchy between structure and history, for when this hierarchy is reversed, only the value attached to the two terms changes: the closed boundary separating them remains intact.

In the way it is used here, the notion of a fundamental,

---

takes up the question of history where the structuralist critique of history leaves it, and thus his theory is of crucial importance in the contemporary discussion of history. The significance of Foucault's theory of history is analyzed in Chapter One.

contradictory historicity of all structures and of all concepts and institutions does not make history into a master discipline or master term in the sense that Sartre, for example, has argued. Though history reveals fundamental differences in structures, concepts, and institutions, the form and sense of history are also differentiated by this fundamental and contradictory historicity: history too cannot be claimed to be at one with itself. To assert the fundamental historicity of history itself, then, is to assert that history is engaged in a never-ending struggle to distinguish itself from nonhistory. As we shall see, this struggle has characteristically been (and this is especially so in the eighteenth century) with a fiction and a literature to which history bears a disquieting resemblance. With respect to illuminating the self-contradictory nature of history, structuralism has had, once again, an important role to play. For the structuralist reader, attentive above all to language, history has become a form of literature that can be distinguished perhaps generically, but not ontologically or logically from other literary forms. Thus the image of history that emerges from both the analyses of a contemporary structuralist such as Roland Barthes and an eighteenth-century philosopher such as Voltaire is one of an entity divided against itself, struggling against itself to transcend its status as language, form, and literature.

Given the emphasis this study places on history, it is important to stress that literature is not here being treated as a mere adjunct. The problem of the specificity of fictional literature has important implications not only for contemporary literature and theory but also for eighteenth-century studies. One could perhaps argue that its neglect in most eighteenth-century criticism is justifiable on the grounds that have already been outlined: the modern distinction not only between literature and history but between all forms of what the eighteenth century frequently called "literature" dates from the nineteenth century and is in a sense alien to the Enlightenment. But if this is granted, the problem then becomes that of discovering how this relatively homogeneous field which

23

comprises what we today would distinguish as philosophy, history, political philosophy (or political science), science, literature, and circumstantial writing should be treated. There is little question that eighteenth-century criticism has relied on a mimetic model for the understanding of literature, conceived in the broad terms provided by the eighteenth century itself. In this mimetic, historicist view, it is history that is imitated—whether history be conceived of in terms of the (ideal) biography of an author, a biography that would record all of his conscious or unconscious intentions, or as the history of the society in which the author lived, itself conceived of as an ideal unity, whether that unity is based on the concept of ideology, of a *Weltanschauung*, or merely of chronology. The present work however, argues that if fiction and literature are already a part of the process by which history constitutes itself, then history cannot serve as the model or example of a "true" copy after which literature, in turn, would model itself as a more or less perfect imitation.

Fiction, moreover, is not just at work in the constitution of history. It "contaminates" all of the entities that might themselves serve as the original for the copy thought to be produced by either history or literature. This is particularly clear in the case of the master origin, nature. Rousseau's treatment of the concept of a state of nature in his *Second Discourse* is exemplary in the way in which an aesthetics of representation is shown to be already assumed as the condition for the elaboration of an "original state." A similar aesthetics is also at work in Condillac's theory of sensation and perception. Concepts such as perception and the state of nature are central to the historical thinking of the eighteenth century, and to its philosophy, epistemology, psychology, and political philosophy as well. These fundamental concepts, however, are never self-evident. As Condillac's and Rousseau's work in particular shows, their definition can only proceed thanks to processes that must be called "aesthetic" or "literary,"[13] because those

---

[13] "Aesthetic" and "literary" must appear in quotation marks, however, be-

processes do not follow from the natural and literal status often conferred in a priori fashion on the fundamental concepts in question.

In this way fiction is as much a center for the present work as history, and it is also, in the form in which it is analyzed here, a principle of differentiation of the natural, the historical, and the perceived from themselves. Fiction does not constitute in its turn a master discipline, however, for it has its own contradictions and its own historicity (its own "fictionality") which stem precisely from the fact that fiction is already "beside itself," already at work in the constitution of other fields and already implicated in their basic assumptions—just as they are in its assumptions. My analyses of Rousseau's *Second Discourse*, his *Emile*, and his *Lettre à d'Alembert* in particular criticize the view that literature is a master discipline, and Paul de Man's extensive writings on Rousseau serve as the point of departure for this critique. De Man's readings of Rousseau do what a long tradition of Rousseau scholarship has never done. They present a coherent interpretation that does not reduce the problem posed by Rousseau's fictional work by analyzing it within the context of a purely mimetic interpretation of literature. But the end result of that interpretation is a defense of literature or of what de Man calls "language."[14] Central to his argument is that the constitutive role of fiction or of "rhetoricity" in the elaboration of the major concepts of Rousseau's philosophy—that is, nature, language, perception, the social contract, the self—is evidence of the priority of fiction and of "unreliable" literary language with

cause in their normal usage they are always conceived of as being derivative with respect to concepts such as nature, perception, origin, and the like.

[14] In de Man's interpretation, language is constitutively metaphorical and hence "unreliable" or "literary." This view of language is articulated in de Man's analysis of Rousseau's theory of the origin of language in "The Rhetoric of Blindness: Jacques Derrida's Reading of Rousseau," *Blindness and Insight* (New York: Oxford University Press, 1971), pp. 102-141, and in "Metaphor *(Second Discourse)*," *Allegories of Reading* (New Haven: Yale University Press, 1979), pp. 147-155.

respect to the nonrhetorical languages of philosophy, political philosophy, and so on. Insofar as their own language becomes "rhetorical," these disciplines too, according to de Man, may be considered "literary" (*Blindness and Insight*, pp. 136-137). Thus he can affirm that when we read Rousseau, "we are reading a fiction and not a history" (ibid., p. 137). In contrast, I argue that it is the participation of fiction in the elaboration of the fundamental concepts of the "disciplines" practiced by Rousseau that indicates the relative lack of specificity not only of these disciplines and their discourses, but of fiction and literature as well. Rousseau cannot write history without writing fiction, but he cannot write fiction without confronting the problem of history.

My debate with de Man concerns not only the work of Rousseau but also the work of Jacques Derrida and its implications for contemporary theorists. Despite the polemic contained in de Man's major essay on Derrida and Rousseau, "The Rhetoric of Blindness," de Man has consistently portrayed Derrida's work as essentially in harmony with his own theory of the priority of "literary language" and of what he calls "rhetoric" over metaphysics, history, political philosophy, and the like. This view of literature and of Derrida's work neglects two points I take to be crucial. First, although Derrida's critique of the concept of presence is also a critique of history insofar as history is inevitably a history of presents, history is also seen by Derrida as serving as a condition of the existence of the present. As such, it always in some sense eludes the grasp of metaphysics. In this second critical sense of history as "*différance*," it has a crucial role to play in the critique of presence. Second, fiction and literature do frequently serve as tools for the critique of metaphysics insofar as they reveal the fundamental impropriety of the language in which the subject tries to reflect and to grasp its own autonomy and presence. But Derrida argues at the same time that the concepts of fiction and literature are also to some degree products of a philosophy of presence, and thus they are always implicated in its history. In critically analyzing de Man's view of literature and

26

of Derrida's work, I hope to make clear that although there is a great deal of criticism and theory being produced that reflects a concern with themes and methods of interpretation elaborated by Derrida, insofar as that work would claim to constitute a Derridean orthodoxy, it should in fact be questioned and challenged on many grounds, but most importantly in terms of the privilege given to the literary text.[15]

The relationship between fiction and history articulated here is one in which neither term can be reduced to the other because each is part of the process by which the other is constituted. This interpretation of their relationship strives to be interdisciplinary in the strongest possible sense, and yet an interdisciplinary approach does not in and of itself guarantee that the complexity of the relationship between ficton and history will be clearly understood. Literary theory and the philosophy of history—indeed, any theory that is concerned with "marking off" the fundamental boundaries of a given field—frequently imply or state a theory concerning the "other" discipline. But with almost equal frequency, that "background" theory idealizes the "other" discipline in a variety of ways in order to permit the theorist to set the boundaries of his "own" discipline, and these boundaries already contain in themselves the most basic assumptions governing the discipline. Thus the most fervent believers in an ideal history are often literary critics and philosophers. The most fervent believers in an ideal of

[15] In connection with this interpretation of Derrida, it would be natural to ask why it is that, accepting the major premises of Derrida's interpretation of what he has called "metaphysics," I have chosen to focus on the problem of history and its relation to fiction in a way he has not. The answer lies in the context in which Derrida's work has been read in the United States, in particular, where the prevailing interpretation considers Derrida's work to be a defense of literature and of a literary text that has "always-already deconstructed itself," and where we have been told "not to take [Derrida] literally, *especially* when his statements seem to refer to concrete historical situations such as the present" (*Blindness and Insight*, p. 137, my emphasis). It is in relation to this context and to this interpretation that the importance of focusing on the problem of history, both as a general problem and as a problem for Derrida, has become clear.

literature are frequently historians, philosophers, and scientists. This idealization of the "other" discipline is just one side of a coin whose reverse is the view that that "other" discipline is unimportant, or lacking in rigor, or excessively logical or dogmatic.

The interdisciplinary relationship on which this work focuses is not based on a simple opposition in which literature and history are seen as sovereign, autonomous entities with the power to institute or curtail movement across their boundaries. Instead, it is a relationship in which the two terms are seen as formally similar because each borrows from the other and each refuses in its own way to acknowledge that borrowing. And yet for the same reasons that history and fiction are not sovereign, they never completely merge. The difference between the two constantly reasserts itself, for though they may be seen from a certain perspective as *formally* identical, their relationship is never purely formal. The aim of this work, then, is to confront history with two related tasks with which the Enlightenment already confronted it: (1) to elaborate a critical theory of itself that would not deny the specific role played by fiction in the constitution of history (deny it in some cases by conceding to it a special prerogative over figural speech, rhetoric, image, form, language, etc.); and (2) to confront the concepts of fiction and literature with their own fundamental and contradictory historicity—that is, not only the historicity of their context, of their various forms, or of their language, but of form-in-general and language-in-general. The status they ascribe to the boundary between history and fiction locates the work of Voltaire, Montesquieu, Rousseau, and Diderot in the Enlightenment. But the form that boundary has since taken and the conflict over who or what should determine its place are also part of our, as well as their, "historical situation."

ONE

(*Voltaire*)
Establishing Rationality in the Historical Text: Foucault and the Problem of Unreason

SINCE the Enlightenment, a concept of reason or of the rational has served as the basis of attempts to write a history—intellectual or other—of that period. At times, reason has been taken as a historical principle that transcends the Enlightenment itself, inasmuch as it is the basis of all human progress toward an ultimate end or ultimate form of reason. At other times, it has been held to be a determined structure, specific to or characteristic of the Enlightenment. But whether one considers history from a rationalist or historicist perspective, the concept of reason remains the condition of possibility of a history of the "age of reason." To question the concept of reason is to question the possibility of a history of the Enlightenment, and, perhaps even more, the possibility of history itself.

Michel Foucault's *Madness and Civilization* is just such a radical questioning of the possibility of a history of the Enlightenment and of history in general, for it not only analyzes the institutions and forms of knowledge that imprisoned and defined "madness" in the classical age, it also questions reason, and, through it, history itself, from the critical perspective provided by the figure of madness.[1] To narrate the story of the "classical age" from the perspective of madness is to break

[1] *Madness and Civilization: A History of Insanity in the Age of Reason*, translated by Richard Howard (New York: Random House, 1965).

with all previous attempts to write its history, for, Foucault argues, all forms of discourse, including history, are grounded in a concept or norm of reason that has never been seriously questioned.[2] Foucault's *Madness and Civilization* is *also* a history of reason, but it is the one history Foucault would claim that reason itself cannot write, because reason, according to Foucault, can never exist outside of itself—it can never assume the radically critical perspective of madness. The concept of madness is crucial for Foucault, not just thematically, but also methodologically, for "madness" coincides with the possibility of an authentic history, that is, a history irreducible to the terms of a philosophical or rational interpretation.

In his essay "Cogito and the History of Madness," Jacques Derrida questions Foucault's use of the term "madness" and argues that he never resolves the problem with which his rejection of the various historical definitions of madness leaves him:

> Foucault, in rejecting the psychiatric or philosophical material that has always emprisoned the mad, winds up employing—inevitably—a popular and equivocal notion of madness, taken from an unverifiable source. . . . It could be demonstrated that as Foucault intends it, if not as intended by the historical current he is studying, the concept of madness overlaps everything that can be put under the rubric of *negativity*. One can imagine the kind of problems posed by such a usage of the notion of madness.[3]

The problematic nature of Foucault's concept of madness is an important issue from the standpoint of the institutions and

---

[2] In "The Discourse of Language," *The Archaeology of Knowledge*, translated by A. M. Sheridan Smith (New York: Harper and Row, 1972), the taboo on politics and sexuality, the opposition between reason and madness, and the opposition between the true and the false are held by Foucault to be the three great "exclusions" that govern all discourse yet are themselves hardly ever objects of discourse.

[3] Jacques Derrida, "Cogito and the History of Madness," *Writing and Difference*, translated by Alan Bass (Chicago: University of Chicago Press, 1978), p. 41.

the forms of knowledge that define and treat madness and of the history that seeks to describe them. But, as Derrida points out, perhaps even more importantly, if "madness" remains a vague notion in Foucault's work, then the critical distinction between Foucault's archaeology and the traditional forms of history he criticizes becomes blurred. Foucault rejects all forms of interpretation, all teleologies, all forms of the subject, and all origins because they are all in his view reductive of history. But if the concept of madness remains vague, then it is always possible to consider it as a subject, an origin, or an end of history, and to consider its silence as the subtext of all discourse.

A problematic concept of "madness" thus not only undercuts the possibility of a history irreducible to philosophy and reason, it also puts into question the *discontinuity* that is a recurring methodological theme in Foucault's work—whether it be the discontinuity of a classical age and a modern age (in *The Order of Things*),[4] of each particular statement (*énoncé*) and its context and all other statements and their contexts (in *The Archaeology of Knowledge*), of the panoptic model and previous techniques of prisoner control (in *Discipline and Punish*),[5] of madness and reason, or, finally, the discontinuity between Foucault's archaeologies or genealogies and all prior histories and philosophies of history. Moreover, if the concept of "madness" is vague and all discontinuities that derive from this concept are as a result unclear, then the concept of "reason" or truth is ultimately problematic as well. In writing as though he "knew what 'madness' means" ("Cogito and the History of Madness," p. 44), Foucault must also write as though he knows what reason means, for, as *Madness and Civilization* itself forcefully argues, knowledge of each is always conditioned by knowledge of the other. Thus the possibility of the history of reason is *the same* as the possibility of a history of

[4] *The Order of Things* (New York: Random House, 1970).
[5] *Discipline and Punish*, translated by Alan Sheridan (New York: Random House, 1977).

madness. In Foucault's work, a "metaphysics" of madness (or reason) that takes for granted the knowledge of madness (or reason) exists side by side with a historicism that argues that a history of madness in the classical age can be written without it being necessary to question the history of the classical age itself (its historical roots in medieval or ancient history) or the relationship between a classical form of madness and a more general form of it, present in more than one period.

The history of the Enlightenment with which Foucault's *Madness and Civilization* seeks to break is the history that the Enlightenment was already writing about itself. Voltaire's *Essai sur les moeurs*, in particular, contains within it the two paradigms according to which the history of the Enlightenment has been subsequently written. It is already a history in which reason is the condition of historical knowledge, the condition of history itself, and the principle of continuity uniting, through its progress, the origin and the end of history. At the same time, the *Essai sur les moeurs* is already a historicist history: it argues that reason is *specific to* the Enlightenment and that the history of reason can only be written if the radical discontinuity between reason and nonreason and between the Enlightenment and all previous historical periods can be established. Ultimately, however, it is not only rationalist and historicist historiography that are both in some sense rooted in Voltaire's historical program. A history of madness of the type Foucault proposes to write is also rooted there. For, as I shall show, according to a logic that is not exclusive to Voltaire, the history of rationality he sets out to write in the *Essai sur les moeurs* is also a history of unreason or of a "madness" that, like Foucault's concept, "overlaps everything that can be put under the rubric of *negativity*." Just as Foucault, writing an archaeology of the silence imposed on madness, will never define madness other than negatively, so Voltaire, writing a history of human reason will never define it except negatively, as the opposite of unreason, of the idiosyncratic, of the fabulous. Just as Foucault sees discontinuity as the mode of existence of madness (and of reason), just as he stresses the disruptive force of madness, so Voltaire will constantly portray reason as coinciding with a radical break with all origins and with all "previous" history. Finally, just as the possibility of history itself hinges on the delimitation of a concept of reason and the complementary delimitation of a concept of madness for Foucault, so for Voltaire *from the opposite perspective*, the delimitation of reason (and thus of unreason) is the condition of history. Foucault may be the anti-Voltaire, but in taking a position "against reason," he remains to a very large extent dependent on the same strategies and the same concepts.

Voltaire's *Essai sur les moeurs* differs in an important respect from *Madness and Civilization*, however. It confronts reason not only as specific to the age of enlightenment but also as it coincides with what Voltaire takes to be the totality of history. In this sense, the *Essai sur les moeurs* raises a question that Foucault does not confront: the question of what "general" condition makes possible the existence of a "specific" form of reason within history. This question has always been rejected by Foucault at the same time as he rejects any form of interpretation that would "reduce" history to the manifestation of a transcendental term or to that which was already present implicitly at the origin of history. Foucault's rejection of this question, to the extent that it obliges him to presuppose dogmatically the existence of madness as a thing in itself, leads him to a historicism more radical than any historicism to date, but a historicism nonetheless. In addition, it causes him to turn his back on a question that no historicism has ever asked and in which the complicity between all forms of historicism and what Foucault calls "interpretation" is evident. The question is whether or not reason is ever at one with itself, whether it ever defines a space or an *épistémè* that would be pure interiority and that as such would be severed—whether for a specified "moment" in history or for all time—from nonreason. If the answer is no—and I would argue it is no—then it is never possible to escape from history in the name of an eternal, rational perspective, but neither would it be possible to remain wholly "within" history or to write a history of reason (or of madness) "in itself." For Foucault now to write a history of madness it must have first been possible at some moment in history to write a history of reason. Voltaire's *Essai sur les moeurs* shows in what sense such a history is possible and in what sense it is not.

VOLTAIRE offers several criteria for determining whether or not a work is to be accepted as history, and, taken together, they give a preliminary indication of the relation between rationality and history in Voltaire's philosophy of history. He begins his article on "history" in the *Dictionnaire philosophique* by distinguishing history from the fable: "History is the narration of facts given as true, in contrast to the fable, which is the narration of facts given as false."[6] This definition proves to be idealistic, however, for in composing his own histories, Voltaire is constantly confronted with sources that in his own view are fables, but that are presented by their authors as history. Thus the essential question is not whether or not an account is given to be historical, but whether or not it is "vraisemblable" or plausible. Philosophy "finds ceremonies, facts, monuments all established in order to verify lies. . . . Monuments prove facts only when these plausible facts are transmitted to us by enlightened contemporaries."[7]

The "vraisemblable" is the ultimate standard of historiography, so much so that it takes precedence over the "vrai," the factually true. It is conceivable for Voltaire that an event that is not "vraisemblable" could have taken place, but it would not be a proper object for history simply because it was true.

[6] "Histoire," *Dictionnaire philosophique, Oeuvres complètes*, vol. 19 (Paris: Editions Garnier Frères, 1878).

[7] *Essai sur les moeurs, Oeuvres complètes*, vols. 11-13 (Paris: Editions Garnier Frères, 1878), cxcvii. Because there are several editions of this work that can with equal justification be regarded as authoritative and because none of them is more widely available than others, references to this work are by chapter rather than page number.

> All of these adventures which have a legendary quality and which are nonetheless quite true, do not occur among civilized peoples who have a regular form of government. (*Essai*, cxc)

> Let us believe in the events attested to by public record, by a consensus among contemporary authors living in a capital, enlightened one by the other, and writing under the gaze of the leaders of the nation. But as for all those little, obscure, and imaginary facts, written by obscure men from the depths of some ignorant and barbarian province, as for those tales loaded with mere circumstance, as for those wonders that dishonor history rather than embellish it, let us leave them to Voraigne, to the Jesuit Causson, to Maimbourg, and the like. (*Essai*, cxcvii)

Leaving the merely "vrai" to men like these, Voltaire excludes it from rational history. The "vraisemblable" is not a category within the true; it is the true that is a category within the "vraisemblable." What is "vraisemblable" may not always be true, but if it is false, it will still participate in ultimate historical truth: "There are historical errors; there are historical lies. . . . When one says that a czar had the hat of an ambassador nailed to his head, it is a lie. But to be mistaken concerning the number and the strength of the vessels of a navy, to attribute to a country a greater or lesser size is only an error, and a very pardonable error."[8] To err is to remain within the realm of historical truth. To "lie" is to be expelled to the barbarous realm of absurd tales where the terms "truth" and "falsehood" can no longer have any meaning.

The "vraisemblable" is the fundamental category of history for Voltaire, but what, specifically, does it mean? As we have already seen, according to Voltaire, an event may take place without being "vraisemblable." History is not the faithful rep-

---

[8] *Histoire de l'empire de Russie sous Pierre le Grand*, in *Oeuvres historiques*, edited by René Pomeau (Paris: Editions Gallimard, 1957), Preface, viii, p. 351.

resentation of all events, but only of certain events. The "vrai-semblable" is thus not only a standard for determining the value of a historical work, but also, for determining which historical events and cultures are worthy of being treated by the historian. In a passage already cited (*Essai*, cxc), Voltaire declares that incidents unworthy of being called historical frequently occur that could not "among civilized peoples who have a regular form of government." Only such a people or civilization with a "regular" form of government is a proper object of history, for only it maintains a relationship to time that Voltaire deems historical. For anyone outside the order such people inhabit, time can only mean change, the purely negative principle often invoked by Voltaire to "explain," or rather, to exclude from the realm of the historical all that cannot be labeled as rational: "All these customs, that time had introduced, have been abolished by time" (*Essai*, xlviii). Voltaire declares the impossibility of establishing any continuity between the present and previous historical ages, for the explanation of the present cannot be found in a past to which its only link is the purely negative movement of time: "It is thus a vain idea, a quite thankless task to want to refer everything to ancient usage and to want to fix the wheel that time causes to turn with an irresistible motion. To what epoch should one have recourse? . . . To which century, to which laws should we return?" (*Essai*, lxxxv).

It is only with the modern era that history becomes possible for Voltaire, for it is only with the emergence of modern political systems of the type instituted by Louis XIV that change ceases to be quixotic and irrational and becomes instead rational change, progress, or history.[9] Before Louis XIV, "for

[9] The close connection between what is rational in the political realm and what is rational in historiography is evident in Voltaire's use of the term "history." Though it is frequently evident from the context that Voltaire does recognize a semantic distinction corresponding to the difference between history as events "in themselves" and history as the narration of events, cases in which Voltaire's term "history" could have either meaning are equally frequent.

nine hundred years, the French genius was almost always restricted under a gothic government, in the midst of divisions and civil wars, having neither laws nor fixed customs, and changing every second century a still crude language."[10] Thus the "vraisemblable" is the rational, or rather, it is the conceptual and methodological dimension of a rationality that has a historical and institutional dimension as well (just as, for Foucault, madness provides *Madness and Civilization* with its subject matter and also with its theoretical basis). But while rational historiography cannot be discussed without a simultaneous discussion of the rational political order, the designation of that order as the only realm in which rational historiography can be produced does not really enlighten us as to the nature of the rational or the "vraisemblable" itself. The *Essai sur les moeurs*, Voltaire's most comprehensive historical work, can be read as an *attempt* to give to the rational the positive content it lacks in his programmatic statements, for the *Essai* is both a chronicle of man's struggle to establish a rational form of social organization and an attempt to establish a point at which historiography could be said to have broken with the fabulous tradition of history writing that preceded it, to become truly rational. What the *Essai* ultimately describes, however, is the successive failure of such attempts: "Thus you will see, in this huge tableau of human dementia, the prejudices of theologians, the superstitions of the masses, fanaticism, ceaselessly varied, but always constant in plunging the earth into stupidity and calamity until the time when a few academies, a few enlightened societies, made our contemporaries blush at so many centuries of barbarism" (lxii). Throughout the *Essai*, Voltaire is occupied less with pointing to the adumbrations of modern rationality than with the exclusion of past cultures and past historiography from the rational order, and thus rationality remains a negative concept. It is defined nowhere in any positive sense, and yet it is active everywhere as a principle of discrimination identical to the historical process itself.

[10] *Le Siècle de Louis XIV*, in *Oeuvres historiques*, chap. 1, p. 619.

In Voltaire's brief descriptions of the origins of history, two contradictory paradigms are already in place. According to them, rationality is both present and absent at the origin of history, and thus the "present" in which Voltaire is writing is both continuous with and cut off from that origin. For Voltaire, the possibility of a rational political order and of a rational historiography dates from the invention of speech by the intellectual elite whose presence in the state of nature guaranteed the immanence of rationality. But almost as soon as rational historiography becomes possible, it ceases to be. Oral historiography quickly degenerates into folk tales, for memory is imperfect and easily distorted by the imagination, and in all subsequent stages of history, the contradiction remains.[11]

[11] If Voltaire poses a difficulty to the modern reader, it is often not because his ideas seem antiquated and bizarre, but because they seem so self-evident as to be banal. Thus what is often required of the reader is not so much the restoration of a literary and cultural context in which the text could have made sense, as the acquisition of a distance from the text that permits its self-evidence to be questioned. Although the current political and intellectual climate is such that the ethnocentrism of Voltaire's view of history no longer appears justifiable, his judgment on the ahistoricity of cultures "without writing," which lends pseudoscientific support to that ethnocentrism, is still widely shared. In fact, the role of oral accounts and of memory in cultures "without writing" cannot be understood by considering their role in cultures that rely on writing for the transmission of all socially important knowledge. The complexity of the technical and cultural information transmitted from generation to generation in the former type of culture reveals that Voltaire's view of these cultures is far from self-evident.

Even more important, as Jacques Derrida has argued in *Of Grammatology*, translated by Gayatri Spivak (Baltimore: Johns Hopkins University Press, 1974), the colloquial definition of writing in the Western tradition (and this is of course Voltaire's) is itself ethnocentric insofar as it implicitly equates writing with phonetic writing. It thus privileges the latter with respect to all other forms of writing on the basis of its proximity to an absolutely privileged (notion of) voice thought to preexist, at least logically, all forms of writing. But, as Derrida has argued, though the priority of a pure voice over all forms of writing is desired, it can never be established: the (concept of) voice is undermined from within and from the start by the (concept of) writing it excludes. In the sense that writing cannot be contained within the metaphysical presupposition that subordinates it to voice, it ceases to coincide with its colloquial concept. From the standpoint of the more fundamental concept of

Reason is both eternal and specific to the Enlightenment whose history Voltaire is already writing. And because of this contradiction, history itself extends back to this earliest period during which speech was invented and *at the same time* can only be said to begin when this period was drawing to a close, and when a new period, inaugurated by the invention of writing (or of printing, or of philosophy) was beginning.

It is with the invention of writing that the defects of oral historiography are overcome, and Voltaire uses this date to establish anew the age of history: "All history is recent. It is not surprising that we have no lay ancient history going further back than about four thousand years. Global upheavals and the long and universal ignorance of the art that transmits facts through writing are the cause of this" (*Dictionnaire philosophique*, "Histoire"). The existence of different types of writing, each bearing a different relation to rational historiography, forces Voltaire to retreat from this "new" position. Voltaire calls hieroglyphs, "des caractères parlants," speaking graphic signs. They represent an intermediate stage between the oral tradition and alphabetical writing, a stage through which all writing systems may have passed. But while the hieroglyph provides a logical link between speech and writing in what, for Voltaire, is the gradual perfection of the techniques of historiography, the historiography that the hieroglyph itself produced would be more accurately described as myth: "It is to these hieroglyphs that we owe fables, which were the first human writings. Fable is much more ancient than history" (*Essai*, Introduction, xliii).

For Voltaire, the Chinese and their symbolic writing represent a more significant stage in the development of rationality. China is initially presented to the reader as the first culture to produce a wholly rational historiography, and so it seems, at least initially, that the invention of symbolic writing

---

writing, revealed only once the "metaphysical" nature of the colloquial concept is exposed, there would be no purely "oral" cultures, no cultures without writing, and, ultimately, none without history.

marks a clear-cut break with the irrationality of the fable. According to Voltaire's interpretation, the rationalization of historiography went hand in hand with the rationalization of Chinese social and political life: "They have no history predating that of their emperors; practically no fictions, no prodigious events, no enthusiast who calls himself a demigod, as is the case with the Egyptians and the Greeks; as soon as this people writes, it writes rationally" (*Essai*, Introduction, xviii). Indeed, Voltaire's China seems to conform in every respect to his ideal of an enlightened society. The Chinese are religious, but their religion has none of those features that lead to the fanaticism Voltaire despises. It has no priesthood and no religious hierarchy distinct from the political rulers. Confucius, the foremost of Chinese religious figures, did not teach the Chinese a new faith. He was a civil servant "who taught the ancient laws" (*Essai*, Introduction, xviii). Chinese society is hierarchical, but there is no nobility in the European sense, government service being the only title to honors (*Essai*, ii).

Given Voltaire's admiration for the Chinese and the apparent similarity between China and enlightened European society, the way in which China and the historiography it produced are ultimately excluded from the historical realm is all the more interesting. In Voltaire's view, it is the same virtues that permitted the Chinese to form a rational government and to produce a rational historiography that have isolated China from the current of history, for they have impeded progress as well as prevented degeneration.

> If one seeks the reason why so many arts and sciences, cultivated without interruption for such a long time in China, have nonetheless progressed so little, there are perhaps two reasons: one is the prodigious respect these peoples have for what is transmitted to them by their fathers, and which, in their eyes, renders perfect everything that is ancient; the other is the nature of their language, the first principle of all forms of knowledge. (*Essai*, i)

The respect of the Chinese for authority and for the ancient has prevented them from making the scientific discoveries that have characterized European progress. With regard to the question of language, this same respect for the ancient has prevented the Chinese from adopting Western printing, for to do so, they would have to abandon symbolic writing in favor of the alphabet (*Essai*, i). In Voltaire's view, so long as writing continues to be restricted to the small and inevitably elderly elite who has mastered the symbolic system only after years of study, the continued stagnation of China's political and intellectual life is assured. China, like the less rationally organized cultures that preceded it, is fundamentally ahistorical in Voltaire's terms, not because its culture and language are determined by accident, custom, sheer change, and the like, but because it is closed to any modification. China has isolated itself from the purely negative effects of time, from pure change, but has succeeded too well, for in doing so it has cut itself off from rational, historical time, or progress.

Voltaire's fundamental lack of appreciation for ancient history extends even to those ancient cultures that he seems at points to admire. Though ancient cultures are arranged by Voltaire on a scale placing those that most resemble modern Europe at the top, though one ancient culture may be progressive with regard to another, none guarantees the production of rational historiography and thus none provides a starting point for a rational history of mankind. Though the subject of the *Essai sur les moeurs* is the history of the world prior to the age of Louis XIV, the *Essai* only serves to confirm a remark by Voltaire in the introduction to the *Histoire de Charles XII* on the futility of most history:

> It seems to me that if one wanted to put one's time to the best use, one would not spend life infatuated with ancient fables. I would advise a young man to have a smattering of ancient history; but I would want him to begin a serious study of history from the age in which it becomes truly interesting for us: it seems to me that this

is toward the end of the fifteenth century. Printing, which was invented at that time, begins to make it [history] less uncertain.[12]

Voltaire renews his effort to establish a historical age starting with the invention of printing. By permitting the widespread diffusion of knowledge and of Enlightenment values, printing proves the superiority of the alphabet over other writing systems (for, among the systems discussed by Voltaire, only the alphabet is adapted to printing) and the superiority of modern Europe over ancient Greece and Rome. But Voltaire admits in his article "Langues" in the *Dictionnaire philosophique* that no modern European language can perfectly express what he considers to be reality, and, in writing on modern history and historiography, Voltaire often declares that both have been less than what he would consider realistic or rational. This admission reveals the arbitrariness of Voltaire's exclusion of ancient cultures and writing systems from the historical realm. If all writing systems, including the alphabet, are only relatively faithful to the "real," then the causes of "irrationality" do not lie in the systems themselves, but rather in the ideologies that dictate the various forms of historical discourse. In discussing the difficulties faced by the rational historiographer in the modern age, it is precisely these problems Voltaire takes up. But he does so only after the exclusion of ancient cultures from the rational on grounds he himself now implicitly rejects as inessential, that is, on the grounds that the "prealphabetical" writing systems are not technically "advanced" enough to ensure a rational representation of the real. For Voltaire, only the "destructive" forces undermining the rational are ideological, and this view effectively precludes any discussion of the exclusion that founds the rational order. For Voltaire—and he is not alone—ideology is only what others are prejudiced by.

Indeed, printing, which permits the broad diffusion of historiography, its public criticism, and the like, and the re-

---

[12] *Histoire de Charles XII*, in *Oeuvres historiques*, pp. 43-44.

sources of modern governments, which permit the printing and storing of chronicles and treaties (*Charles XII*, "Nouvelles considérations sur l'histoire"), do not in themselves guarantee that historiography is rational, even though they permit it to be factual. As I have already noted, in Voltaire's view facts alone do not constitute history: "If we wanted to use reason rather than memory and examine rather than transcribe, we would not infinitely multiply the number of books and errors; we ought to write only things that are new and true. What is ordinarily lacking in those who compile history is the philosophical spirit" (*Charles XII*, "Remarques sur l'histoire," p. 43). Once again Voltaire attempts to found an age of rational historiography, this time coinciding not with the modern age (post-fifteenth century) and the invention of printing, but with the advent of what he calls philosophy: "In all nations, history is disfigured by fable, until finally philosophy arrives in the midst of this darkness" (*Essai*, cxcvii).

Like all previous guarantees of the rationality of historiography, however, philosophy is threatened from all sides. Speculation on the broader sense of history does not, for Voltaire, necessarily represent an advance over mere fact finding. In attempting to go beyond factual accuracy the historian risks being caught up in his own speculations to such an extent that they no longer reflect historical reality, but rather, become an intellectual fiction of the philosopher-historian's creation. This, it seems, was the case of Boulainvilliers, described by Voltaire as "the most learned gentleman of the kingdom on the subject of history, and the most capable of writing that of France, if he had not been too systematic" (*Louis XIV*, "Catalogue des écrivains français," p. 1142). The overly systematic historian is, for Voltaire, a more sophisticated version of the providential historian who interprets history from a narrow cultural, religious, or even personal perspective. Such, according to Voltaire, were the Jewish historians who could interpret world-shaking events only as being for their particular edification, and such are the European historians who blithely ignore the four-thousand-year-old Chinese empire to assert that the monarchy who is paying them to write its history is the oldest in the world.

Furthermore, not all of Voltaire's contemporaries shared his philosopher's view that the principal value of ancient historiography, which Voltaire considers "as false as it is obscure and disgusting" (*Essai*, Introduction, lii), is to heighten the reader's thankfulness to be living in the age of enlightenment. Traces of their opinions can be found in Voltaire's attacks on them. Some, though they too may have perceived past historiography as largely unscientific, still felt that these "fables" deserved the attention of rational historiographers as documents of past values. In Voltaire's view, those who believe the "fables" recounted by ancient history are bad enough—"irrational and stupid," but "perhaps the most stupid of all are those who want to find a sense in these absurd fables, and thus place reason in madness" (*Essai*, Introduction, vi). Still others, more critical of present institutions, looked to the past for models that might serve for reform. Voltaire accuses them of desiring the impossible, that history would reverse itself (*Essai*, lxxxv). For him, the only rational attitude toward the past is one of rejection: "What greater fruit can be reaped from all of the vicissitudes gathered in this *Essai sur les moeurs* than to convince ourselves that every nation has always been unhappy until the laws and the legislative power were established without contradiction?" (*Essai*, lxxxii).

Voltaire's critique of his contemporaries restricts further and further the field in which rational historiography is possible: ultimately, it may only be possible in the present in which Voltaire himself is writing. But if in the present history realizes its ultimate, rational destination and essence, in another, equally important sense, it ceases to be history. A rational history that has retreated to the pure present is robbed of any historicity. And without historicity, without change and transformation, rationality itself cannot be, as Voltaire's interpretation of China clearly reveals. Before this end point is reached, however, Voltaire will try to establish still another "rational period" that could be considered to be continuous with the present, thanks to its rationality, but at the same time past, that is, just barely past. Voltaire implies that it is impossible to live up to his own definition of rational historiography in the greater part of the *Essai sur les moeurs*, for its subject is the ancient and feudal cultures, which, both as producers of historiography and as subjects for later historiographers, are sources of irrationality. In the age of Louis XIV Voltaire finds a subject worthy of the rational historiographer, for in it rationality appears to have been established without contradiction, and thus the *Siècle de Louis XIV* becomes the first and last chance for rational historiography.

One of Voltaire's most frequent criticisms of existing historiography is its preoccupation with events of primary concern to the aristocracy and the monarchy, and of little importance to the larger audience which Voltaire designates as "mankind":[13] "Thus I here consider the fate of men in general rather than the upheavals of a dynasty. It is to the human race that attention ought to have been paid in history: it is there that each writer should have said *homo sum*; but most historians have described only battles" (*Essai*, lxxxiv). "I would like to discover what human society was like at the time, how one lived within the family, what arts were cultivated, rather than repeat so many misfortunes and so many combats" (*Essai*, lxxxi). But the notion that true history is made by the class of people engaged in commerce, industry, the arts, and sciences is directly contradicted by the notion that Louis XIV was the cause of the great political and intellectual achievements of his day. Voltaire's project of describing the state of "mankind" in the preceding century is at odds with his decision to characterize the century in question as that of *Louis XIV*: "But above all, be a bit less angry with me for my calling the last century the age of Louis XIV. . . . Not only were great things done during

[13] Such a conception of "mankind" would not include the peasants, who in the eighteenth century made up the vast majority of France's population but whose illiteracy "naturally" excluded them from Voltaire's audience.

his reign, but it is he who did them" (*Louis XIV*, "Lettre à milord Hervey," p. 608).

Voltaire's insistence that the role of Louis XIV is all-important in rationalizing intellectual and political life contradicts his claims concerning the historical importance of the bourgeoisie. But both an insistence on the importance of the bourgeoisie and a contradictory insistence on the historical primacy of *Louis XIV* are necessary if the age of Louis XIV is to be seen both as historical, that is, as continuous with what Voltaire sees as the economic and social progress of the bourgeoisie from the Middle Ages through the eighteenth century, and as rational, that is, as discontinuous with all previous periods in political and intellectual history. In the sense that the rational can only be introduced by means of a radical break with an irrational past, Voltaire's emphasis on the agency of Louis XIV is essential, for in his view, Louis embodies just such a radical break. René Pomeau notes that Voltaire minimizes the accomplishments of previous governments in order to portray Louis XIV as the originator of all institutional reform.[14] By the same logic, Voltaire never portrays the change instituted by Louis XIV as the result of a prolonged struggle between the monarch and reactionary historical forces. The reforms that initiate rational history cannot be themselves historical, they must be immediate and virtually spontaneous if rationality is to be established without contradiction. Voltaire portrays the most radical political changes as coinciding with the will of Louis XIV. He speaks once, and the *parlement* of Paris, which Voltaire sees as a perennial fomenter of destructive, factional disputes, is silenced for an indefinite period. He dominates the nobility—a constant source, in Voltaire's view, of violence and political irrationality—by bringing them all to Versailles where they are wholly under his influence. He wills it, and, with Colbert as his instrument, French trade and industry flourish and a navy is created overnight. Indeed, Voltaire argues that Colbert's accomplishments were not his own,

[14] In Voltaire, *Oeuvres historiques*, p. 22.

but should be credited to Louis XIV: "What could a Colbert have done under another prince?" ("Lettre à milord Hervey").

In the *Siècle de Louis XIV*, the figure of the monarch becomes synonymous with rationality itself. It is thus of the utmost significance that the rational principle Voltaire has isolated in this figure becomes the source of the *failure* of the *Siècle de Louis XIV* to live up to Voltaire's programmatic statements concerning rational historiography and to give rationality a positive content. Ironically, Louis XIV's patronage of commerce, science, arts, and letters comes to justify the importance of his actions in spheres that for Voltaire himself are only indirectly, or even negatively, related to the above. The preponderant role ascribed to Louis XIV in the "positive" achievements of his reign forces Voltaire to emphasize the military and aristocratic matters that preoccupied Louis XIV much more than the arts and sciences, or even commerce. Thus by far the better part of the *Siècle de Louis XIV* deals with aspects of history that, according to Voltaire, have already received too much attention, and from the point of view of which the age of Louis XIV is much like any other.[15] Though Voltaire frequently laments the fact that "most historians have described only battles," the first twenty-four of a total of thirty-nine chapters comprising the *Siècle de Louis XIV* are concerned with military history. Voltaire himself seems aware of the incongruity when he writes at the beginning of chapter 11: "It is necessary to say to those who might read this work that they must remember that this is not a simple record of military campaigns, but rather a history of the morals and manners of men" (pp. 722-723). Indeed, it is necessary for Vol-

[15] The age of Louis XIV is, according to Voltaire, the most illustrious of the four great ages of which he writes: "It should not be thought that these four ages were exempt from unhappiness and crime. The perfection of the arts cultivated by peaceful citizens does not prevent princes from being ambitious, the people from being seditious, priests and monks from at times stirring things up and behaving knavishly. All ages are alike from the standpoint of human wickedness; but I know of only those four ages that are distinguished by great talents" (*Louis XIV*, pp. 617-618).

taire to state what is far from obvious, for aside from his protestation to the contrary, nothing substantial distinguishes his account of Louis XIV's conquests and reverses from the military history he repeatedly declares to be irrelevant to rational historiography.

Four out of the thirty-nine chapters are devoted to anecdotes. And yet in his "Nouvelles considérations sur l'histoire" Voltaire himself declares they are only of ephemeral interest: "There are books that apprise me of the anecdotes—true or false—of a court. Whoever has seen court life, or has wanted to see it, is as avid for these illustrious bagatelles as a provincial woman who wants to know the news of her small town: at bottom it's the same thing with the same value. . . . All these little portraits stay around for a generation or two, and then perish forever" (*Charles XII*, "Nouvelles considérations," p. 47). According to Voltaire, anecdotes, like battles, are all alike. Once again, he reveals an awareness that he is including material that does not support his contentions about the rationality of Louis XIV's reign. At the same time he attempts to justify himself by invoking a uniqueness of Louis XIV that the anecdotes themselves cannot reveal: "I would even like to think that these court intrigues, foreign to the state itself, ought not to enter into history if the great age of Louis XIV did not render everything interesting" (*Louis XIV*, xxvi, p. 929).

Five chapters of the *Siècle de Louis XIV* are devoted to religious disputes. Here Voltaire himself points up the contradiction between what he sees as the enlightenment of the age and the ignorance and narrowness of the antagonists. Moreover, Voltaire clearly recognizes that these disputes cannot simply be dismissed as historically insignificant in view of the role of Louis XIV himself in aggravating them. Voltaire views Louis XIV's role in the debate surrounding Jansenism as of little consequence, for he views Jansenism itself as more or less impotent (*Louis XIV*, xxxvii). But the violence of the government's policy against the Huguenots, culminating in the *dragonnade*, and the active role of Louis XIV in the formulation of that policy are, for Voltaire himself very real and even disturbing:

> It is a strange contrast that, from the bosom of a voluptuous court where a gentleness of manners, the graces, and the charms of society reigned, such hard and pitiless orders were given. ... "His Majesty desires that those who do not wish to become members of his religion be treated with the ultimate severity; and those who have the stupid ambition of wanting to be the last to give in must be pushed to the ultimate extremity." (*Louis XIV*, xxxvi, pp. 1053-1054)

The conflict between Louis XIV's interests and the interests Voltaire is promoting as those of "mankind" persists in the chapters on government finances and the arts that are in principle devoted to the positive accomplishments of Louis XIV's reign. In Voltaire's view, the wars conducted by Louis XIV had an ultimately negative effect on France's economy (*Louis XIV*, xxx). Moreover, in many cases, the exigencies of war brought about the abolition of reforms made in the early years of Louis XIV's reign. Though elsewhere Voltaire insists that Louis XIV deserved ultimate credit for the accomplishments of Colbert, the chapters on finances show Colbert time and again resorted to economic practices he deplored in order to finance Louis XIV's grandeur: "Colbert, in order to meet the expense of wars, of construction, and of court amusements, was obliged to reestablish, toward the end of 1672, what he had wanted originally to abolish forever: taxes on land, rents, new offices, and the augmentation of salaries; in short, those things that sustain the state a while and encumber it for centuries" (*Louis XIV*, xxx, p. 987). Louis XIV's preoccupation with his grandeur had a negative effect on art and architecture analogous to its effect on finances and the economy. Though Voltaire claims that the consumption of articles "de luxe" had a stimulating effect on French industry, he deplores Louis XIV's decision to concentrate art and luxury in his own capital, Versailles, rather than in Paris, where the result would have been accessible to a greater number of citizens (*Louis XIV*, xxix). Like the wars conducted by Louis XIV, Versailles, the symbol of his grandeur, became, "an abyss that swallowed up all the sources of abundance" (*Louis XIV*, xxx, p. 989).

Voltaire declares that the age of Louis XIV "most closely approaches perfection" and that Louis XIV was directly responsible for the great accomplishments of his age. What the *Siècle de Louis XIV* reveals is that the specific actions and preoccupations of Louis XIV were, more often than not, in conflict with the philosopher's notion of perfection or rationality. In the light of this conflict, Voltaire tries to retrieve the ultimate sense of Louis XIV and his reign by maintaining that Louis XIV's relationship to the projects that exalted him at the expense of the "nation"—the third estate—was one of fundamental detachment, that is, that his essence as rational monarch was not fundamentally implicated in any of the specific actions or policies that were in apparent conflict with the ideal of rationality.

There is a parallel to be drawn between the rational historiographer and the rational monarch. In principle, the former produces a historiography free of ideological distortion. He scrupulously avoids interposing his personal point of view or any speculation that is the product of his imagination and not a faithful reflection of the "real." To do otherwise would be to lose his objectivity, to become implicated in an ideology and thereby to cease to be rational. According to Voltaire, the rational historiographer must "paint rather than judge," and he finds in a portrait of Pope Gregory VII the model the rational historiographer must strive to imitate: "All the portraits, whether flattering or odious, that so many writers have given of him, are to be found in the painting of a Neopolitan artist, who depicted Gregory holding a crozier in one hand and a whip in the other, trampling scepters under his feet, with the nets and the fish of Saint Peter at his side" (*Essai*, xlvi).

Only the rational order over which Louis XIV rules maintains a relationship to itself through time that, in Voltaire's view, can be termed historical. Thus in maintaining the rational order, Louis XIV produces history in much the same way the philosopher produces historiography. His production, like that of the rational historiographer, must be free of any ideological distortion that might result from the predominance of one faction within the political order. Though there may be an apparent divergence between the interests of his grandeur and those of the nation, he must maintain that in fact his grandeur and the interests of the state are one, that his relationship to the rational order is perfectly disinterested. The rational order that takes the form of a tableau when presented by the philosopher-historian also takes a visual form when presented by the monarch. The reign of Louis XIV is a spectacle played to all of Europe. His marriage is celebrated by the representation of an Italian opera in which the king and queen both dance. In 1662 a carrousel is presented across from the Tuileries in which the king figures prominently. Louis plans his military expeditions much as he stages these spectacles. Taste and magnificence are evident even in his military camps. The scenario for the military debut of Monseigneur is carefully written by his father: "Everything had been foreseen and disposed in order that the son of Louis XIV, who was contributing his name and his presence to this expedition, received no affront. The maréchal de Duras was the actual commander of the army" (*Louis XIV*, xvi, p. 772). Louis XIV's own campaigns are equally well staged: "The king, with so many advantages, sure of his prospects and his glory, brought with him a historian who was to write his victories" (*Louis XIV*, x, p. 713).

Though he may participate in the historical spectacle that is his reign, Voltaire assures us that the monarch himself is never caught up in the spectacle; and thus his participation never endangers his absolute status as monarch. In this sense, Voltaire's portrait of Louis XIV contrasts explicitly with that of Charles XII of Sweden. The latter best typifies Voltaire's definition of the "glory seeker" or the ruler who can achieve only a "vain" or "false glory" because he has become excessively enamored of "the apparatus of representation" (*Dictionnaire philosophique*, "Glorieux"). Charles XII seeks out the most dangerous situation on a given battlefield to better demonstrate his own heroism. His ardor contrasts with Louis XIV's detachment: "One did not see in him [Louis XIV] . . . the impulsive courage of François I and Henri IV, who sought out all sorts of dangers. He contented himself with not fearing any danger and encouraging everyone to throw themselves ardently into battle for him" (*Louis XIV*, ix, p. 702). Charles XII abandoned his specific duties as ruler of Sweden in his quest for personal glory. But the brilliant court amusements that reflect Louis XIV's personal glory "took nothing away from the continuous work of the monarch" (*Louis XIV*, xxv, p. 908). Significantly, Voltaire tells us that as soon as it occurs to Louis XIV that his participation as an actor in the plays and operas produced for the amusement of the court detracts from his dignity as sovereign, he ceases to appear on the stage.

Louis XIV is thus not distinguished from the monarchs preceding him by specific policies he may or may not have promulgated and implemented. There is no essential difference between his wars, his court, his personal intrigues, and the wars, courts, and intrigues of rulers of the supposedly less rational political orders portrayed in the *Essai sur les moeurs*. The rationality of Louis XIV's monarchy lies in Voltaire's affirmation—an echo of the affirmation of Louis XIV himself—that Louis XIV's actions were fundamentally disinterested, that whatever he did, he always represented, not himself, or a class, but the state. In the final analysis, Louis XIV's reality and rationality are purely formal, for no specific action or long-term policy can negate the rational, nothing concrete can disprove the purity of Louis XIV's intentions and actions.

BY VOLTAIRE'S DEFINITION, the *Siècle de Louis XIV* represents a privileged moment in history and historiography, one in which the rational and the "vraisemblable" are more than ideally conceivable as the organizers of "history."[16] But in fact,

[16] As René Pomeau notes (in Voltaire, *Oeuvres historiques*, p. 20), the

nothing specific distinguishes Louis XIV from other monarchs, and there is no substantial thematic difference between the *Siècle de Louis XIV* and the *Essai*. The reign of Louis XIV exemplifies rationality, but like all preceding ages, it does so only negatively. Having silenced and excluded from history and rationality such elements as the *parlements*, the "reactionary" factions of the aristocracy, and certain religious groups such as the Jansenists, the regime of Louis XIV then excludes itself from the rational order by the irrational nature of the undertakings making up its own history—wars, aggravation of religious disputes, deficit spending, court intrigues. Though the reign of Louis XIV may be different in degree from previous ages, it is not different in kind; despite Voltaire's claims, it does not represent any radical break with the past. Rationality, then, is only negatively connected to the texts of Voltaire's histories, and in this sense all of his histories could just as well be considered chronicles of the "irrational," the "invraisemblable," and the persistent misery of an "inhuman" humanity. Voltaire can only write the history of reason by writing the history of unreason, that is to say of a *negativity* that includes everything from specific forms of writing to the political and intellectual achievements of entire civilizations, to groups and ideologies within "modern" history.

This history of "(un)reason," however, poses the same type of difficulties as Foucault's history of madness. The irrational remains a vague concept for Voltaire—so vague as to include the whole of history. It lacks any specific content, for, like rationality, it can only be defined as the negative of its opposite, the negative of its negative. Indeed, had Voltaire been able to overcome the vagueness of the concept of irrationality, he would have been able to write the history of reason that the *Essai* and the *Siècle de Louis XIV* both strive to be. Because the two concepts are inseparable, there can be no history of

---

"progress of the human mind," which has such a restricted place in the *Siècle de Louis XIV*, is even more summarily evoked in the *Précis du Siècle de Louis XV*.

reason that would not also be a history of unreason, no history of unreason that would not be a history of reason.

If ultimately Voltaire could not write a history of reason in itself, it is because there is a radical tension at the heart of reason itself. As both the *Essai sur les moeurs* and the *Siècle de Louis XIV* argue, reason can only be itself if it has a history. A reason that has none quickly becomes unreason, as Voltaire's interpretation of China is designed to show. History is the indispensable condition of the existence of reason in and for itself. But as we have seen, the definition of reason that emerges from this history is highly contradictory. Reason *is* and *is not* present in all of the specific ages that make up history, for if it were simply present in any of them, then each age would be the beginning and end of history—that is, there would be no history, but only an undifferentiated present. But if reason were simply absent in every specific period, then rationality would have no history, and without history, rationality itself cannot be.

The radical nature of Foucault's "antirationalist" historical project is perhaps clearest when one compares it to Voltaire's historiography, because for the *philosophe*, history is synonymous with reason itself. The necessity that leads Foucault to combine a search for a radically critical historical method with an attempt to let madness speak or, at least, to let its silence be heard, is evident in negative form in Voltaire's *Essai sur les moeurs*. In *Madness and Civilization*, Foucault seems to tell us that as long as we continue to accept reason either as the voice of history itself or even as the voice of the classical age, we will continue to write history as it has always been written, as Voltaire wrote it; and, in some fundamental sense, the historical itself will continue to elude us. We will be rationalists, perhaps even philosophers, but not true historians. The nature of Foucault's historical project appears somewhat less radical, however, when one situates it in terms of Voltaire's attempt to define reason through and in history. The vagueness of Foucault's concept of madness parallels the vagueness of Voltaire's concept of reason, and this parallel results not from a superficial similarity between the two, but rather from the fact that both terms in both contexts are dependent on the precarious opposition separating them from each other. Foucault's concept of madness is as dependent on a concept of reason against which it negatively defines itself as Voltaire's concept of reason is on the irrational it attempts to negate and transcend. Foucault is certainly not the Voltaire of the twentieth century, nor is Voltaire the Foucault of the eighteenth; but insofar as Foucault's aim in *Madness and Civilization* is to be a "new" or even antihistorian, the historian of the silence of madness and thus in this sense the anti-Voltaire, his project and critical strategy can be linked to Voltaire's. Foucault's project of breaking with rational, philosophical history and establishing the historical itself on a new footing and Voltaire's project of establishing rationality as the ground and essence of history are both determined by their attempts to fix and respect the boundary separating reason from unreason, philosophy and history from madness. What can be learned from a critical study of both Voltaire and Foucault is that neither reason nor unreason as such can be considered a simple origin for either traditional or "new" history, for neither ever exists in itself; and no matter how loquacious or silent either is considered to be, neither remains on the side of the boundary assigned to it.

One could also argue, then, that the *Essai sur les moeurs* exceeds its own concept of reason, for in it, reason is not just one thing as historical accounts of the Enlightenment from Kant, to Herder, to Foucault have argued or implied. In revealing the fundamental contradiction "within" reason, the *Essai* also reveals that both rationalist and historicist history, despite their differences, are rooted in the "same" concept of reason and that both belong to the tradition of the *Essai sur les moeurs*. But the *Essai* can also be considered as a beginning for another type of history that does not take reason as given, to be one thing in one age or one thing for all ages. It shows against Voltaire's intentions, against his rationality, that reason can never be either a specific object among others for history, nor a condition of history outside of history itself. The contradictory historicity of Voltaire's *Essai* and in fact of all history is evident in the instability of the rationality in which they are rooted, and this is true whether the object of history is reason or its other, unreason.

TWO

(*Voltaire*)
The Question of Genre:
White, Genette, and
the Limits of Formalism

HISTORY has almost always been conceived in mimetic terms as a relation of a discourse to a referent, a picture to a subject, words to things. From this perspective, the form of history has been considered to be of secondary importance or even irrelevant to the ultimate nature of history. The crucial problem is thought to be the referent, not the way in which the referent is presented. Citing the work of diverse continental thinkers and certain Anglo-American philosophers of history as signs that this traditional view is being challenged, Hayden White's *Metahistory* takes direct issue with it.[1] White proposes to analyze historical writing itself rather than the relationship between historical writing and the reality it purportedly represents. He thus redefines all histories as "purely verbal structures" and examines the "prefigurative linguistic protocol" responsible for their "explanatory affect" (pp. 4-5).

Though he seeks to shed light on the problem of historical knowledge as it has been considered traditionally, White argues that only a new method—new, at least, in the context of the philosophy of history—can effectively analyze history from the perspective he has adopted. However, as White himself acknowledges, his method is a traditional formalism and is the result of a choice he has made among numerous and contend-

---

[1] *Metahistory: The Historical Imagination in Nineteenth-Century Europe* (Baltimore: Johns Hopkins University Press, 1973).

ing philosophies of form that traditional and contemporary theory has bequeathed us. Given the historical dimension of the problem of form and the formal categories White uses, a critical consideration of his system cannot accept it as he presents it, that is, as metahistorical, as an ultimate explanation and radical reversal of traditional historiography. Any analysis of the form of history should begin by confronting the question of form-in-general (in history, but also in literature, philosophy, or language-in-general), a question that by right should be raised before any practical, formal analysis is carried out, that is before categories are "applied" either to history or literature.

It is not a simple matter to reverse the traditional pattern of historiography and analyze the significance of the form of history, for once one begins to investigate the problem of historical form, one is confronted not with *a* form but a plurality of forms. History writing does not make use of only one style, one narrative technique, or one mode of argumentation, but several. History is not a genre, it encompasses several genres, and this is perhaps nowhere more evident than in the Enlightenment. One of the most striking features of the historiography of Voltaire, for example, is the variety of forms or genres it comprises. His earliest historical work is also a poetic one—the epic poem the *Henriade*. His *Histoire de Charles XII* has been treated as a mock epic that uses epic conventions and satirizes them at the same time.[2] His *romans* and *contes* have typically been viewed as a literary restatement of the theses of his philosophy of history, an *Essai sur les moeurs* in another form.[3] Simply to acknowledge the diversity of the forms

[2] Lionel Gossman, "Voltaire's *Charles XII*: History into art," *Studies on Voltaire*, vol. 25 (1963).

[3] As Henri Bernac puts it: "Thus, to write a commentary on the tales, it usually suffices to refer to Voltaire's historical works: they give us, with all its nuances, the idea whose tip alone is evident in the tales; the historical works show us at the same time the transition from the abstract to the concrete, from reasoning to the symbol, and therein lies all of Voltaire's art" ("Présentation," in Voltaire, *Romans et contes* [Paris: Editions Garnier Frères, 1960], p. ix).

adopted by Voltaire to set forth his history and his philosophy of history, as most interpreters have been content to do, is not enough, however, for this diversity raises two essential questions concerning form itself: first of all, why are there several forms for what is assumed to be one historical truth? And second, if there is a plurality of "historical" genres, how are they related to and distinguished from each other?

Though White's *Metahistory* is a rare attempt by a historiographer to address the problem of the form of history, it is of no direct assistance in analyzing the formal plurality of Voltaire's historiography. For White is above all interested in categorizing or synthesizing the work of a given historian in terms of one dominant trope rather than analyzing the dynamic and often contradictory nature of the form of any single work or the formal diversity distinguishing various works of a single author from each other. Like traditional critics of Voltaire, White is for the most part content merely to acknowledge the plurality of form as a first step in an attempt to categorize each writer in terms of an ultimate unity; the difference between White and traditional critics is that this unity is now one of form rather than of sense or intention. In the final analysis, however, the question of form-in-general and with it the very possibility of understanding history in formal terms both rest on the outcome of the attempt to situate and categorize the plurality of form within *a* formal system, and from the standpoint of this general problem, White's *Metahistory* is exemplary in its scope, rigor, and the difficulties it confronts. Ultimately, the plurality of form will pose the greatest problem for White's or any other formalism, if plurality can be shown to be the condition for unity, if it can be shown to resist the imposition of unity and thereby to reveal the arbitrary nature of any unified, finalized concept of form.

White claims that all history writing is preformed by a limited number of fundamental formal choices. *Metahistory* divides these formal choices into four levels, but the two of greatest interest here are the level of explanation by emplotment and the level that White considers to be the "deepest"—

the tropological level. On the first level, White distinguishes four "genres" of history—Comedy, Tragedy, Romance, and Satire. On the "deepest" level, he distinguishes four major tropes which he claims preform all history writing and, by implication, all the other levels of his analysis: Metaphor, Metonymy, Synecdoche, and Irony. White's system of classification comports two elements typical of formal systems of classification in general. First, it implies a *hierarchy* among the forms. This hierarchy is implicit rather than explicit, for White constantly affirms that from the point of view of the system itself there is no reason for preferring one genre or one trope to another. Nonetheless, underlying White's fourfold system is a binary opposition which contrasts Irony with Metaphor, Metonymy, and Synecdoche (and Satire with Romance, Comedy, and Tragedy).[4] Thus White speaks of European historical thinking as being "plunged into the Ironic condition of mind which seized it at the end of the nineteenth century" (*Metahistory*, p. xii).[5] This plunge only repeats, in White's view, an earlier "fall" into Irony which culminated the historical thinking of the eighteenth century. Irony can create such a crisis in historical thinking because it is both the possibility of history and a threat to it. For White argues that it is through Irony that the historian achieves the awareness that history is formal or poetic in nature rather than literal and realistic. But the result of that awareness is paradoxical in that, although it can liberate the historian-poet and safeguard the formal pluralism that White considers essential for the production of history, it can also

---

[4] For just as White opposes Irony to the other tropes, so Satire is opposed to the other genres: "But Satire represents a different kind of qualification of the hopes, possibilities, and truths of existence revealed in Romance, Comedy and Tragedy respectively" (*Metahistory*, p. 10). Because of the close parallels between these two levels of White's analysis, it seems fair to say that White's tropology is also a genre theory in which all that White says of Irony can be applied to Satire.

[5] Or, again, White writes that "in the 'realism' of Burckhardt, one witnesses the *fall* once more into that Ironic condition," and "Marx . . . provided . . . more than ample grounds for the *descent* into Irony" (*Metahistory*, p. 40, my emphasis).

paralyze him by casting suspicion on the ability of all historical forms to capture the real. The capacity of Irony to produce
such a crisis, then, is the source of the master division in White's
tropology which opposes Irony to the other tropes.[6]

The second element common to White's system and to formal systems in general is that it assumes a distinction between
"literal" and "figurative" language. White goes against conventional wisdom when he declares that history is in essence
figurative rather than literal, but he respects that wisdom insofar as he maintains that "science" is a nontropological, nonliterary, purely descriptive language, and that, as such, it can
be opposed to both literature and history.[7] Moreover, White's

[6] In "On Tropology: The Forms of History," *Diacritics*, vol. 6, no. 3 (Fall
1976), David Carroll points to the special status White gives to Irony and
the serious nature of the contradiction that this special status introduces into
his tropology: "Irony, the fourth trope, is ultimately, as White admits without
drawing the radical conclusions his statement suggests, metatropological. . . .
For, if the tropological level is the metahistorical level, what is the status of
a metatrope and where can it be situated? Irony not only undermines the
epistemological foundations of history but also the substantiability and specificity (the properness) of the three other tropes. In fact, the existence of a
metatrope puts into question the whole taxonomy" (p. 61).

[7] As it is in the following passage, in which White equates the formal and
ideological components of history and contrasts history with science: "There
does, in fact, appear to be an irreducible ideological component in every
historical account of reality. That is to say, simply because history is *not* a
science, or is at best a protoscience with specifically determinable nonscientific
elements in its constitution, the very claim to have discerned some kind of
formal coherence in the historical record brings with it theories of the nature
of the historical world and of historical knowledge itself which have ideological implications for attempts to understand 'the present,' however this 'present' is defined" (*Metahistory*, p. 21). One of White's major arguments justifying his use of a fourfold tropology is that such a system permits one to see
continuity between poetic (mythic) consciousness and prosaic (scientific) consciousness (p. 32). White's own conception of science and of the poetic,
however, is ultimately founded on an opposition between the two, which
clearly distinguishes science from history and which leads to a surprising
statement about the nature of science: "The most important of these problems
was created by the fact that the student of the historical process was enclosed
within it or involved in it in a way that the student of the natural process was
not" (p. 45).

own formalist project claims to a certain extent to be scientific and literal. For a formalist language is, in White's view, the only one that can fully account for the essentially tropological nature of history writing. If we accept his premises, White's tropology is a system upon which a science of history writing could conceivably be founded.[8]

There is an intimate relation between the hierarchy implicit in White's system and the distinction it assumes between figurative and literal language, and without an understanding of this relationship, it is impossible to understand the contradictions in *Metahistory* and the necessity dictating them. Indeed, the hierarchy between Irony on the one hand and Metonymy, Synecdoche, and Metaphor on the other *is itself* an opposition between the literal and the figurative, inasmuch as White first affirms that "Irony, Metonymy, and Synecdoche are all kinds of Metaphor" (p. 43), and then goes on to subtract Irony from the group by asserting that it represents a negation of Metaphor: "The Ironic statement . . . presupposes that the reader or auditor knows, or is capable of recognizing, the absurdity of the thing designated in the Metaphor, Metonymy, or Synecdoche used to give form to it. . . . Irony . . . is deployed in the self-conscious awareness of the possible misuse of figurative language. Irony presupposes the occupation of a 'realistic' perspective on reality, from which a non-figurative representation of the world of experience might be provided" (p. 37). It is because Irony negates Metaphor and presupposes a "realistic" (i.e., nonfigurative) perspective that it is considered to be "metatropological" (p. 37) by White, and it is because of its metatropological status that he gives Irony both the "lowest" and the "highest" position in his tropology,

[8] By characterizing his work as *consciously* Ironic (*Metahistory*, p. xii), he endows it with the attributes he gives science. For Irony *is* metatropological; it dominates and transcends the poetic, and, moreover, like science, Irony has no ideological dimension: "Existentially projected into a full-blown world view, Irony would appear to be *transideological*," writes White, even though it may be used "*tactically*" in defense of Liberal or Conservative ideological positions" (p. 38).

62

claiming even that his own *Metahistory* is an Ironic work: "It may not go unnoticed that this book is itself cast in an Ironic mode" (p. xii). Irony in this sense is firmly grounded in the literal.

If Irony is both figurative and the negation of the figurative at the same time, White's own attempt to write a poetics of history is ironic in the same way: it acknowledges the poetical nature of history in order to transcend the poetical by defining it, by fixing it in a formal system. Underlying White's formalism—indeed, I would claim, underlying all formalisms—is a theory of literal language whose dream is to dominate "metaphorical" language by reducing it to a system of categories in which metaphor can be literally presented. If the question of the mimetic relation of history to reality is no longer central from White's point of view, still another mimetic relationship is: that between the tropes of history (the referent) and the linguistic-formal system with which White "literally" describes those tropes. The concept of Metaphor is thus scientific and literal in White's system and in any formal system. For the formalist who can define and delimit the various tropes (all figurative uses of language) can also presumably define and delimit the literal and the scientific.

White insists that a formal approach to the work of a historian, or, at any rate, of a "great" artist-historian, can uncover the fundamental unity of historical writing: "In every case, dialectical tension evolves within the context of a coherent vision or presiding image of the form of the whole historical field. This gives to the individual thinker's conception of that field the aspect of a self-consistent totality. . . . The problem here is to determine the grounds of this coherence and consistency. In my view, these grounds are poetic, and specifically linguistic, in nature" (p. 30). Thus White's answer to the problem posed by the existence of a plurality of forms in the work of an individual historian is that a given plurality is only apparent; in reality, form constitutes unity. The unified and unifying nature of form is evident not just in White's treatment of individual artist-historians, however, but in his treatment of form in relation to history in general, and this is why White's tropology is only apparently plural. Underlying its fourfold categorizations is an opposition between figurative and literal language, and any distinctions between the various forms are ultimately of secondary importance next to this master opposition between language that is essentially formal in nature and language that is essentially referential and, as a result, cannot be subjected to formal analysis. *Metahistory* would exempt from formal analysis nothing but its own language and the reasons for choosing one form over another. In White's view the existence of a specific form represents the "free choice" of the artist-historian—that is to say, it is always an arbitrary act that escapes formal analysis. This "free choice," however, is what guarantees the integrity of form, and it too is situated in "reality" itself, outside of tropology.

Formalists frequently claim to be able to capture a timeless essence of the object of formal study, and this claim is consistent with the view that formal variety is subordinate to the unity of form in general, even if both the plurality of form and the notion of its historicity argue at least to some extent against its overriding unity. White too makes such a claim, when he states that his aim is "to establish the uniquely *poetic* elements in historiography and philosophy of history in whatever age they are practiced" (p. x). Following Northrop Frye, White considers the tropes to be "archetypal." For him, their scientific value in classifying historical writing lies in their transhistorical (and nonideological) nature. He thus raises the important question of the significance of form in history, but in doing so presumes that the history of form itself is ultimately insignificant and that formal systems are by their nature free of contradiction.

In contrast to White and other formalists such as Frye, Gérard Genette has argued that formal categories, and specifically the genres, *do* have a history—one characterized not by uniformity and harmony, but by suppression, betrayal, and mystification. His point of departure is a critique of precisely those literary theorists such as Frye whose systems White takes as his models. Genette's attentiveness to the historicity of form in his *L'Architexte* makes that work in particular extremely important for any attempt to understand how the problem of form might be related to the philosophy of history and to history writing without obfuscating the historicity of form itself.[9] Ultimately, however, Genette's attentiveness to the historicity of form represents an attempt to rescue formalism from its own historical contradictions, and in this sense, his formalism is as traditional, as metahistorical, and as determined to defend the unity of form as the formalisms it criticizes.

L'Architexte presents a brief history of formal systems of classification from Plato and Aristotle to the moderns, a history in which Genette's own formalism is implicated in a complex way. The two features central to White's tropology—a hierarchy among the tropes (and among their corresponding genres) and a theory of language based on a distinction between the figurative and the literal—both play a major role in the poetic tradition as interpreted by Genette. His analysis shows that despite what he considers to be a highly significant break, coinciding with the genre theory of the Romantics, the history of poetics from the ancients to the moderns consistently orders the formal diversity represented by the different modes and different genres into a hierarchy of some kind. Thus Plato, Aristotle, the classical aestheticians, the Romantics, and modern literary critics all privilege *different* genres or modes, but all of their systems of classification do privilege some genre or mode over the others—and even Genette himself tentatively gives lyric preeminence as the most quintessentially literary of all the genres. In the history of formal systems of classification none seems to be without hierarchy, and yet the very fact that the content of that hierarchy has so often shifted in the history of literary theory indicates that hierarchy is not "natural" or "self-evident" in any formalism. Indeed,

---

[9] *Introduction à l'architexte* (Paris: Editons du Seuil, 1979), was originally published under the title "Genres, 'types,' modes," in *Poétique* (November 1977).

though no formalism exists without hierarchy, no hierarchy can be accounted for in purely formal terms. It always refers back to assumptions that permit the formal system to function but that are not themselves formal. These assumptions may be about language as Genette argues is the case with the ancients, or they may be about the existence of archetypal, psychological attitudes as he argues is the case for the moderns. Thus no formalism is ever innocent or purely descriptive of form; all formalisms are caught in a contradiction between their formal "object" and the extraformal criteria that permit the hierarchization and differentiation of forms.

The second feature prominent in White's formalism—a distinction between figurative and poetic language on the one hand and scientific and literal language on the other—is also evident in Genette's analysis, for it provides the larger framework in which the poetic tradition is considered in *L'Architexte*. While Genette shows that poetics from Plato to the Romantics is consistently hierarchical, he considers it even more significant that there are two distinct "periods" in the history of genre theory—the ancient and the modern. The former extends from Plato and Aristotle to the eighteenth century. The latter is inaugurated by the Romantics. Genette's aim in *L'Architexte* is polemical with respect to both. Initially, he states that he seeks to demystify the poetic tradition that holds that the tripartition of the genres (epic, tragic, lyric) originates with the ancients. He argues that the major "formal" categories of the ancients were in fact not generic, but modal—that is, they were based on the *mode of enunciation* of a given text. The moderns, according to Genette, have sought to "naturalize" the genres, but in fact, they are not a priori categories—rather they either involve thematic specification or are arrived at inductively. The modal categories of the ancients, on the other hand, "legitimately" enjoy the privilege of being considered natural in that they are categories not of literature but of language.[10]

[10] "Thus one sees here the theoretical disadvantage of a fallacious attribu-

The result of Genette's double-edged polemical stance is to leave the formalist caught between two equally unsatisfactory ways of grounding his method. The modes provide him with "natural forms" (p. 69) in the sense that they are derived from linguistics. But, for that very reason, they are neither immanent nor "properly literary." The genres, on the other hand, "are properly literary categories" (p. 68), but they are not strictly *formal* categories, in that their definition "inevitably includes a thematic element, no matter how vague it might be" (p. 66). Thus there is no properly literary form in Genette's ironic formalism, for the genre, which is properly literary, is thematic, and the mode, which is properly formal, is linguistic.[11] This point does not get the emphasis it deserves from Genette, who persists in his formalist project even after he has undercut the assumptions that would make it realizable. Modern formalists have consistently maintained that a formal definition is the only one immanent in literature, the only one to examine literature "on its own terms," and thus to guarantee the integrity of literature as a discipline.[12] Genette's demystifica-

---

tion [of genre theory to the ancients] . . . : this attribution projects the privilege of naturalness that belonged *legitimately* . . . to the three modes . . . onto the triad of genres" (*L'Architexte*, p. 74).

[11] Nor is White's formalism purely literary. He too gives it a linguistic basis: "In addition, I maintain, they [histories] contain a deep structural content which is generally poetic, and specifically *linguistic*, in nature" (*Metahistory*, p. ix).

[12] In their *Theory of Literature* (New York: Harcourt, Brace and World, 1956), René Wellek and Austin Warren defend what they call "the intrinsic study of literature" (this is the title of part 4 of their work) and argue that genre theory is central to this intrinsic study, inasmuch as "the center of literary art is obviously to be found in the traditional genres of the lyric, the epic, and the drama" (p. 25). Genre, they go on to argue, is primarily a formal category: "In general, our conception of genre should lean to the formalistic side" (p. 233). In the *Anatomy of Criticism* (Princeton, N.J.: Princeton University Press, 1957), Northrop Frye writes of an undertow that carries the student of literature away from it and into philosophy or history, or both (p. 12). The stated goal of Frye's *Anatomy* is to stem this undertow by establishing literary criticism as "the systematic study of the formal causes of art" (p. 29) based on three systems of formal classification: modal, symbolic, and generic.

tion of genre theory, his thesis that genre is ultimately a historical rather than a natural concept, leads to the conclusion that *form itself is extraliterary.*

Ultimately, however, even Genette's ironic formalism is faithful to the basic tenets of formalism. For Genette's irony is a function of the distinction he makes between modes and genres, and that distinction is ultimately rooted in the fundamental, traditional distinction between the properly literary (the figurative) and the properly linguistic (the literal): " 'properly literary' here signifies . . . proper to the aesthetic level of literature that it shares with the other arts, as opposed to its linguistic level that it shares with other types of discourse" (p. 68). This basic opposition determines the outlines of Genette's analysis of the history of poetics, and it is in terms of it that he makes his own "modernist" critique of ancient poetics for its prejudice in favor of mimetic literature. For if Genette insists that the genres as such are not present in classical poetics, he is equally insistent that the literary as such is virtually unknown to the ancients, inasmuch as they confounded the literary and the mimetic.

In Genette's interpretation, the mimetic view of literature leads to a poetics that suppresses all of the forms connected with lyric poetry (the dithyramb and pure narrativity) and ultimately to the suppression of lyric itself within ancient poetics. The lyric is nonrepresentational in Genette's view, and as such it is not, at least not immediately, contaminated by the anthropological and thematic specification that contaminates the formality of the other genres or modes. In this crucial sense, the lyric is quintessentially literary;[13] it stands at the opposite pole from the quintessentially linguistic, the "natural languages" from which the modes derive. In his statements on

[13] "To the extent that all distinctions between genres, or even between poetry and prose, have not yet been effaced, our implicit concept of poetry merges entirely . . . with the ancient concept of lyric poetry. To put it another way: for more than a century, we have considered as 'more eminently and peculiarly poetry' . . . precisely the type of poetry that Aristotle excluded from his *Poetics*" (*L'Architexte*, p. 64).

the lyric, Genette comes close to reversing the hierarchy of the ancients and replacing it with a modern hierarchy in which the lyric would be privileged. But he stops short because, as he puts it "an absolute reversal is perhaps not the sign of a true emancipation" (p. 65). Indeed, such a reversal could not lead to an emancipation from mimetic theory, for the distinction between the literary and the linguistic, which is the key element of Genette's valorization of the lyric as well as of his analysis of the distinctions between genres and modes, is profoundly linked to the concept of mimesis. It is only once a literal or natural language that mimetically reproduces the real has been constructed and defined that the figural or literary can be determined. If Genette refrains from reversing the hierarchy between lyric and the other genres and if he hesitates to choose between a "purely literary" and a "purely linguistic" system of analysis, he nevertheless clearly shows that all formalisms imply a hierarchy between the two sets of concepts. In Genette's history of genre theory, as in White's *Metahistory*, the hierarchy of forms (or of genres) *is also* a hierarchy of literal and figurative language.

How is it, then, that some form of hierarchy, although never analyzed or theorized by the various formalisms, is so persistent within the history of formalism? If, as White argues, there is no reason for preferring one trope to another, or if, as Genette argues, there are no formal reasons for valorizing lyric poetry over epic or vice versa, then how are such hierarchies introduced into formalism, even into the ironic formalisms of Genette and White? Many modern formalist critics have noted that formal systems are indeed based on hierarchies and have presented theories of the origins of such hierarchies, theories designed to rescue their own formalism from the "impurity" that they feel hierarchy introduces into it. In his *Anatomy of Criticism*, Northrop Frye states that formal hierarchies—what he calls literary value judgments—are in reality "projections of social ones. . . . Rhetorical value judgments usually turn on questions of decorum, and the central conception of decorum is the difference between high, middle, and low styles. These styles are structured by the class structure of society" (p. 22). Just as Frye rejects mimetic and historical views of art, so he rejects a rhetoric whose conventions are social in origin. Oddly enough, however, Frye adopts a modal system that differs insignificantly from those he is criticizing in the passage just quoted. Frye's authority for his own system is Aristotle, but he offers no arguments as to why a hierarchy that he considers elsewhere to be a naive reflection of social values has, in Aristotle, a purely "figurative" (i.e., neither moral nor political) sense.[14]

Genette's reading of the history of genre theory also traces the hierarchy of generes back to Aristotle, but, unlike Frye, Genette sees Aristotle's own generic hierarchy as a reflection of moral and political ones. However, Genette is like Frye in that his reading of Aristotle assumes that it is nonetheless possible to keep the social and political meanings of hierarchy distinct from their "properly poetic" meaning, and this despite the fact that his own definition of genre will ultimately reveal that there is no such thing as "properly literary" or "properly poetic" meaning.

Genette summarizes Aristotle's justification of the hierarchy among genres by referring them to a hierarchy among men and comments in a note that these categories of superiority and inferiority are clearly of a moral or, more properly, social nature. He takes the position that this hierarchy constitutes another side of the *Poetics*, that it is distinct from the formal side that interests him and thus lies beyond the scope of his investigation. And yet the question of the political and social side of the *Poetics* comes back to haunt Genette when he writes of Aristotle's "failure" to differentiate between a formal and a thematic sense of the term "tragic." There are, in Genette's view, two distinct senses attached to this term in the *Poetics*, but unfortunately, according to Genette, Aristotle does not always take pains to make this clear:

[14] Frye, *Anatomy of Criticism*, p. 33.

Thus the tragic could exist outside of tragedy. . . . In fact, of course, what we have here are two distinct realities; one generic, . . . which is the noble or serious drama. . . . The other is purely thematic and of an anthropological rather than poetical order: it is the *tragic*, that is to say, the sense of the irony of destiny or of the cruelty of the gods. . . . From all evidence, Aristotle successively adopts now one sense now the other without concerning himself very much with their difference, and without suspecting, I hope, the theoretical imbroglio his insouciance would create several centuries later for a few poeticians caught in the web of this confusion.[15]

Genette's own logic here is extremely contradictory, but the contradiction is projected onto Aristotle rather than being acknowledged by Genette as his own. First, Genette decides not to consider what he calls the moral and social (or political) side of the *Poetics* or what, in the passage just quoted, he calls the thematic or anthropological order. Having himself excluded these spheres from his consideration of form, he then charges Aristotle with insouciance for having "extended" his definition of tragedy beyond the proper (that is, Genette's own) limits of a formal and generic definition. But, even more significant and ironic, Genette's own conclusion on the question of the various genres reveals that they *always* involve a thematic element: "their definitional criteria *always* comport, as we have seen, a thematic element that escapes a purely formal or linguistic description" (p. 69). Genette's essay, which sets out to show the way in which the moderns have distorted the ancients in order to provide the tripartition of genres with a legitimacy and a universality that it does not in fact possess, in the end itself constitutes a mystification of the ancients. The thematic and anthropological specification characteristic for

[15] "Genres, 'types,' modes," pp. 397-398. Genette slightly alters the wording of this passage in *L'Architexte* (pp. 24-25), striking out "generic" the first time it appears in the paragraph, but retaining it further on.

Genette of *modern* generic categories is already present in Aristotle's *Poetics*, as Genette reveals in spite of himself.

In Genette's analysis of the Aristotelian conception of tragedy, it becomes evident that his own attentiveness to the "historicity" of formal categories is seriously limited. If he insists on the historicity of the genres, it is in order to preserve language as a natural entity and linguistics (and a formalism rooted in linguistics) as a transhistorical and scientific discipline. Despite this position, however, Genette's reading of Aristotle reveals that there is no purely formal definition of form, inasmuch as the "purely linguistic" modal categories of Aristotle are *already* thematic, historical, and political as well. This historicity of form—even of a form rooted in language—indicates that form is always in some sense extraformal; it is always defined by rhetoric, by linguistics, and by philosophy, and implicated in politics and history. The distinction between form and its "others" is, like all distinctions within formalism, never neutral. It is inextricably linked to historical, philosophical, and political hierarchies which are themselves repeated "within" the formal system as hierarchies among genres, tropes, and so on. Formalism needs to define a sphere in which language functions as a passive reflection of reality in order to define by opposition its own distinctive domain— that governed by a rhetoric considered to be in some sense immanent in "poetic language." Formalisms thus do not exclude the possibility of mimetic theories of art; in fact, the two imply each other. Debates between formalists and thematic or "realist" critics are at bottom debates about the territorial rights of each approach within a general system of mimesis and hierarchy.

The attempt by formalists such as Frye and Genette to purify formalism of hierarchy by showing that it is derived from extrapoetic, extraformal spheres reveals instead that form is itself in some sense extraformal. From this it also follows that the hierarchy of forms and the ultimate hierarchy between literal and figurative language from which the former hierarchy derives are not themselves derived simply from political and social hierarchies. For if form is at once philosophical, political, and historical as well as formal, then the philosophical, the political, and the historical can themselves be considered to be "contaminated" by questions of form. Indeed, formalism has two forms: one, banal, which denies the political and historical nature of art or language, and a second, normally unrecognized, which denies the formal characteristics of the political and historical spheres. Taken together, the hierarchy of forms and the hierarchy between literal and figurative language constitute a point around which all systems of formal classification are organized, but those systems are rarely if ever explicitly theorized or defended in terms of such hierarchies. Indeed, they cannot be until an analysis is made of the formal processes of those domains that up until now have been considered to lie beyond the reach of formalism. But this "extension" of formalism to the "extra formal" sphere must inevitably "corrupt" the concept of a pure form and underscore the contradictory historicity and plurality of such a concept.

FROM a formalist perspective all texts, no matter how much they might ignore or even deny their formal nature, are subject on their most fundamental level to formalist analysis. That certain types of texts such as the realist novel and most history and philosophy seem unconcerned with the problem of form only makes them all the more suitable for formalist analysis, for the formalist can show that what is proposed as a reflection of the real is really a certain formal construction producing an "effect of reality," or that what distinguishes the work of one historian from another is not just a different view of history but, more important, a different way of *writing* it. But it is not always true that historians, in their pursuit of the "real," necessarily ignore questions of form. In fact to an important extent, that pursuit, even in some of the most traditional historians, is explicitly formal. Even a militant rationalist such as Voltaire grappled openly with the problem of form as an important component of his attempt to establish a rational historiography. It could even be said that his entire project rests as much on his ability to establish precise formal, generic distinctions between rational historiography and other "less elevated" forms of discourse as it does on his success in distinguishing between reason and unreason.

Indeed, Voltaire, like White and Genette, must discover a basis for the distinctions between genres. For Voltaire, this means distinguishing between the "highest" genre, history, and the "lesser" genres, epic and satire. And though one could say that it is Voltaire's intention that these distinctions ultimately derive their validity from an extraformal, rationally ordered reality, it is also apparent that for Voltaire, if form is to be truly rational, then the distinctions between the genres must be immanent and the form of history rational "in itself," as rational as the reality it is supposed to reflect. Voltaire's rationalism thus places him in the same position with respect to form as with respect to history—the rational must *also* be historical if it is to be truly rational, and yet rationality must at the same time struggle against the irrational in history to preserve itself as reason. Just as the rationalist philosopher is constantly confronted with the problem of unreason in history, so the rationalist historian is constantly confronted with the problem of the plurality of the forms of history, of how to distinguish the form of rational history from all others. The distinction between (rational) history and the other forms of discourse does not just have to do with the content of history, then, but also with its form.

Despite his rationalism, or perhaps because of it, Voltaire confronts the same problem as Genette and White, the problem of formal distinctions (no matter what their basis), and what many of his texts narrate, and none more forcefully than the *Histoire de Charles XII*, is the struggle and, as we shall see, the ultimate failure to establish such distinctions on purely formal grounds.[16] Voltaire's failure to establish a (rational)

---

[16] Voltaire, *Oeuvres historiques*, edited by René Pomeau (Paris: Editions Gallimard, 1957), p. 55. All references to the *Histoire de Charles XII* are from this edition and will be given hereafter in parentheses in the text.

formal hierarchy or, even more fundamentally, (rational) generic distinctions will force him outside the formal sphere, where he will continually attempt to fall back on an extraformal historical sphere within which reason can in principle be more easily defended. But because Voltaire has implicitly acknowledged that form is as intrinsic to reason as history is, no "return" or retreat to an extraformal sphere can extricate him from the impasse created by his failure to establish rational generic distinctions in themselves. Indeed, as we shall see, the "reality" to which Voltaire seeks to return in the *Histoire de Charles XII* is itself in many respects "formal," that is, contaminated by questions of form and genre, questions that have become conditions of experience and reality themselves. This contamination of reality by questions of form and genre is complex and much more fundamental and radical than the very controlled relationship between the represented and representing elements prescribed by a classical, mimetic theory of art or history. In fact, this radical contamination represents the greatest possible threat to such a theory. But it also represents the ultimate threat to formalism by showing that the formal is always "beside itself," that is, always radically and fundamentally implicated in the so-called extraformal spheres.

In the *Historie de Charles XII*, Voltaire's attempt to establish formal criteria that would fix the relationship of history to the other genres hinges from the outset on the relationship between the two principals of the history—Charles XII and Peter the Great. Voltaire claims that both Charles and his rival are objectively great men and thus both are in principle proper objects for history, but still it is clear that in Voltaire's view the two rulers are not themselves equally historical. The conqueror (here Charles XII) by definition remains outside of history conceived of as a process of transformation, accumulation, and progress. This is made explicit in "L'Homme aux quarante écus," in a conversation between the central figure of that tale and a group of his friends who marvel that the public is more interested in the adventures of the conqueror than in the feats of the nation builder and who label Charles

XII the "Don Quixote of the North."[17] The conqueror is thus outside of history in the way that fiction is outside of history: both may capture the imagination but neither is completely rational and progressive. Like Don Quixote, Charles lives by a heroic code that perhaps corresponded at one time to a historical world but that has become anachronistic in the world into which he is born, an empty form deprived of whatever content or meaning it might once have had. In contrast to Peter, Charles believes in the decisive nature of the actions of the individual hero-king—in this case, of his own actions. His belief reflects what for Voltaire is Charles's essentially fictive, even fabulous nature, and it also reflects an interpretation of history that makes it into a form of literature. Voltaire shows us that Charles interprets history in terms of the heroes of antiquity after whom he has modeled himself, and thus his interest in history is confined to Caesar's *Commentaries* and the *History of Alexander*. For Charles, then, history has become an epic, dominated by the actions of the epic figures he takes as models. Voltaire indicates that Charles's interpretation of modern European history is equally superficial and equally a function of his own mystified view of himself: he has an aversion to the rational monarch Louis XIV and a religious respect for his grandparent Gustavus Adolphus, which is based on the latter's military prowess. Charles's tendency to privilege the great men of history as individuals contrasts clearly with Voltaire's own view of what history is, as well as with his view of individual greatness. Peter's individual accomplishments are indistinguishable from the transformation he brings about in Russia. Charles's accomplishments are personal. As Lionel Gossman remarks, he, unlike Peter, could have been king of any country; it would not have substantially altered history.[18]

The question of form (of generic specificity) in rational history is thus thematized by the figure of Charles XII. He personifies the view that history is essentially epic in nature and

---

[17] *Romans et contes*, p. 342.
[18] "Voltaire's *Charles XII*: History into art," p. 692.

that the criterion of historical importance is essentially aesthetic; in other words, he confuses genres. Voltaire, the rational historian, does not attempt to defeat Charles XII and the view of history he represents, however, by simply subjugating him to different extraformal criteria. Like Peter, Voltaire adopts the strategies of his opponent; he does battle with Charles on Charles's own, epic terrain in the hope of gradually luring Charles onto the terrain of rational historiography, where he can be defeated.

Voltaire's first tactic is thus to accentuate and heighten the effects that give Charles an epic quality not only in his own eyes but in those of any student of history. Voltaire stresses Charles's view that his life has already been predetermined by a special, heroic destiny, even though Voltaire considers such a view to be the sign of a false historical consciousness, of an inherently aesthetic conception of the historical process. In the same vein, Voltaire emphasizes Charles's iron discipline, his refusal to alter his routines even in circumstances in which they seem totally inappropriate, characteristics that affirm not only his indomitable will but also his fatalistic view of life and his corresponding belief in his own heroic destiny. Voltaire then validates that fatalism by narrating Charles's several brushes with death, in which those fighting alongside Charles are killed while he survives without a scratch, and, most of all, the incident in which he deliberately places himself in view of a cannon to protect the life of a colonel whose brightly colored uniform seems bound to attract a shot, only to have the man with whom he has just changed places be mortally hit (p. 85). Charles's belief in his own special destiny, a belief that Voltaire seems to corroborate to an important extent, underscores his affinity not only with the quasi-mythic heroes of antiquity, but also with the heroes of tragedy. Voltaire relates that during his captivity, he is read the tragedies of Pierre Corneille and of Racine, and points out that his favorite tragedy is *Mithridate*, "because the situation of this king, defeated and full of projects of vengeance, was analogous to his" (p. 175).

Charles, then, is a hero of literature turned loose in a historical world, and the critical task of the historian is to present Charles in such a way that the distinction between Charles's own essentially aestheticist apprehension of himself and the historian's apprehension of him, though initially blurred, emerges clearly in the end. Voltaire has two tools for making this distinction and thus ending the confusion of genres. The first is a formal device: satire. Time and again Charles is brought low by a Voltaire who reveals that Charles XII is not the hero he imagines, but rather a mock-hero, a Don Quixote. Voltaire takes pains to point out that the life of Charles cannot ultimately even be conceived as epic, and to indicate to the reader that if the historian has underscored the uncanny aspects of Charles's story and reinforced the reader's initial impression that Charles is indeed an epic (or tragic) hero ruled by a special destiny, it has only been to highlight better, through contrast, the fundamental vulgarity revealed by Charles's anticlimactic death. Charles's epic status is further undercut by the contrast between the epic battles he fights up to his defeat at Pultava and the mock epic battle of Bender. Indeed, it is in the Bender episode that Voltaire is most explicit in suggesting that irony and satire represent as great a menace to Charles XII as Peter the Great does. For though his courtiers console Charles by reading him tragedies, "when they read him the line of the eighth satire" of Despréaux, "in which the author treats Alexander as crazy and senseless, he tore up the page" (p. 175). What is more unbearable to Charles than even his defeat at the hands of Peter is the idea that that defeat is a chapter, not in an epic or tragedy, but in a vulgar satire.

The contrast between epic and satire is essential to Voltaire's historical program, for it is through satire that Voltaire discredits epic and any pretension it might have to be the truly historical genre. But the purely formal nature of satire is a problem; it is a literary form that can point up the emptiness of epic, but it remains itself formal in a purely negative sense, that is, without formal specificity. Satire is parasitical; it lives off the other genres, turning them inside out, leaving them without secure boundaries. Indeed, the victory of reason (and

thus history) over Charles XII is jeopardized by the nature of
the weapon Voltaire has used to achieve it. That victory could
just as well be seen as an assertion of the no longer epic, but
now satirical nature of history, thus blurring the boundaries
of history once again and even more seriously.

Voltaire clearly intends that Peter the Great should be the
ultimate victor in the battle between Charles the hero and
Charles the fool, between epic and satire. He is Voltaire's second weapon in distinguishing "true history" and its form from
epic or even from satire, because in Voltaire's view Peter's
greatness and rationality elevate him above both the vulgar
(satire) and the heroic (epic) prince. Peter understands and
capitalizes on the sources of economic and political strength
he has inherited, whereas such concerns do not even exist for
the epic hero Charles. For Peter, political and military action
is in principle a school in which to learn rather than a stage
upon which to perform brilliantly, and it is his ability to learn,
to progress, that ultimately brings him victory over Charles.
Charles's losses, though they are few, do irreparable damage
to his epic stature. But Peter's losses do not detract from his
historical importance, which is not based on a heroic invinci-
bility, but rather on an ability to survive defeat, to learn from
the very military disasters in which Charles has made him appear the most ridiculous. It is thus Peter's story that reestab-
lishes the distinctions between the different genres, because it,
much more effectively than the story of Charles's epic adventures, can resist the power of satire to recast all history in its
own ironic mode. It is the story of Peter's patient, shrewd
progress toward his triumph over Charles that constitutes true
history for Voltaire.

But while in many ways it is clear that for Voltaire Peter is
the actual hero of the *Histoire de Charles XII* and that the
historical genre has thus triumphed over other genres, Charles
is never completely overshadowed by his rival. The triumph
of history and the differentiation of history from the other
genres is not decisive. There are two related senses in which
the issue between Peter and Charles is left in doubt. At a

dinner held for the captured Swedish generals after the battle, Peter proposes a toast "to his masters," the Swedes themselves. Just how much Peter is indebted to his enemy for his victory becomes even more evident in the triumphal procession he stages in Moscow. His years of struggle have taught him not only how to beat Charles in battle, but also the importance of "staging" his victories, of creating a spectacle in which he himself and his policies appear in the most heroic light. The procession crowning Peter's victory is but one of the spectacles he gives as ruler. As Lionel Gossman has argued, all of Peter's policies and his transformations of Russia have this spectacular quality: they all deal with the visible aspects of life in Russia, from the cutting of beards to the creation of St. Petersburg, the showplace of the civilization he has brought to Russia.[19] Like Charles, Peter the Great acts as though history were a stage, and, like Charles, Peter does and must play to an audience composed of both his subjects and the historians who will determine his place in history. In his emphasis on and attention to the theatrical, it is apparent that the actions of Peter too are dictated by the requirements of the epic genre and that he is thus in principle as vulnerable to satire as Charles.

Even after Peter's defeat of Charles at Pultava, the triumph of history is left in doubt. The victor in a battle always has a second, more significant battle to win in Voltaire's view: the battle to determine how the military battle and the events surrounding it will be recounted to present and future generations. If this second battle is lost, the effects of the first battle are nullified. It is for precisely this reason, for example, that Voltaire views the barbarian invaders of the Roman Empire and the Moguls who conquered China in the Middle Ages as "losers." Peter the Great is already engaged in the preliminary skirmishes of this second battle when he stages his triumphal procession in Moscow. But he cannot win it, in Voltaire's view, without the cooperation of the historian, and the his-

[19] "Voltaire's *Charles XII*," pp. 704-705.

torian himself cannot win it for Peter without emphasizing the epic and satirical elements of his composition and neglecting to some extent the "purely historical" elements. As the narrator of "L'Homme aux quarante écus" ruefully remarks, people would rather read "the history of Charles XII, who spent his life destroying, than that of Peter the Great, who spent his creating."[20] From this standpoint, the literary devices Voltaire uses to undercut his hero are dubious weapons. For in educating his public as to the true sense and form of history, he writes an epic or a satire and thus defines only negatively a history that should in principle be a distinct genre. In the process he only reinforces the prestige of Charles and despite his intentions makes Charles as much and perhaps even more of a "historical subject" than Peter. Voltaire writes the *Histoire de l'empire de Russie sous Pierre le Grand*, but he also foresees that it is not this work but rather the *Histoire de Charles XII* that will be read and discussed by present and future generations. Charles XII, the mock-epic hero, will "live on" in history thanks to Voltaire's portrait of him; his Peter the Great, the "truly historical" subject, will be forgotten. Paradoxically, then, Voltaire has been able to defend the formal integrity of history only by blurring the distinctions between it and the "lesser" genres.

VOLTAIRE'S explicit concept of form is, of course, classical and mimetic. For him, form exists to serve the ideals of his philosophy of history. Form, however, is a dangerous tool that always threatens to be unfaithful to the intentions with which it is employed and, ultimately, to undermine the rationality that is for Voltaire its proper end. As a result, Voltaire constantly defines form in terms of a hierarchy, for the function of the hierarchy is to master the formal element itself. The historical genre supposedly dominates the hierarchy, but it cannot do without the other, "lesser" genres, without epic and even satire, the "lowest" of genres. Voltaire's *contes* or tales,

[20] *Romans et contes*, p. 342.

and *Zadig* in particular, are like the *Histoire de Charles XII* in that they play an important role in establishing the hierarchical relationship between history and the other genres. As the "least elevated" genre, the tale has the function of contributing to the negative definition of a (nonfigurative) history by stating in an indirect, figurative way and in inappropriate, trivial, or even burlesque language issues that are weighty and serious and that history, if it could be totally separated from the other genres, would state truthfully and directly. The tale constantly calls attention to its own "impropriety" and to the "trivial" nature of its own form. But though the definition of the tale as a lesser genre, like the definition of genre and of form in general, remains the prerogative of the philosophy of history and reason, the tale poses a threat to both. The impropriety of the tale must always be controlled, so that it does not in the end obscure or even obliterate the "proper history" whose definition is its ultimate task.

In the "Dedicatory Epistle" of *Zadig*, Voltaire identifies both the proper end of the tale and the risk it faces in its journey toward its destination. *Zadig* purports to be written by a sage, and in the dedicatory epistle a second sage cites the wisdom of the supposed author as evidence in support of the rational and educational value of the tale. But *Zadig* must compete for the reader's attention with other representatives of the same genre that do not represent the same value. The fictive author of the epistle in question contrasts *Zadig* with *A Thousand and One Nights* and declares that in this form, the tale is a menace to reason and historical truth. Unlike *Zadig*, it represents the inherent triviality and insignificance of the tale form. It is, writes the sage, "without reason and [it] signifies nothing" (*Romans et contest*, p. 2). Inherently, then, the tale is so frivolous and insignificant that it must overcome what Voltaire sees as the limitations of its own genre in order to serve his historical project.

Just as the question of form or genre in the *Histoire de Charles XII* is a problem both for the historian and for the political "men of action" whose careers Voltaire narrates, so the form of the tale is a political and historical question as well as a formal and aesthetic one. The philosopher who writes the tale must "find" an audience; and, indeed, as the dedicatory epistle makes clear, the audience for which it is ultimately destined is a key element in the tale's own definition of itself. According to the epistle, the two different types of tale imply the existence of two different sorts of audiences, one composed of a group of women (the harem wives of Ouloug-beb) whose frivolity and superficiality are apparent in the preference they give to *A Thousand and One Nights* over *Zadig*, the other, of those who resemble the sultaness Sheraa to whom *Zadig* is fictively dedicated and who accept the rational values represented in Voltaire's portrait of her. In discriminating between its own inherently frivolous nature and the worthiness of the rational and philosophical goals of its fictive author, the tale at the same time discriminates between the two audiences. The trivial nature of the tale corresponds to the marginal nature (marginal with respect to Voltaire's ideal of rationality) of a whole segment of society preoccupied with what Voltaire views as trivial matters: fashion, polite conversation, and a literature devoid of reason and truth. The correspondence the dedicatory epistle establishes between the frivolous form of the tale and the superficiality of this segment of society indicates that the aim of orienting the tale toward rational ends coincides with a political program: to imbue the tale's audience with "progressive" values and to isolate the frivolous segment of that same audience and show that it, like the tale, is marginal with respect to rational history. Reason dictates that language ought not to mislead, nor exaggerate, nor trivialize, that figure be subservient to sense, just as it dictates that particular, idiosyncratic, or extravagant historical forces be harnessed in the service of the rational goals of progress and enlightenment. Reason is thus the nonfigurative end of all figurative language; in other words, its transcendence.

The same program that assigns a proper sense to the figural tale assigns women their place and function. It is important to note that femininity is not an empirical (and thus not a purely thematic) concept for Voltaire. It is a group of harem wives who prefer *A Thousand and One Nights* to *Zadig*, but they stand for a whole group of readers who might have the same preference. By the same token, *Zadig* is dedicated to a princess who can "reason better than old dervishes with long beards and pointed caps," so that the frivolity and superficiality of the harem wives here characterize the dervishes, and the philosopher's wisdom, the princess. Because femininity does not correspond to an empirical reality, it is a fundamentally metaphorical or improper concept, and the profound affinity of Voltaire's concept of femininity and his conception of the tale can be traced back to their common "impropriety." Like the tale in relation to historiography, the "woman" represents an element potentially disruptive of the rational order, but also like the tale, femininity has an important, albeit a negative, function in defining reason. When this feminine element is simply repressed, history stagnates, rationality degenerates into lifelessness and rigidity, and progress and reason are both inhibited.[21] Thus just as the tale provides an arena in which the potentially menacing nature of the figural can be dispelled, so it also provides such an arena for the negation and sublation of femininity.

The dedicatory epistle of *Zadig* evokes a second major theme characteristic of the tales as a group, and like the theme of femininity, it determines (overdetermines) the function of the tale, as a satiric genre, with respect to history. That theme is the Orient. Like femininity and the tale itself, the Orient has a dual function. If it is evoked so consistently in all of Voltaire's tales, it is because it occupies a subordinate position in the scheme of Voltaire's philosophy of history. The cultures

[21] Thus Voltaire writes to Sir Falkener in the "Seconde Epître dédicatoire" to *Zaïre*: "Society depends on women. All the peoples who are so unhappy as to sequester them are unsociable," and he goes on to explain that England's civil wars had the effect of inhibiting social intercourse between men and women and thus prevented England from attaining the same degree of civilization as France, which "of all the nations . . . is the one that has most completely experienced social existence."

of the Orient may point the way toward the triumph of rationality, but the march of rational history leaves them behind as it moves toward the West. It must be pointed out that, like femininity, the Orient is not limited to the cultures of what could be called the empirical Orient.[22] Even when the age dominated by India, China, Persia, and Egypt is past, as it clearly is for Voltaire, something that could still be called the Orient persists in occidental culture, and affects it from within. The Orient "repeats" itself throughout history because it is in some sense repressed by history, and it must constantly be repressed because it is constantly being repeated. Voltaire's Occident, like his concept of rational historiography, is an ideal that must be constantly reaffirmed and that Voltaire will never put into question as such. In the case of the Orient too, Voltaire's ideal of rationality and propriety is responsible for the creation of two Orients—one benign, the other pernicious. In seeking to demonstrate the universality of the rational, Voltaire creates a picture of the Orient as a place where a few wise men are misunderstood or even persecuted by an irrational majority. Ironically, this picture resembles point for point his description of European culture. Though the distinction between the Orient of the sage and the irrational Orient is intended to secure the ideal of rationality, it in fact poses a new threat by revealing the Occident to be a repetition of the Orient rather than its ideal other, that is, its negation and transcendence.

Ultimately the Orient, the woman, and the tale share a trait that, because it is common to all three, defines them as a genre. For Voltaire, all three are inherently improper, that is to say they are inherently metaphorical. Just as Voltaire underscores

[22] Indeed, in his *Orientalism* (New York: Random House, 1979), Edward Said argues that there is no such thing as an empirical Orient: "I have begun with the assumption that the Orient is not an inert fact of nature. It is not merely *there*, just as the Occident itself is not *there* either. . . . As both geographical and cultural entities—to say nothing of historical entities—such locales, regions, geographical sectors as 'Orient' and 'Occident' are man-made" (pp. 4-5).

the metaphorical nature of femininity by portraying women as avid readers of tales that signify nothing, so he underscores the metaphorical character of the Orient each time he discusses oriental language. The opening lines of the dedicatory epistle to *Zadig* and, in a sense, of the whole cycle of tales sum up through caricature what is for Voltaire the essence of the Orient: "Charm of the eye's pupil, torment of hearts, light of the spirit, I do not kiss the dust of your feet because you do not walk, or rather, because you walk on Iranian carpets or on roses." "Oriental language" is presented as being *essentially* figural, and in Voltaire's terms, this means it is an irrational nonlanguage. In the Orient, according to Voltaire, reason does not dominate metaphor and ensure its ultimate propriety. The figure, deprived of sense, is simply grotesque and ridiculous in his view, as myriad allusions to oriental literature in general and to the Bible in particular indicate. The predominance of the Orient and of femininity in the tales, then, underscores their status as figurative and irrational fictions. At the same time, their function is also to call attention to the role of the figural in rational history and to be a step toward the achievement of the ultimate formalist and rationalist goal of history, the transcendence of figure and form.

It could be argued that *Zadig* is intended to illustrate the subordination of form to reason through an analysis of the concept of *destiny*, and just as Voltaire's philosophy of history strives to subordinate form to rational ends, so, in *Zadig*, that same philosophy strives to distinguish itself from a heroic or epic conception of destiny which, as we have seen in Voltaire's satire of Charles XII, is associated with an imaginary view of the place of the subject in the world. The tale attaches more than one sense to the concept of destiny. The first is a false sense which places the individual subject at the center of the historical world, much as Charles's epic conception of himself places him at the center of all events. Though clearly the object of criticism, this false sense of destiny still represents an attempt to impose an order on events and phenomena and thus constitutes a twisted form of history, a misguided phi-

losophy of history. The second sense of destiny is defined negatively with respect to the first. It is an ironic destiny which
constantly undercuts the heroic-epic illusions of the subject
and his relation to the world. Destiny in this second, satirical
guise represents the argument that historical necessity rigorously conceived leads to the conclusion that "great" events
frequently prove to have "trivial" causes. Like the conflict between Charles's epic and vulgar natures, the function of the
antagonism between these two senses of destiny is to unveil a
third, properly historical and rational sense.

Zadig can easily be interpreted as constituting an *Essai sur
les moeurs* in miniature, burlesque form, for Zadig's exile from
Babylon at the end of the chapter entitled "Jealousy" is an
exile into history. His wanderings bring him into direct contact with many cultures of the ancient world and with representatives of those he himself does not visit. As a stranger,
Zadig's position remains marginal with respect to all of these
cultures, but what is equally responsible for his alienation is
his inherent rationality. Indeed, as a rational man, Zadig is
fundamentally an outsider even in his native city of Babylon.
The path he takes, then, is that of history and rationality, and
the cultures he visits only become historical because Zadig
touches them in his travels.

What is particularly significant about the lack of rationality
and the ahistorical nature of the cultures touched upon by
Zadig, however, is that their ahistorical character is itself
grounded in what for Zadig is a parody of historical consciousness. Slavish respect for religious and social custom is
the particular subject of two episodes, one in which Zadig
saves a young widow from having to throw herself on her late
husband's funeral pyre and another in which representatives
of all the "great" civilizations of ancient history dine together.
In both cases, customs that appear arbitrary and senseless to
an outsider are justified by the claim that they are ancient or
even that they have existed since the beginning of history. As
Zadig's friend Setoc sarcastically comments: "For more than
a thousand years women have had the right to burn them-

selves. Who among us dares change a law that time has sanc-
tified? Is there anything more respectable than an ancient
abuse?" (pp. 29-30). In "The Supper" too, the notion that an
ancient custom is by definition legitimate (rather than arbitrary) and that any custom that could be traced to the origin
of history would be absolutely legitimate is the underlying
assumption shared by all the guests as they decry each other's
table manners and argue over which of the civilizations they
represent is the oldest. None of the cultures visited by Zadig
is without historical consciousness, but in all of them, that
consciousness is falsified, perverted by custom and superstition. As a result, what is viewed by the Indian, the Egyptian,
or the Greek as representing the culmination of history is, for
Zadig and Voltaire, only a chapter in the philosophy of history. Just as *Zadig* is a parody of the *Essai sur les moeurs*, so
this ethnocentric historical theory which takes an imaginary
part for the rational whole is a parody of the rational theory
of historical causation and necessity which it is the job of Voltaire's analysis of the concept of destiny to unveil.

Voltaire's ideal of rationality is like the false historical consciousness he criticizes in that it denies the existence of chance.[23]
There is, then, an important affinity between rational history
and the mythic view of history espoused by the cultures of
the ancient world as they are portrayed in *Zadig*, but having
once affirmed this affinity, Voltaire sets about trying to reestablish the distinction between a mythic conception of destiny
and his own, rational conception. Significantly, the weapon
Voltaire uses to criticize this mythical history is once again
satire. The ironic character of Zadig's own history is a continual reminder that it would be folly to conceive of destiny in
the epic or heroic terms of myth. Zadig is about to be impaled
for a heretical opinion concerning griffons, when he is saved
by the good offices of his friend Cador and "a lady-in-waiting

[23] In the article entitled "Destiny" in his *Dictionnaire philosophique*, Voltaire
writes: "Philosophers have never needed either Homer or the Pharisees to be
persuaded that everything happens according to immutable laws, that all is
arranged, that all is a necessary effect."

by whom he [Cador] had had a child, and who had a good deal of pull in the college of the magi" (p. 10). On the point of being executed for having allegedly written a seditious poem against the king, he is saved when the missing half of the tablet on which the poem is written is miraculously picked up by a parrot and carried to the king, so that the true sense of the poem—written in his praise—is restored. As Zadig's speech of thanks to the parrot sarcastically indicates, if his destiny is more than chance, it is still clearly something less than the noble destiny of a mythical hero or people.

Appropriately, as the circle of his story is about to close, that is, as Zadig is returning to Babylon to rule the city in which he was a marginal figure prior to his exile, Voltaire directly confronts the problem of the necessity governing Zadig's story and the historical order. The appearance of the angel Jesrad imposes an order and a sense upon Zadig and Babylon's history. But because the angel is also the instrument of the burning down of a house and of a young man's drowning, the order represented by the angel seems little different from the violent, arbitrary "order" of superstition and custom. In the last instance, one must ask, with Zadig, if the providence embodied by the angel Jesrad is not simply another form of the "false" historical consciousness that accepts things as they are because they were "destined" to be. Providence would be more encompassing than any particular, culturally defined conception of destiny; nonetheless, this ultimate principle of rationality in history would do essentially what "false" historical consciousness does: it would justify and legitimize all forms of abuse and "irrationality" by declaring that there is no chance, and that all that is must be.

If Zadig is destined to rule Babylon, is that destiny any less of an illusion than the "destiny" that, from a narrow, culture-bound perspective, is thought to justify what is for Voltaire prejudice and parochialism? Zadig's right to rule is determined by his performance in two tests that reveal much about the nature of his destiny. The first is a tournament: Babylon's king must be a great warrior. But considered from the point of view of Voltaire's philosophy of history, the tournament represents the rituals of the medieval nobility and as such is a relic—charming and decorative perhaps—of what is for Voltaire the high-water mark of irrationality. Moreover, it is clear that tournaments and their modern (in Voltaire's sense) counterpart, dueling, represent a hopelessly outmoded method of resolving political or even personal issues. Even its value in demonstrating the candidate's skill as a warrior is irrelevant to the question of who will make the best ruler, for Voltaire sees the warrior-king Charles XII as a relic of the past, whereas a modern monarch, such as Louis XIV, has no need to demonstrate such heady courage. Thus from all points of view, the tournament represents a refusal to recognize what for Voltaire are the laws of history—change and progress—and a desire to cling to a conception of history that sees it as encapsulated within ritual and repetition and decisively influenced by the heroic qualities of a few important men. Voltaire's use of the tournament as a testing ground for the future philosopher-king Zadig undercuts the historical and rational nature of the necessity that ultimately brings him to power.

Zadig's second test is to answer a series of riddles. This test, like the first, is highly conventional in nature—though the convention in question is somewhat different from the epic convention of the tournament. Zadig's situation—exiled from the city by a king who is fearful that Zadig is trying to take his place and now returning to that city to be united at last with the king's widow—is in many ways that of Oedipus, and Voltaire's use of riddles to test Zadig's readiness to be king only underscores the resemblance. Tragedy, like epic, corresponds to a certain theory of "historical" necessity, but that necessity is repetitive rather than progressive, "formal" rather than "historical." Like the tournament, the riddle undercuts the rational and historical nature of the process that places Zadig on the throne and endows it instead with a ritualistic and aesthetic character.

The culture-bound individual whose view of himself and his culture places both at the center of the world is like Charles

XII in giving a heroic dignity to what is in fact a marginal and vulgar chapter in the history of the world. But Voltaire's position in pointing out parochialism and vulgarity is like his position when he seeks to bring Charles XII low through his use of satire. He can only undercut this inherently "irrational" view of history by calling attention to its similarity with epic and tragedy, and yet in the process, he also calls attention to the epic (and even satiric) character of the triumph of reason itself. He can only undercut the heroic illusions of the false historical consciousness by making a hero of Zadig or through a satire of the epic and the tragic. In *Zadig*, Voltaire does both.

I have discussed the ways in which the two contests raise Zadig to heroic heights. It is also important to underscore the ways in which they serve, at the same time, to undercut the epic and tragic conventions from which they derive. The key figure in the two contests to decide who will be king of Babylon and ultimately Zadig's most significant rival is the vain, pompous Itobard, not so much because he poses a direct threat to Zadig's eventual triumph, but because his presence undercuts the heroic and tragic effects of the two contests. Because Itobard steals Zadig's armor and the rest of his costume after Zadig has triumphed in the tournament, Zadig is obliged to answer the riddles and, ultimately, to fight a second duel against Itobard in the only clothes left to him—a nightcap and a dressing gown. It is this second duel, fought under these burlesque circumstances and in a totally ridiculous costume, that decides that he will be king. Thanks to the presence of Itobard, then, the contests degenerate into mock heroism and comedy. It is in vanquishing Itobard that Zadig's superiority over even the heroes of tragedy and epic, to whom in many respects he is compared, becomes evident—just as the eventual victor in the struggle between the heroic and mock heroic natures of Charles XII is Peter the Great. Clearly, however admirable the third contestant, Otmane, may be, his courage and valor are impotent against an Itobard; to harm such an incompetent fool would be sheer cruelty.

Itobard, however, is not only a character *in* the tale, he is the character who *is* the tale as it provides the stage for Zadig's triumph. Zadig reigns, but the world in which he has triumphed is the world of Itobard. Reason dominates, but in the vulgar and irrational world of the tale. There is ultimately no form of control sufficient to ensure the definitive triumph of history and reason when, figured or (un)dressed in the dressing gown and nightcap of the tale, they confront the representatives of the "inferior" genres whose garb history and reason have assumed in order to ensure their own ultimate triumph. Though, from the standpoint of the philosophy of history, the tale represents an apparently insignificant genre, one whose triviality appears to promise that nothing can undermine the rationality of the philosopher of history who manipulates it as further confirmation of rationality and as an additional form for the expression of rational truth, the tale in fact represents an ultimate menace. Reason and history are damned if they do not triumph over their puny enemy and damned if they do.

Zadig's triumph could be called the triumph of the forces of reason and history over the irrational, the anachronistic, the antihistorical, but, it represents in addition the triumph of that same reason over the plurality of genres. Indeed, since generic differences are always defined within a hierarchy predetermined by a philosophy of form, Zadig's triumph represents the triumph of formalism over form itself. In this way, the forms in which history presents itself are dominated and controlled. The relation of form to history remains a complex one, however. Inasmuch as form is always determined by (the) philosophy (of history), philosophy cannot fail to triumph over form. But insofar as form, in its plurality, situates the philosophy of history, that same philosophy is always to some extent constituted and defined by form. For this reason, no triumph of reason over form is ever any more definitive than the triumph of the rational in history. The philosophy of history must constantly *repeat* its triumph

Is it possible then for a formal theory to define Voltaire's historiography, to categorize it with respect to other "genres"? Voltaire's own use of different forms and different genres in the elaboration of his philosophy of history is always tactical. History is epic and tragic when compared to the accounts of memorialists, burlesque when compared to tragedy and epic, and at still other times, when its rationality is affirmed, a completely distinct genre, different even from the other "elevated genres." The writer who, like Voltaire, constantly transgresses the law of generic definition within the frame of a single work points up the relative naiveté of attempts to classify a given work in terms of a fixed set of formal categories. Ultimately, however, those transgressions are in their own way affirmations of the distinctions they defy. The triumph of history over epic, tragedy, and satire reveals the participation of these forms in the elaboration of the philosophy of history and reason. Just as form is both the defining and the defined element of Voltaire's philosophy of history, so is its twin, reason, both the defining and the defined element of form.

As a critical investigation of formalists such as White and Genette shows, a philosophy of history that has not yet confronted the formal nature of history and historiography will always be naive and incomplete. But a philosophy of history that has confronted the formal nature of history and historiography will also be naive and incomplete as long as it fails to recognize the extraformal, philosophical, and historical nature of form. A truly critical approach to form in history must, then, confront the contradictory nature of form, and thus it can no longer be either formalist or philosophical in the sense in which those two terms have been understood traditionally or continue to be understood in the formalist systems proposed today that claim to reverse tradition. If, even in the work of a rationalist like Voltaire, reason (philosophy) never triumphs easily and completely over form, it is also clear that formalisms never triumph completely over (situate) philosophy or history in the way they claim to. Voltaire's struggle to transcend form and ensure the triumph of reason thus communicates curiously with White's struggle to transcend history and ensure the triumph of form (tropes). What may be most interesting in both is the "failure" of the two projects and the critical perspective on form, history, and philosophy such "failures" force us to assume.

THREE

(Montesquieu)
The Cultural Boundaries of History:
Lévi-Strauss, Structuralism, and
the Paradoxical Situation
of the Outsider

IN PERIODS of historical crisis when the traditional form of history is challenged, the question of the relationship between history and culture inevitably arises. Historians and philosophers become interested in exploring the limits and boundaries of their fields and are no longer content just to work within those established by tradition, and this leads them to ask if the limits of a given form of history are not those of the culture that produced it. Thus the nineteenth century saw the "rational" historiography of the Enlightenment as the expression of a particular culture and not as the culmination or the last chapter in a universal history embracing and subsuming all cultures. But the Enlightenment itself already coincided with a crisis in historical thinking, and it too confronted this crisis and sought to resolve it through an investigation of the relationship between culture and history. The history it inherited was for the most part dominated by the orthodoxy of the Catholic church and thus by a certain judeo-christian tradition. In challenging that tradition, the Enlightenment looked to other cultures with other traditions and orthodoxies— Chinese, Egyptian, Indian, Persian, Greek, North American Indian—in order to point up the parochiality of previous historical thinkers. This was facilitated by a body of ethnographic literature that had begun as a trickle in the Renaissance but that by the eighteenth century had become a flood, and the works of the major figures of the age reflect both the practical and methodological significance of the expanding ethnographic corpus.

By raising the question of the relationship between culture and history, the *philosophes* created a crisis in historical thinking, but in the view of many of them, that crisis contained the basis of its own resolution. For Voltaire, for example, reason is not the exclusive property of any one culture. In its ultimate form it is the result of a series of confrontations in which what is specific to each culture—superstition, custom, religion, myth, and fable—is discarded, but what is common to culture in general—reason—is retained. Thus Voltaire's philosophy of history has an anthropological dimension: Zadig in particular could be seen as representing the philosopher-historian as anthropologist, and his journey across the ancient world as prompted by the view that history must confront cultural diversity if it is to be something more than the "myth" of a given tribe or people. But one could also argue that the perspective of Zadig as he moves from culture to culture remains that of an "outsider" who looks at all cultures including his own from a "safe," rational distance. Surely it is only from a perspective "outside" any specific culture that history and rationality can be reconciled with cultural diversity and claimed to be universal or transcultural.

To relativize history by rooting it in specific cultural concerns is always to run the risk, however, of contaminating the rationality posited as universal, of making it just another cultural "myth," and thus of making the crisis in history permanent. Montesquieu's *Lettres persanes* figures just such a crisis in history, for, like Zadig, Usbek, the Persian hero of that novel, will leave his own culture to enrich and broaden his understanding of philosophy and history, but unlike Zadig's journey, his does not lead him back home. Instead, it reveals that his position as an "outsider" is untenable, for it becomes increasingly evident that he is bound to and limited by his own culture, and his contact with a foreign culture will only heighten his unhappy consciousness of that limitation. In this case the outsider will prove not to be an outsider at all, but very much within a specific culture. But that this "outside" inevitably ends up being a projection of the "inside" and universality, another cultural myth or "prejudice," does not negate the initial critical aspect of this confrontation with other cultures.

In the celebrated chapter of *The Savage Mind* entitled "History and Dialectic," the anthropologist Claude Lévi-Strauss testifies to the existence of a contemporary crisis in historical thinking that like previous crises has come about as a result of a confrontation between history and culture.[1] In this modern crisis, Jean-Paul Sartre plays the same role for Lévi-Strauss that church history did for the Enlightenment and that Voltaire did for the nineteenth century. According to Lévi-Strauss, Sartre's privileging of dialectical thought or history over every other type of thought reflects a profound ethnocentrism, for it causes Sartre to reduce to a special and in some ways subhuman status all cultures in which historical thought is not the dominant means of reflection. Lévi-Strauss suggests that Sartre is at worst in the position of a colonialist and at best in the position of a tourist when he views cultures "different" from his own and specifically those cultures traditionally identified as being "without history." For Sartre takes his cultural prejudices with him when he considers these cultures and thus refuses to describe them on their own terms. According to Lévi-Strauss, Sartre has adopted a position that he implicitly claims to be outside of culture in general, and from this position he passes judgment on all cultures, including his own. But, Lévi-Strauss argues, in reality Sartre is a prisoner of his own culture, and his defense of history is merely a defense of that culture's prevailing myth: "There is little difference between the way in which this opposition [between primitive man and historical man] is formulated in Sartre's work and

[1] Claude Lévi-Strauss, *The Savage Mind* (Chicago: University of Chicago Press, 1966).

the way it would have been formulated by a Melanesian savage, while the analysis of the practico-inert quite simply revives the language of animism" (p. 249). Moreover, Lévi-Strauss adds in a note to this passage, "it is precisely because all these aspects of the savage mind can be discovered in Sartre's philosophy, that the latter is in my view unqualified to pass judgment on it. . . . To an anthropologist, on the contrary, this [Sartre's] philosophy (like all the others) affords a first-class ethnographic document, the study of which is essential to an understanding of the mythology of our time" (p. 249). Because there is no outside not already determined by the inside of culture, it is the anthropologist who is the proper judge of the philosopher and historian, not the reverse. Thus the crisis caused by the confrontation between history and philosophy has a resolution for Lévi-Strauss, as it does for Voltaire, but the solutions are in some respects opposites. History, for Lévi-Strauss, although not bound to disappear, will no longer dominate the human sciences. It will be replaced by anthropology, and historical culture will be given its proper status as just one element among others in "the system of . . . differences and common properties" of the different historical or geographical modes of human existence (p. 249).

The claims Lévi-Strauss makes on behalf of anthropology in his debate with Sartre over the place and sense of history raise two particularly important issues. One concerns the status of the "peoples without history" whose empirical existence provides him with the point of departure for his critique of history in general and of Sartre's historical idealism in particular. As Lévi-Strauss himself admits in an earlier work, *Race et histoire*, the determination that a culture is "without history" is never empirical, but depends instead on how one defines history.[2] Thus there is always a danger that even the anthropologist, who studies and normally values very highly such cultures, will in some sense already have discriminated against them when he adopts a naively ethnocentric definition of his-

[2] *Race et Histoire* (Paris: Editions Gonthier), pp. 32-33.

tory and then uses it to determine that history is "lacking" in this or that culture.[3] Seen in this light, the "empirical" existence of peoples who lack what the anthropologist and philosopher call history does not in the least safeguard against the idealism or ethnocentrism that are for Lévi-Strauss characteristic of history and dialectical thought in general.

A second issue is that of the manifest persistence of the classical figure of the outsider in the work of Lévi-Strauss, and of various theorists who, like Lévi-Strauss, have transposed the methods and presuppositions of structural linguistics into other fields, and into literary criticism and psychoanalysis in particular. The object of their theories is described from a perspective that, although it no longer belongs to the historian, is that of an "outsider" nonetheless. Roland Barthes, for instance, in his *L'Empire des signes* lists the advantages of being an outsider to a given culture: "What a relief to be in a foreign land! There I am protected from stupidity, vulgarity, vanity, mundaneness, nationalism, normality. The unknown foreign language, whose respiration, emotive aeration, in a word, whose pure signification creates a gentle vortex around me . . . carries me into its artificial void, which exists only for me."[4] Barthes thus describes the formal aspect the alien culture takes on for the traveler and in doing so evokes a situation fundamental to structuralism. The traveler, seemingly cut off from the social

---

[3] Lévi-Strauss's view that there are peoples "without history" is analogous to his view that there are peoples "without writing." In *Of Grammatology*, translated by Gayatri Spivak (Baltimore: Johns Hopkins University Press, 1974), Jacques Derrida argues that Lévi-Strauss can only view certain cultures as being "without writing" because he has an ethnocentric view of writing: "If writing is no longer understood in the narrow sense of linear and phonetic notation, it should be possible to say that all societies capable of producing, that is to say of obliterating, their proper names, and of bringing classificatory difference into play, practice writing in general. No reality or concept would therefore correspond to the expression 'society without writing.' This expression is dependent on ethnocentric oneirism, on the vulgar, that is to say ethnocentric concept of writing. The scorn for writing, let us note in passing, accords quite happily with this ethnocentrism" (pp. 109-110).

[4] Roland Barthes, *L'Empire des signes* (Paris: Skira, 1970), p. 18.

and political conflicts that might define him in his native land, experiences Japan as a totality, albeit one devoid of the sense and depth that politics or history might give it.[5] Just as the traveler experiences the alien culture as a totality, so he experiences the alien language as "pure signification," undivided by any reference to an outside reality or by any "sens plein"— by any meaning in the traditional sense. This experience belongs to the traveler alone ("exists only for me"). The Japanese's relationship to his own culture, Barthes indicates, would not be as neutral, as formal as that of the outsider. The Japanese would be as uneasy in Japan as the European traveler indicates he is in Europe. Like the European, he would look to a foreign land for the same kind of "relief."

Barthes's description of Japan draws deliberately and heavily on the work not only of Lévi-Strauss but of Ferdinand de Saussure as well. The latter, by "bracketing" the existence of the real world in his consideration of language already places the linguist in the position of Barthes's tourist. Like him, the linguist is confronted with a system in which sense is constituted not by a relation between an element of the system (sign) and something external to the system (referent), but between a signifier and a signified held to be two faces of the same, *linguistic* coin. Signification, then, is interior to language and thus purely a function of the differences between one signifier (and hence its signified) and another. Barthes's Japan is also an analogue for culture-in-general as Lévi-Strauss defines it. Just as Barthes argues that the elements of Japanese culture (gestures, costume, language) have no meaning or function

---

[5] Barthes uses the same formal procedures to describe student activism in Japan as he does to describe Japanese cooking or the physical arrangement of Tokyo and charges that attempts to apply "Western-style" political criteria to the students' political activities are evidence of ethnocentrism (ibid., p. 139). In an earlier work, however, he takes a very different and more critical position: "To be a *tourist* is to have a marvelous alibi: thanks to this status, it is possible to see without understanding, to travel without interesting oneself in political realities" ("La Croisère du *Batory*," *Mythologies* [Paris: Editions du Seuil, 1957]).

outside a system of relationships, so Lévi-Strauss argues that a given culture is not merely an agglomeration of biologically constituted families, but rather that the family in fact presupposes the existence of culture, conceived as a system of exchange. Lévi-Strauss argues that the rules governing social exchange are codified in a kinship system, and that, like language, this system cannot be explained with reference to any natural (biological) or historical reality either outside itself or reflected within it. Barthes's Japan, and particularly the capital, Tokyo, thus exhibit what is the essential characteristic of the structural object or system as it is considered by all three theorists: "The city I speak of offers this precious paradox: it does indeed possess a center, but that center is empty" (p. 44).

As important as his use of structural method for his analysis of Japan, however, is the link Barthes establishes between the structuralist view of his object as a discrete totality that is significant but not meaningful in any traditional sense and the special situation of the cultural outsider. In fact, Barthes's frequent allusions to Europe continually remind the reader of his special status, and it is the contrast with Europe that gives sense to his description of Japan. The special situation of the traveler-anthropologist is also a major theme of Lévi-Strauss's *Tristes Tropiques*, where the author confesses that his own culture has accompanied and even haunted him in his search for cultures that, unlike his own, can be described purely in terms of structure:

> What *is*, in point of fact, an anthropological investigation? . . . Did my decision to become an anthropologist bespeak a profound incompatibility vis-à-vis my own social group? Was I destined, in fact, to live in ever greater isolation from my fellows? The strange paradox was that . . . when I was traveling in areas which few had set eyes on . . . I found that neither people nor landscape stood in the foreground of my mind. This was occupied, rather, by fugitive visions of the French countryside from which I had cut myself off, or fragments of music and poetry

which were the perfectly conventional expression of a civilization against which I had taken my stand: such, at any rate, was how I must interpret my actions, if my life were to retain any sense of purpose.[6]

The structural anthropologist describes not just any culture, but, rather, one perceived as fundamentally different from the historical cultures that, as anthropologist, he rejects and yet continues "even despite himself" to represent. Thus he remains an outsider to culture in two related senses. He is outside history and outside the Western culture whose myth history is because he has rejected them; he is also outside the cultures he considers to be "without history" because he carries the values of his own culture with him no matter what he does. Moreover, it is his alienation from both that maintains the theoretical boundary between Western culture and "primitive" cultures, between history and culture; for though, like Lévi-Strauss, the outsider may seek to reduce the distinction or boundary between culture and history, his position as outsider *presupposes* that distinction.

Jacques Lacan's reinterpretation of the status of the unconscious intentionally parallels Lévi-Strauss's description of culture and Saussure's description of language and provides further insight into both the status of the outsider and the opposing systems that define him. Just as Barthes's Japan takes on sense in opposition to Barthes's Europe, so Lacan's redefinition of the unconscious takes on much of its sense in opposition to the "ego psychology" that according to Lacan, dominated psychoanalysis prior to his delivery of "The Function of Language in Psychoanalysis" (1953), and continues to dominate the profession, particularly in America.[7] Thus he criticizes the ego psychologists and their view of the uncon-

<hr />

[6] Claude Lévi-Strauss, *Tristes Tropiques*, translated by John Russell (New York: Atheneum, 1961), pp. 374-375.

[7] Jacques Lacan, "The Function of Language in Psychoanalysis," *Speech and Language in Psychoanalysis*, translated by Anthony Wilden (Baltimore: Johns Hopkins University Press, 1968).

scious and the instincts as substantial entities that function as the referent and ultimate source of the subject's discourse. In contrast, he asserts that what the analyst in fact discovers in the unconscious is the very structure of language. In a similar vein, he criticizes the view that the goal of psychoanalysis is to restore and strengthen a substantial ego. The ego is, he argues, an imaginary construct, and thus its strengthening cannot result in a cure, but only in the reinforcement of the Imaginary, which he holds to be the realm of alienation. There can be a cure only when the subject comes to terms with the order of language (the Symbolic) through the recognition that he and the analyst are not the sources, but only functions of language (signifiers not the signified).

As Lacan himself makes clear in a passage from "The Function of Language in Psychoanalysis," his description of the Symbolic and the Imaginary has an anthropological and historical dimension that corresponds clearly to the distinction made by Lévi-Strauss and Barthes between the societies they study and the societies they represent as observers:

> The law of man has been the law of Language since the first words of recognition presided over the first gifts—although it took the detestable *Danaoi* who came and fled over the sea for men to learn to fear deceiving words accompanying faithless gifts. Until that time, for the pacific Argonauts—uniting the islets of the community with the bonds of a symbolic commerce—these gifts, their act and their objects, their erection into signs, and even their fabrication, were so much part of the Word that they were designated by its name. (p. 35)

For Lacan, as for Lévi-Strauss, there can be no deviance and no deception within the cultural-linguistic order constituted by the so-called primitive societies. Only with the emergence of modern man (whose forerunner is the *Danaoi* of the passage just cited) does deviation from that order become possible, and thus only with the emergence of modern man do both alienation and the Imaginary come into existence.

103

The opposition between the Symbolic and the Imaginary is of special interest here, for within its framework Lacan goes much further in analyzing the scientific civilization that shapes the perspective of the outsider than either Lévi-Strauss or the Barthes of *L'Empire des signes*, whose references to that civilization remain, for the most part, tacit. For Lacan, the "modernity" of modern man lies in his positing of his ego as the condition of his relationship to language and to others. Thus, ironically, the very norms that govern him and his society determine that he will be alienated and neurotic. But if alienation from the cultural-linguistic order (Lacan's Symbolic) has become "normal," then how can modern man break with his alienation and gain access to an order made remote by ideology and history? In his "Propos sur la causalité psychique," Lacan dates modernity from the beginning of the seventeenth century and takes Molière's misanthrope Alceste as his model for egocentric modern man: "The ego of modern man . . . has taken on its form in the dialectical impasse of the 'beautiful soul' who does not recognize his very own *raison d'être* in the disorder that he denounces in the world" ("The Function of Language," p. 44). Lacan points out the futility, or rather the spuriousness of Alceste's attempt to overcome his alienation, for, according to Lacan, Alceste denounces the egotism of others only because his own ego is more demanding than the average. Not content with conventional signs of recognition, he demands absolute sincerity. This demand is the perfect alibi for the ego, for it permits Alceste to reject as insincere signs that are, in fact, only unflattering.

Lacan's own interpretation of *Le Misanthrope* opens with a critical allusion to the traditional reading of the play. In Lacan's view, interpreters of Molière's comedy have been incapable of understanding the author's critique of Alceste because they are themselves "modern," or, as Lacan also puts it, they are themselves "beautiful souls." This means that they valorize the spurious form of authenticity represented by Alceste (without recognizing it as spurious) and hence deplore the ridicule it necessarily provokes from others. But a close look at Lacan's own analysis of *Le Misanthrope* reveals that the situation of the "beautiful soul" is equally a problem for him and not just for the "beautiful minds [or wits] nourished by humanistic study" whom he criticizes. Though Lacan points out that Alceste benefits from the "disorder" he denounces, Lacan too sees the society around Alceste as "disordered" by the dominance in it of the function of the ego. Alceste is the "beautiful soul," that is, he is mad, not because his analysis of the disorder of society is wrong, but because it applies to him as well as to the others: "To be precise, he is mad . . . because he is caught up in . . . the narcissism that affects the leisured class and that furnishes to every period the psychological structure of its 'world' which is paralleled here by that other narcissism which manifests itself more particularly in certain periods by the collective idealization of love."[8] But although he points out that Alceste is in fact governed by the narcissism he denounces in others, Lacan nevertheless makes the same claim for psychoanalysis that Alceste does for his virtue. Just as Alceste claims to speak for an impersonal, impartial ideal, uncontaminated by the egotism, vanity, and hypocrisy of his peers, so, according to Lacan, the psychoanalyst speaks from a position totally dominating the Imaginary, "madness," and the scientific civilization whose norm is alienation.[9]

The work of both Lévi-Strauss and Lacan defines a closed

[8] Jacques Lacan, "Propos sur la causalité psychique," *Ecrits* (Paris: Editions du Seuil, 1966), p. 173. The "beautiful soul" is, of course, a concept borrowed from Hegel's *Phenomenology* and, specifically, from the section dealing critically with Kant, Fichte, and the German Romantics.

[9] Lacan states that the analyst himself enjoys no special privilege, but that he, like the patient, is merely a function of language (a signifier), not a source of language (a signified): "the signifier . . . is what represents a subject for another subject" (Preface, *Ecrits*, vol. 1 [Paris: Editions "Points," 1970], p. 11). But the fact that both the patient and the analyst are functions of language does not lead to the equality between them one might anticipate. In one fundamental respect, their relationship is not reciprocal. The patient can be mad, but not the analyst: "It seems to me that in keeping watch over the just maintenance of the human distances constituting our experience of madness, I have conformed to the law that, according to its letter, causes the apparent 'givens' of madness to exist: without which [conformity], the doctor, like one who tells the madman that what he says is not true, raves no less than the madman himself" ("Propos sur la causalité psychique," p. 177).

system which presumably has no exterior referent, but which is constituted by the differences between its elements. But the closed cultural-linguistic order is only describable thanks to the positing of an opposed system (the Imaginary, modern scientific culture, the Occident) and, ultimately, thanks to the privileged position of an outsider—the anthropologist-psychoanalyst who, like Barthes's traveler to Japan, participates in and yet remains aloof from both systems. And yet questions remain as to the validity of both the psychoanalyst's claim that his situation is fundamentally different from that of Alceste and the distinction between authentic and inauthentic systems that gives sense to the analyst's discourse and to the anthropologist's journey.

In referring his own analysis of the Imaginary to *Le Misanthrope*, Lacan roots the problems confronted by structural psychoanalysis in a classical age that is still, in his view, contemporary. In a similar way, Lévi-Strauss regards Rousseau as the founder of modern anthropology and cites him as the authority for the view that it is from those cultures least like our own that we can learn the most about culture and man in general (*The Savage Mind*, p. 247). Both Lacan and Lévi-Strauss trace the origins of their own methods back to a classical age they hold to be the first to theorize man's alienation from his own culture and the first to understand the methodological significance of such alienation. In their view, then, their own structural theory of language, culture, and the unconscious does not emerge in a period radically distinct from the classical age. The classical and modern periods are in many ways stages of a single modernity, and both confront history in a state of crisis brought on by the coming into prominence of the question of culture.

Montesquieu's *Lettres persanes* is a classical text that addresses itself in a particularly direct way to the symptoms and effects of this historical crisis, precisely because the "return" to rationality and to history, which for Voltaire will resolve the confrontation between culture and history and put an end to the "alienation" of history, is missing from it. Usbek, the hero of the novel, is a Zadig in perpetual exile. As such, he is similar to Molière's Alceste and thus to "modern man" as described by Lacan; he also resembles the philosopher-historian criticized by Lévi-Strauss. The limits culture imposes on him seem to indicate that Montesquieu is in many ways a Lévi-Strauss before the fact, bearing witness to the way in which all history and philosophy are already determined by culture. As in the case of Alceste, critics of the *Lettres persanes* have made Usbek the undisputed hero of the novel and defended him in the name of the ideal, Enlightenment values he represents and which, to an overwhelming extent, humanist critics share. Lacan's diagnosis of "méconnaissance," the failure of recognition that permits such critics to interpret Alceste as the tragically misunderstood hero of *Le Misanthrope*, raises the possibility that, like Molière's play, the *Lettres persanes* may in fact be a critique of the ideals that have previously served as the basis for interpretation of the novel.

But it is equally important to note that Usbek *also* closely resembles the structural anthropologist and psychoanalyst. For even though Usbek's voyage from Isphahan to Paris is based on a rejection of his own culture, he will remain an outsider with respect to the foreign culture as well. He will search for a differently structured social order (of the kind Lacan sees as existing prior to the emergence of "modern man") in order to give philosophical and scientific rigor to his denunciation and value to himself. And if the *Lettres persanes* do go on to offer a critique of Usbek, it will not only be a critique of Usbek the "historian" but also of Usbek the "anthropologist." The critique of Usbek's idealism does not, however, imply the existence of an authentic position free of the contradictions it denounces as the impasse of the "beautiful soul." In putting into question the position of Usbek, the traveler-*philosophe*, it is not merely some "spurious" claim to authenticity that is being undercut in the novel. It is rather the very position of the outsider, who, because he purportedly participates in two cultural systems and at the same time remains aloof from both, is at the center of a classical or modern order based on reason and history and *also* at the center of a structural order based on the unity of language and culture.

As has already been indicated, critics of the *Lettres persanes* have tended to equate the aim of the novel with the tasks set by Usbek for himself, but they have not seriously investigated whether or not such a literal interpretation is justified in the light of the various points of view offered by the novel. Jean Starobinski, for instance, sees the *Lettres persanes* as a satirical device designed to liberate Occidentals from certain prejudices in order to permit the unveiling of a more universal conception of man. "The trial by mask is a test of the truth. Characters in costume and masked must enter upon the stage in order that the true nature of men be *unmasked* in their presence. . . . The real Orient has no role in all this. It serves as a spectacle that occidental men give themselves in order to liberate themselves from the traditional values of the West."[10] Starobinski's description of the novel closely parallels Usbek's description of his motives for undertaking a voyage to the West: he is determined to liberate himself from the traditional values that have heretofore circumscribed his knowledge: "Rica and I are perhaps the first among the Persians to have left their country out of a desire to know. . . . We were born in a flourishing kingdom; but we did not believe that its boundaries and those of knowledge were one, and that the light of the Orient alone should illuminate us."[11] But indications exist from the first letter that Usbek, the *philosophe*, is in fact a "beautiful soul," and that it is not just the cultural mask that is being criticized by the *Lettres persanes*; it is the agent of the unmasking as well. From the very outset of his voyage, we see Usbek in a posture he will hold for the rest of the novel. Like the structural anthropologist, he is not merely looking ahead to the experience that awaits him in other cultures, but back to the society whose conventions he claims will not cir-

[10] Jean Starobinski, *Montesquieu par lui-même* (Paris: Editions du Seuil, 1953), p. 63.

[11] *Lettres persanes, Oeuvres complètes* (Paris: Editions du Seuil, 1964), letter I.

cumscribe his knowledge: "Keep me informed of what is being said about our trip; don't flatter me; I don't expect there will be a great number who approve" (*LP*, I). Usbek's own account of his decision to travel to the West reveals that his quest for knowledge is motivated as much by his position in Persian court society as by a disinterested attachment to science:

> I appeared at court at a tender age. I can tell you that my heart was not corrupted by it; I even conceived of a great ambition: I dared to be virtuous there. As soon as I was introduced to corruption, I took my distance; but I later approached it in order to unmask it. . . . But when I saw that my sincerity had won me a number of enemies; . . . that, in a corrupt court, I was only weakly sustained by virtue, I resolved to leave it. I feigned a great attachment for science, and, by feigning it, I acquired it in reality. (*LP*, VIII)

Usbek's unmasking of corruption reveals his paradoxical position vis-à-vis the court society he shocks and amazes by his desire to be virtuous. Usbek's actions imply that the Persians are at once too corrupt to reform themselves but virtuous enough to recognize his unmasking of their corruption as an act of disinterested virtue. Usbek's desire and need to leave Persian society are thus a logical outgrowth of his attempt to reject the prevailing morality of Persian court society, and, moreover, these two projects imply a similar contradiction in Usbek's position. His desire to reform and later to leave his own society is determined by that society; he will continue throughout the novel to seek recognition within the Persian world he appears to abandon at the outset.

Usbek's position as an outsider thus implies a position "within" his society as well: that of the reformer who rejects his society in its present state. As a reformer and a man of virtue, Usbek recalls the Roman dictator Sulla, portrayed in Montesquieu's "Dialogue de Sylla et d'Eucrates."[12] Like Us-

---

[12] *Oeuvres complètes.*

bek's desire to reform Persian society, Sulla's desire to reform Rome implies a contradiction, for, as he tells his interlocutor, Eucrates, his love of absolute freedom has prompted him to become a dictator. He has used his power to terrorize the Roman population in the hope that this will make it possible for him to restore by force the republican institutions it has abandoned. But as his interlocutor indicates, Sulla's forcible liberation of the Romans ultimately only reinforces their enslavement and thus only reinforces his isolation as a free individual from the society he rules. The freedom he had sought to establish on a broader base than his own person is thereby undermined, and, clearly, his attempt to restore the Romans to their former independence will disappear with him. Similarly, Usbek's forcible unmasking of vice does not make the courtiers more virtuous, but only personalizes the virtue he seeks to impose. Court society can only interpret his virtue as the ruse of a supremely ambitious man. Like Sulla's freedom, Usbek's virtue comes to reside in his person alone. It is supremely vulnerable, for it can be extinguished by a mere assassin.

The similarities between the Persian *philosophe* Usbek and the dictator Sulla reveal another crucial dimension of Usbek's character. Not only is he an anthropologist obsessed with his own culture who loves virtue and freedom and professes a desire to live in a society without deception, but as it becomes increasingly clear from the letters he exchanges with his wives, his eunuchs, and his other slaves, he is also a dictator who imposes deception on those around him. His ideals are in essence republican; his actions and attitudes are despotic. Indeed, as we shall see, Usbek's seraglio is a form of despotism in miniature, in which the essence of Montesquieu's description of despotism in *De l'esprit des lois* is already apparent.

The parallels between Usbek the despot and Lacan's description of "modern man" are as striking as the parallels between Usbek the traveler and the structural anthropologist. Though Montesquieu does not emphasize the historical status of the three types of government he defines in *De l'esprit des lois*, still they do imply a certain chronology. He states that the monarchy is the specific contribution of the "modern" age to the typology of governments (for it, unlike despotism or the republic, is not found in antiquity), but, in fact, despotism is in an important sense even more modern. Though it is present in antiquity, it also represents the wave of the future, for every monarchy is a potential despotism, but no despotism is a potential monarchy: "The greater part of European governments are monarchies, or rather, they are called thus. For I do not know if there have ever really been any; at least it would be difficult for them to have subsisted in their purity for very long. This is a violent state, which always degenerates into despotism" (*LP*, CII). The modernity of despotism is not the only trait it shares with the Imaginary as described by Lacan. The despot, like Alceste of *Le Misanthrope*, is radically cut off by the course of history from the ancient world in which ideal, republican virtues still existed. Even in the case of Sulla where the "modern" age he inaugurated is only a few years old, the separation from the ancient world of republican virtue is nevertheless absolute. Thus in attempting to impose republican virtue on a modern society, it is not that virtue Sulla is actually promoting, but rather the arbitrary power he exercises in seeking to impose it. Like Alceste, the despot is a perfect reflection of the society from which he isolates himself in order to reshape it in his own image. In imposing his will or his virtue the despot creates terror and a slavish mentality in his subjects, thus radically negating the essence of the society he rules. "In the despotic [government], an individual, without law and without rule, carries away everything by his will and his caprices."[13] "Education, which principally consists in living with others . . . is thus in a manner of speaking nonexistent [under a despotic government]" (*EL*, IV, 3). The reduction of his subjects to slavery and the destruction of all social relationships are ultimately a reflection of the nullity of the despot himself and of any value—egotistical or altruistic—

---

[13] *De l'esprit des lois, Oeuvres complètes*, Book II, chap. 1.

111

he might represent. He becomes a prisoner, in his own house, of his own power, as much a slave as any of his subjects: "these seraglios of the Orient; . . . these places where artifice, viciousness, ruse, reign in silence, and cover themselves with impenetrable darkness; where an old prince, having become more of an imbecile every day, is the first prisoner of the palace" (EL, V, 14).

Montesquieu's despot is very much like Lacan's Alceste, who is "mad" because his analysis of the disorder around him determines him first of all, and no doubt but what this composite portrait describes Usbek, particularly in his relationship to his seraglio. The order Usbek creates there is purely a reflection of his will. Having once imposed it, he then denounces transgressions of that order as the fault of his eunuchs or his wives; in fact, however, those transgressions are a direct result of the absolute nature of the order Usbek has created. No one does more to undermine the authority of Usbek than does Usbek himself by his insistence that his order be strictly policed, and indeed, as the course of the novel reveals, the more ruthless the enforcement, the greater the disorder. Usbek's authority is absolute only when he commands absolute fidelity from his wives. For that very reason, his authority is threatened by the slightest indiscretion: "When we confine you so severely . . . it isn't because we fear the ultimate infidelity; it's rather because we know that purity cannot be too great and that the slightest stain can corrupt it" (LP, XXVI). Because they are domestic slaves and because, in this sense, their "love" for Usbek is prescribed by the law, there is no sign by which his wives can express a sincere attachment for him. The reign of Usbek's "virtue"—that is, of his will—thus becomes the reign of hypocrisy, for clearly, Usbek's law, by commanding absolute fidelity, creates a situation in which all are potentially unfaithful and in which there is practically speaking no way he can determine whether they are "truly" faithful or not. Given Usbek's position, there is nothing either his wives or his eunuchs can say to allay his suspicions, and thus he is devoured by a jealousy that is the inevitable correlate of the absolute status he claims for himself (*LP*, VI). Like the despot, Usbek is the first and last victim of his own absolute will.[14]

When he is considered in the light of his relationship to his seraglio, what emerges is a view of Usbek—and ultimately of the *Lettres persanes*—that differs importantly from the one traditionally held by critics who see Usbek as the unquestioned hero of the novel and the spokesman for Montesquieu. And, indeed, even Roger Laufer, who, unlike most scholars, is critical of the values represented by Usbek, nonetheless considers him to be the direct representative of the author.[15] Once the impasse Usbek creates for himself in relation to his wives is analyzed, it becomes evident that Usbek's "failure" to resolve the contradiction between his philosophical ideals and his repressive policies is more than the result of some contingency of theory and practice. Indeed, Usbek's ideals are not "hollow," as Laufer has noted in criticizing him and as other critics have acknowledged with appropriate expressions of regret; it is precisely these ideals that order the disorder of Usbek's seraglio. Montesquieu's novel is in fact a forceful critique of this central figure. For the *Lettres persanes* shows that the universal values Usbek claims to embody in his opposition to Persian society and expects his voyage to the West to confirm, when they are enforced on his seraglio in the form of "virtue," create disorder and repression.

In contrast to Usbek, Rica and his descriptions of society have been viewed as representative of the "frivolous" or "superficial" side of Montesquieu's nature. Even those critics who view the *Lettres persanes* as primarily a social satire have not considered Rica's satirical letters to be of significant philo-

---

[14] Usbek himself argues that an absolutely perfect God, if he existed, would be destroyed by the contradictions inherent in his perfection: "The most sensible philosophers who have reflected on the nature of God have said that he is a supremely perfect being. . . . They have enumerated all the different perfections . . . and heaped them upon the idea of divinity, without realizing that often these attributes cancel each other out, and that they cannot subsist within the same subject without destroying one another" (*LP*, LXIX).

[15] Roger Laufer, *Style rococo, style des "lumières"* (Paris: J. Corti, 1963).

sophical consequence. In taking this stance, critics have neglected the character of Rica and the systematic nature of the
contrast between Rica and Usbek. And yet the opposition
between Rica and Usbek not only further underscores the untenable nature of Usbek's position, it seems to hold out the
possibility of an alternative to his impasse. Indeed, Usbek's
voyage to the West only intensifies the contradiction inherent
in his idealism. As he pursues a knowledge free of cultural
prejudice, the jealousy that attaches him to his own culture
and his own seraglio causes the self that his idealism supports
to crumble: "I live in a barbarous climate, present to everything that disturbs me, absent from everything that concerns
me. A somber sadness grips me; I fall into a terrible state of
despondency: it seems to me that I am destroying myself"
(*LP*, CLV).

For Rica, the loss of his Persian "identity" and his assimi-
lation into French society are gradual and painless: "I go a
great deal into society, and I seek to familiarize myself with
it. My mind is gradually losing its Asian aspect, and it conforms effortlessly to European manners and morals. I am not
surprised to see a house with five or six women and five or
six men inside, and I find that such gatherings are not at all a
bad idea" (*LP*, LXIII). The contrast between the two characters reflects an essential difference in their attitude toward the
alien culture, and ultimately, toward their own. "Rica is writing you a long letter; he has told me that he speaks to you a
great deal about this country. The vivacity of his mind causes
him to grasp everything promptly. As for myself, I think more
slowly and am not in any state to tell you anything" (*LP*,
XXV). Because he seeks a profound understanding of what he
sees, Usbek deprives himself of the immediate reactions that
are the subject of Rica's first letters. In the long run, his relationship to this alien world becomes as uneasy as his relationship to Persia, for just as he goes to Paris to understand Persia
better, so he must retreat to the countryside to gain a better
perspective on Paris. But Rica, like Barthes's traveler to Japan,
because he seeks nothing, no universally valid principle, is ca-

pable of immediately capturing the alien culture as an ordered, if meaningless system. In contrast to Usbek, who is continually retreating to gain a better understanding and who for that reason, continually defers the understanding that is his stated goal, Rica is able to describe society in a way that cannot be dismissed as "frivolous" and "purely satirical." In fact, the theory underlying Rica's attitude toward culture is as coherent, or rather, is no less coherent, than Usbek's idealism.

The coherence of Rica's position can perhaps be more readily grasped if, bearing in mind that Rica's letters from Paris describe a monarchy, one refers to Montesquieu's definition of this form of government in his *De l'esprit des lois*. Like Barthes's Japan, the monarchy is, at least in Montesquieu's theory, an order whose center is empty in an important sense. According to that theory, the "nature" of the monarchy lies in the existence within it of a nobility (*EL*, II, 4), and the fundamental "principle" of that class and hence of the monarchy itself is the code of honor that distinguishes the nobility from the rest of the nation. Honor is the false virtue that brings about the same results as would true virtue, if it existed: "*Honor*, that is to say, the prejudice of each individual and of each condition, takes the place of the political virtue of which I have spoken, and represents it everywhere. It can inspire the noblest actions; it can, by reinforcing the laws, achieve the ends of the government as if it were virtue itself" (*EL*, III, 6). Honor is a "prejudice"—it is rooted in social convention alone and not in any transcendent value. But honor regulates the monarchy just as well as a transcendent virtue would, or rather, it reveals that the conventions of the monarchy are self-regulating, and that as a result they form a system that has no need of a substantial center in order to function. Thus to understand monarchy, and perhaps, ultimately, any society, there is no need to look beyond convention to a natural or historical reality: "The discussion of public law invariably begins with meticulous research into the origin of societies, which seems to me ridiculous. If men formed no societies, if they separated from and fled each other, then it would be necessary to ask why [societies are formed]. . . . But [men] are all born linked to one another" (*LP*, XCIV).

If there is no need to look beneath or beyond culture in order to understand it, it is because culture itself ought to be recognized as natural. This, then, is the thesis that underlies Rica's position, and it finds an echo in Lévi-Strauss's formulation of the theoretical bases of structural anthropology in *The Elementary Structures of Kinship* as well as in Barthes's description of Japan.[16] There is no doubt that structuralism has created a situation in which the coherence of the specific aspects of Rica's description of Parisian society and the absence of any natural referent for that description become almost self-evident. As portrayed by Rica, Paris is an "empire des signes" where nothing is above social convention: "They say that man is a social animal. From this standpoint, it seems to me that the Frenchman is more a man than the others; he is man par excellence, for he seems to be formed solely for society" (*LP*, LXXXVII). "La mode"—in the sense of both fashion and convention—regulates all aspects of life in the Paris discovered by Rica. In the absence of any value not subject to "la mode," it becomes absolute, and this absoluteness is, for Rica, the surprising corollary of its arbitrariness: "I don't know how to reconcile their furious attachment to their customs with the inconstancy that causes them to change every day" (*LP*, C).[17]

[16] See Claude Lévi-Strauss, *The Elementary Structures of Kinship*, translated by James H. Bell, John R. von Sturmer, and Rodney Needham (Boston: Beacon Press, 1969), pp. 8-9, where he concludes that the incest taboo is the one social rule found in all societies, that is, the one social rule that is natural. Since for Lévi-Strauss the incest taboo generates the kinship system that structures and makes possible the existence of all societies, his observation that it is "natural" is tantamount to the proposition that society itself is natural.

[17] Rica describes fashion and convention with the same paradox used by Saussure to describe the sign. The temporal dimension of language ensures its immutability, in the sense that the speaking subject is not free to invent a new language, but rather can only inherit the old. At the same time, however, time also causes language to be altered, thereby revealing its mutability (Ferdinand de Saussure, *Course in General Linguistics*, translated by Wade Baskin [London: Peter Owen, 1960], pp. 73-74).

In the Paris described by Rica, no value escapes from this radical relativization. All value is illusory, and there are in Paris as many trades and callings as there are illusions to create. Rica lists those illusions in letter LVIII: wealth, spiritual exaltation, knowledge of the future, virginity, beauty, health. The absoluteness of "la mode" is such that there is, at least in theory, no activity that it does not regulate, including the activity of trying to understand the society ruled by "la mode." Usbek would clearly like to exempt the pursuit of knowledge from the rule of convention, since his flight from Persia indicated a refusal to accept the social interpretation put on his quest for knowledge (that he, like the other members of the court, seeks recognition). But as Rica's letters reveal (LIV, LXVI, LXXIII), knowledge and intelligence are illusions to be created like the others, and being a philosopher, that is, being recognized as a philosopher, is a question of mastering one of the styles consecrated by the many social groups and institutions who set them. The absolute nature of "la mode" precludes the existence of any metalanguage not governed by its laws.

It is not only Usbek's claim to represent universally valid philosophical principles that is undercut by the Parisian context of his speculation. Applied to the question of the status of women in society and to relations between the sexes, the equation between "la mode" and "la loi" has implications as disquieting for Usbek the despotic husband as for Usbek the *philosophe*. And just as in the case of structuralism a reconsideration of the function of language and culture is inseparable from a revision of the existing theory of sexuality and the unconscious, so Rica's observations on Paris seem to imply a sexual order very different from the one Usbek has created in his seraglio. In apparent contrast to the Persian woman, the Parisian woman views virginity as an illusion among others, one that she creates as consciously as her beauty. To borrow the language of *De l'esprit des lois*, though there might be virgins in Paris, virginity is alien to the "principle" of the Parisiennes; it is accidental and not systematic: "Among the peoples of Europe, the first quarter-hour of marriage resolves all difficulties. . . . European women don't behave like our Persian women, who resist sometimes for several months; there is nothing so august about their acquiescence; if they lose nothing, it is because they have nothing to lose" (*LP*, LV). In Paris, jealousy can exist only after the fact; it is always too late to lock up one's wife. Husbands, then, are by definition cuckolds, but the jealous husband who refuses to accept this situation is, worse, a ridiculous fool. Among the Parisians, Rica notes, "there are . . . unhappy men consoled by no one: jealous husbands. There are men everyone hates: jealous husbands. There are men held in contempt by all their fellows: jealous husbands" (*LP*, LV).

In Montesquieu's Paris, a constitutive absence of virginity thus undermines all forms of authority, creating an equality of the sexes founded on their equal capacity for infidelity. In the ensuing exchange of partners, all losses are compensated. "In order for a man's complaints about the fidelity of his wife to be justified, there would have to be only three people in the world; but they will always find a way as long as there are four" (*LP*, XXXVIII). Usbek, who is legally entitled to take extraordinary precautions to ensure his wives fidelity, has only to exercise his rights as husband to please his wives who, presumably, are in no position to make comparisons, favorable or unfavorable. But in Paris it is only the jealous husband, the most ridiculous of all men, "who abuses his legal rights in order to make up for the charms he lacks" (*LP*, LV). The Parisian of either sex must seduce a partner who remains free to go elsewhere. Thus neither can invoke the law; instead each strives to create an illusion that will captivate the other—she, of beauty, he, by his "badinage," or playfulness, of potency: "In order to please women, a certain talent is necessary that is different from the one that pleases them even more: it consists in a kind of playfulness of the mind that amuses them in that it seems to promise at every moment what one can give only too infrequently" (*LP*, LXIII). Just as the political virtue of the monarchy is honor, which is, "philosophically speaking," a false virtue, so the sentimental virtue of the monarchy is not love, but gallantry. "Our relationship to women is founded on the happiness attached to sensual pleasure, on the charm of loving and being loved, and ... on the desire to please them, because they are very enlightened judges of certain things that are constitutive of personal merit. This general desire to please produces gallantry, which is not love itself, but rather the delicacy, the capriciousness, the perpetual lie of love" (*EL*, XXVII, 22). Inauthenticity becomes impossible or at least only relative in the Paris described by Rica, if only because there is no aspect of Parisian life not determined by culture and, hence, there exists no ultimate measure of authenticity.

As Usbek's and Rica's absence from Persia lengthens, Rica adapts to French life while Usbek grows increasingly anxious about the state of his seraglio. Usbek complains that the westernized Rica has no sympathy or understanding for his emotional plight (*LP*, CLV). Ironically, Usbek's rejection of Rica's Paris causes him to cling to the despotic values of which his own voyage was to be the negation, for that rejection, as well as his estrangement from his fellow Persian Rica, constitutes an inverted recognition that the values he represents are threatened not only in France, but also where he is most vulnerable, in his seraglio in Isphahan. Though Usbek holds himself as aloof as possible from French society, the interpretation that the latter society would place on his own behavior is nevertheless inescapable. The Parisian's acceptance of the social code preserves him from playing the ridiculous role of the jealous husband. But the Parisian code is obviously unacceptable to Usbek, whose relation to his wives is defined, as he himself admits, solely by jealousy. From the French perspective, Usbek's relationship to his wives is that of a man who imposes himself, who abuses the advantages given him by the law in order to compensate for a lack of "personal merit." Thus Usbek's extreme subjugation of his wives becomes a sign of his impotence. Indeed, Usbek has attempted to secure the interests of his own potency through the castration of his male slaves; but his and Rica's observations on relations between the sexes in France reveal that the potency Usbek values in himself is of secondary importance. Usbek's own observations on this subject come back to haunt him when they are remembered by one of his wives and included in a letter that reaches him in Paris: "I have heard you say a thousand times that eunuchs know a kind of sensual pleasure with women that is unknown to us, and that nature compensates for losses. . . . One has a kind of third sense, and as a result one has, in a sense, only exchanged certain pleasures for others" (*LP*, LIII). And just as his eunuchs "know a kind of sensual pleasure with women" that Usbek can only imagine, so his wives also know a form of pleasure he is incapable of experiencing: "Nonetheless, Usbek, don't imagine that your situation is happier than mine; I have tasted here a thousand pleasures unknown to you; my imagination has been ceaselessly at work telling me of their worth; I have lived, and you have only languished" (*LP*, LXIII).

Thus while as husband and master Usbek manipulates the relationship between his eunuchs and his wives to suit his own purposes, the letters he receives from Asia as well as Rica's descriptions of French society reveal the possibility of a system of pleasure independent of the potency Usbek valorizes and from the point of view of which the women and the eunuchs are "natural" accomplices. Usbek, unlike Rica, resists the process of becoming French and never gives up the idea of returning to Persia. But as his absence lengthens, as "disorder increases in the seraglio," as Usbek's jealousy grows stronger and his health fails, it becomes clear that no return to Asia could restore the "order" that would be a sign of his presence. Usbek was always implicitly absent and impotent, and the sign of both his absence and his impotence is his jealousy, which transforms him into just another slave in his own seraglio:

> I will confine myself within walls more terrible for me than for the women who are there. I will take with me all of my suspicion; their attentions will do nothing to reassure me; in my bed, in their arms, my only "pleasure"

will be my anxieties; at a moment so unfavorable for reflections, my jealousy will find a way to express itself.
Unworthy rejects of human nature, vile slaves whose hearts
have been forever closed to all feelings of love, you would
not bemoan your condition if you knew the unhappiness
of mine. (*LP*, CLV)

It would seem that Rica's Paris provides the ultimate alternative to the despotic social forms constructed by Usbek's
egocentric desire. It would seem too that the contradictions
inherent in Usbek's seraglio have been liquidated in Rica's
Paris. With the "real" potency on which Usbek based his despotic rule negated, despotism would no longer be possible.
The roles played by all members of society would become
fundamentally indistinguishable in that all would be conventional.

It is precisely the work of structuralists like Barthes, Lacan,
and Lévi-Strauss that draws attention to the coherence of culture and language and to the redundancy of the natural and
historical "realities" traditionally invoked to explain their existence. And yet neither Lévi-Strauss nor Lacan would accept
the "culturalist" label his work might at first glance seem to
merit. As I have already argued with reference to Lévi-Strauss,
the anthropologist is, by his own definition, an outsider to
both the historical culture he rejects and the "primitive" culture he valorizes. Despite the anthropologist's rejection of the
alienation and prejudices that are the norm in his own culture,
he cannot simply adopt the "norms" of the "primitive" culture
without ceasing to be an anthropologist. Though the societies
he observes are, in theory, radically different from his own,
his position is essentially the same with respect to each—the
anthropologist defines both the "primitive" and historical cultures, but neither defines him. Similarly, Lacan, in criticizing
Karen Horney and other feminist psychoanalysts, refuses the
culturalist label he applies to them: "It is not a question of
the relation between man and *language as a social phenomenon*,
there being here no question even of something resembling

the ideological psychogenesis with which we are familiar" (my emphasis).[18] Lévi-Strauss and Lacan both resist "going native," that is, abandoning the position outside the cultural and linguistic order from which their own discourse describing that order takes on its sense. The positing of an authentic cultural or symbolic order does not liquidate the problem posed by the ego and the idealism that is its ideological support, for this order becomes authentic only when the transcendent position of the subject (anthropologist, psychoanalyst) in relation to that order is maintained.

One must also, in a similar way, qualify Montesquieu's "culturalism." As the *Lettres persanes* demonstrates, the revelation that Usbek's despotic power is illusory does not dispel once and for all the threat of "despotism" any more than the positing of an authentic cultural, linguistic, or Symbolic order resolves the problem posed by historical idealism or by the alienation of "modern" man. Indeed, Usbek's despotic nature does not prevent him from reaching "culturalist" conclusions in his speculation on the nature of society (*LP*, XCIL). Nor is the alienation represented by Usbek absent from French life, for France is a virtual despotism. Rica's letters reveal that the illusory power of the monarch can have the effects of the "real" power of the despot. The figure of the despot is very much present in French society—in the personage of Louis XIV: "They say that he possesses to a very high degree the talent of making himself obeyed: he governs his family, his court, his state all with the same genius. He has often been heard to say that, of all the governments of the world, that of the Turks or of our august sultan would please him the best, so highly does he esteem oriental political systems" (*LP*, XXXVII). Louis XIV is a despot, not because he disregards social convention, but because he manipulates it. Montesquieu's description of social man fits Louis XIV as well as or

[18] Jacques Lacan, "The Signification of the Phallus," *Ecrits*, selected and translated by Alan Sheridan (London: Tavistock Publications, 1977), p. 285.

better than anyone else. While others create the illusion of beauty or wisdom, Louis XIV creates the illusion of power:

> He has been seen undertaking and sustaining great wars, without any other form of credit besides titles to sell, and, thanks to the marvel of human vanity, his troops were paid, his strongholds provisioned, and his navies equipped. . . . He has the same authority over the very minds of his subjects: he makes them think as he wishes. If he has only one million *écus* in his treasury, and he needs two, he has only to persuade them that one *écu* is worth two, and they believe it. If he has a difficult war to wage, and he has no money, he has only to put it into their heads that a piece of paper is silver, and they are straight away convinced. (*LP*, XXIV)

The Law system was, in Montesquieu's view, a continuation of despotism on an economic plane. While many of Montesquieu's contemporaries saw money as having an intrinsic value—the value of the metal of which it was made—Montesquieu considered that it had value only as the sign of wealth. He deplored the Law system, not because it substituted paper money with no intrinsic worth for gold or silver, but because the conventional value of the paper money was manipulated in such a way as to ruin the classes that were, in Montesquieu's view, the mainstay of the monarchy. Like the political illusions created by Louis XIV, the economic illusions created by Law did have real effects, for they destroyed the fortunes of many members of the traditional ruling class and created a new wealthy group overnight (*LP*, CXXXVIII).

Montesquieu's social man—the aristocrat—is invulnerable to an attack on his essential values, for he has none that is in Montesquieu's sense, essential. He is, on the other hand, highly vulnerable to the despots who attain their goals by playing upon that sense of honor and by manipulating the conventions by which the nobility is ruled. Montesquieu is forced to appeal to values he has elsewhere criticized in order to preserve the conventional order represented by the aristocracy from the ambitious monarch. Though the idealism inherent in philosophy constitutes the mainstay of despotism, it is precisely to that idealism—in the form of philosophy—that Montesquieu is forced to turn to guard against despotism. For the nobility to have a moderating effect on the monarchy and to prevent it from becoming a despotism, the nobility needs more than a code of honor, more than the conservative weight of social convention to defend its prerogatives: "The ignorance that is natural to the nobility, its lack of attentiveness, its contempt for civil government, require that there be a body that tirelessly retrieves the laws from the dust under which they would otherwise be buried" (*EL*, II, 5). The occidental despot who can achieve his ends working within the constraints of the aristocratic code cannot be stopped by the idle aristocrats who understand their own interests less well than does the despot. He can only be stopped by an enlightened magistracy. Even in *De l'esprit des lois* Montesquieu states (in apparent contradiction with his declaration that nobility equals monarchy) that it is the enlightenment of the king and his ministers that distinguishes monarchy from despotism (*EL*, III, 10).

Rica's analysis of Paris constitutes an implicit critique of the political structure of Usbek's own despotically organized seraglio. But despotism and idealism are themselves implicit in the political structure Rica describes. Similarly, though Rica's description of relations between the sexes makes apparent the ways in which Usbek's slaves (his wives and his eunuchs) are still free to "pervert" the moral order he seeks to impose on them, so the seraglio's structure reveals something about the French society analyzed by Rica. French society demonstrates that sexuality is independent of the potency Usbek valorizes in himself, and thereby reveals that the relationships whose purity Usbek had sought to guarantee through the castration of his slaves are in fact sexually charged. But what indeed is the nature of the relationships existing between the slaves and the women in Usbek's absence? Like the relationship between men and women in French society, it is theoretically a relationship between equals, for there is no "real" upon which a claim for the supremacy of masculine potency can be based, which could be interpreted as giving a monopoly on sexuality to some while excluding others from it. With the "real" abolished, sexuality can no longer be a question of identity, but one of role, with women and eunuchs playing alternately the "masculine" or dominant role and the "feminine" or submissive role. In fact, however, this apparent bisexuality of the actors is a sign, not of a liberation from sexual stereotypes, but of the triumph of a unique measure of sexuality to which some will conform, from which others will deviate, but according to which all will be judged. Thus in a letter to a fellow slave, the head eunuch describes the reversal of roles between Usbek's two sets of slaves—his wives and his eunuchs: "They do not lack pretexts for getting me to do what they want. In such situations a blind obedience and an unlimited compliance are necessary; . . . if I hesitated to obey them, they would have the right to punish me. . . . There are moments when I am not listened to, moments when nothing is refused them, moments when I am always wrong" (*LP*, IX). A letter to Usbek treats the same subject: "I always remember that I was born to dominate them, and it seems to me that I become a man once again on those occasions where I do indeed dominate. But all that . . . is nothing without the presence of the master. What can we do with this vain phantom of an authority that never communicates itself entirely?" (*LP*, XCVI). Insofar as the women rule the chief eunuch, they exercise an authority borrowed from Usbek. Insofar as he rules them, the eunuch becomes like his master—"I become a man once again." Thus though the master-slave couple may be comprised of Usbek and a eunuch, Usbek and a wife, or a eunuch and a wife, each alternately occupying the dominant or submissive role, the "equality between the sexes" that permits the various "actors" to exchange roles is apparent only from the point of view of the absent, ideal man represented by Usbek. For it is from this point of view that women, eunuchs, and ultimately Usbek himself appear as "castrated" versions of that ideal.

The despotic idealism represented by Usbek dominates the

cultural order from which the "real" is absent as effectively as it did a "natural" order in which "the real, whatever upheaval it is subjected to . . . is at all times and in all cases in its place."[19] Indeed, just as Montesquieu is obliged to appeal to Enlightenment values he systematically criticizes in order to prevent the monarchy from being transformed into despotism, so it is only enlightenment—that is, the same idealism that rationalizes Usbek's attachment to a self-serving virtue—that prevents the European from taking greater advantage of the privilege that the most culturalist of societies attaches to the male role. Though the enlightened European deplores the state of affairs, nonetheless, like his oriental counterpart, he still views it as in some sense "natural": "The authority that we have over them is a veritable tyranny; they have only let us have it because they are more gentle than we" (*LP*, XXXVIII). The *Lettres persanes* shows that the debate on the place of women in society remains a debate among men; for the barrier that constitutes conventional society as a closed system in opposition to despotism reflects a transcendent perspective from which the potency and autonomy claimed by the despot and renounced by social man are retained as an ideal of man.

Like Barthes's Tokyo and the structuralist "object" in general, the *Lettres persanes* has a center, but that center is empty. Rica cannot occupy it, because he represents an immersion in culture so complete that the outline of a given culture and the question of culture in general are apparent to him only in the necessarily fleeting moments between his arrival in the West and his adaptation to it. Nor does Usbek provide the novel with a center, because his effort to discover the meaning of culture and thereby to transcend it is rooted in and limited by the specific cultural values he represents. Usbek is like Molière's Alceste in that he is as much a product of his culture as those he condemns and criticizes for accepting the limitations of Persian society and seeking only to conform to them. La-

[19] Jacques Lacan, "Seminar on 'The Purloined Letter,' " *French Freud, Yale French Studies*, no. 48 (1972), p. 55.

can's critique of Alceste thus also applies to Usbek. But from the standpoint of structural anthropology and Lacanian psychoanalysis, Usbek's character is a knife that cuts both ways, for the dilemma he represents is in fact as central to structuralism itself as to the classicism of Molière and Montesquieu. Usbek's "modernity"—to use Lacan's term—is also that of structuralism. Paradoxically, structuralism's attempt to account for culture by freeing it from its subordination to a historical center leads to a resubordination of the cultural and the recreation of a center: that provided by the perspective of the outsider.

Montesquieu's *Lettres persanes* represents an attempt to understand the cultural per se, to respect its specificity and its claims. In this sense, it forcefully undermines the position of any historian who might claim that history is by right and in essence free of cultural determination. From the standpoint of the *Lettres persanes* no less than that of *The Savage Mind*, such a view of history is a myth, the myth of a specific culture bent on denying cultural differences by claiming universality for itself and its ideals. But the *Lettres persanes* also argues (and in this way it offers a critical perspective different from that of structuralist anthropology) that the ideal of culture is also a myth, whether of an outsider or of a culture of outsiders. For the cultural order is *an order* with closed boundaries only for the outsider, and the absence of contradiction within that order is based on the outsider's illusion that he is indeed outside all cultural limitations, that his position determines the boundary between cultures as well as the boundary of the cultural in general. The aim of the outsider, no matter how critical his perspective, is thus to accomplish the impossible: to ensure his continued alienation and at the same time to find a more congenial homeland, to renounce his own historical culture but to occupy the position outside of culture that universal history also claims for itself. It is in the interests of the outsider as much as the insider to keep the boundary between culture and history as determined, as closed as possible, in the interests of the structuralist as much as the historicist. For if history is the myth of a specific, Western culture, still the perspective that places culture beyond history offers no escape from this myth: it corresponds to the transcendent perspective of an idealized outsider who is in fact as much inside both the cultural and the historical as outside.

FOUR

(*Montesquieu*)
Idealism and History: Althusser and the Critique of Origins

To WRITE a history of history writing, it is first necessary to have a concept of history. This necessity is implicitly and sometimes even explicitly denied by historians who argue that the sense of history can only emerge from the practice of history itself, from the accumulation and analysis of historical data, which, it is claimed, arrange themselves according to their own logic, to laws inherent in the historical process itself rather than according to a theory of history imposed on the material by the historian. Historical events are treated by such historians as discrete moments in a unified and continuous temporal sequence. Historical periods are treated as natural divisions which by and large follow calendar divisions, and history is seen as an evolutionary process with the end of the process never explicitly stated or investigated—although it is in each case assumed. All investigation of the concept of history itself is considered to be abstract, philosophical (or, by some, literary) speculation of no use to the practical historian and even a threat to "true history." Such historians attempt to maintain at all costs the boundary between the *theory* and *practice* of history, between the philosophy of history and "true history." In a very general sense, theirs is an empiricist view of history that avoids the question of how the categories, operations, and even form of historical practice are to be defined if history itself has not first been defined.

It is highly ironic that so much of the history written on the Enlightenment is naively empiricist, inasmuch as the historiography of the Enlightenment itself gives such a prominent place to reflection on the concept of history. In his portrait of the memorialists, Voltaire criticizes historians who, as contemporaries of the events they described, exhibit a similar desire to record what happened simply because it happened and thus fail to develop a concept of history. At the same time, Enlightenment philosopher-historians such as Voltaire and Montesquieu also recognize that the absence of explicit reflection on the concept of history does not mean that such a concept is wholly absent, even in the work of the least reflective memorialist. Instead, an interest in the past is always an interest in a *specific* past, and religious, cultural, social, or personal factors motivate the choice of a historical subject and the manner in which it is presented. In such cases a concept of history is indeed present, but it is a naive concept that fails to express the specificity of history, reducing it instead to an implicit set of religious or cultural values. Thus history, far from being a record of things past becomes a reflection of the ideology of the historian and of his time.

Louis Althusser's "Montesquieu, Politics and History" stands out in contrast to the great majority of studies concerned with the historical thinking of the Enlightenment, for where they are dominated by the assumptions of the traditional history of ideas, it raises fundamental questions about the possibility, scope, and nature of history.[1] His interpretation of history and of Montesquieu's De l'esprit des lois is based on the premise that history can only be proper history if it produces its own concept of itself, and that, moreover, once it succeeds in doing this, history becomes a science. To produce its own concept of itself and its corresponding object is no easy task for history, however; it requires constant vigilance and struggle. One

[1] Louis Althusser, "Montesquieu, Politics and History" is included in a volume of Althusser's essays entitled *Politics and History: Montesquieu, Rousseau, Hegel and Marx*, translated by Ben Brewster (London: New Left Review Press, 1972). This essay appeared originally in French as a separate work, *Montesquieu, la politique et l'histoire* (Paris: Presses Universitaires de France, 1964).

could say that in this struggle as it is depicted by Althusser, the enemy of the historian and philosopher is idealism, for "idealism" and "abstraction" are the two terms used interchangeably by Althusser to characterize the approaches Montesquieu must forcefully reject in order to produce authentic history. Althusser argues that Montesquieu is unlike Spinoza, Grotius, and Hobbes before him, in that he proposes, not a theory of the essence of society, but a theory of "real history." Like them, he wants to establish a science of politics, but whereas they never discovered or constructed an object corresponding to their demand for scientific rigor, Montesquieu does when he proposes to study "all the concrete societies of history" ("Politics and History," p. 20). This construction of a new object and its theoretical and methodological ramifications are what, in Althusser's judgment, make Montesquieu both the first political scientist and the first scientific historian, the "most determined adversary of [the] abstraction" of the political philosophers and the moral and theological historians who preceded him ("Politics and History," p. 20).

Clearly, in Althusser's work on Montesquieu, idealism is not just a specific movement in the history of philosophy nor is it a label applicable only to a handful of philosophical thinkers. The struggle against idealism is so difficult precisely because it exists in so many guises. Although he does not exhaustively enumerate all of these, Althusser does characterize its dominant forms: "In order to begin to be scientific, the necessity which governs history must stop borrowing its reasons from any order transcendent to history" (p. 21). This means, first of all, that morality and theology must both be rejected as the basis of (scientific) history. More surprising than this rejection of theologians and moralists, however, is Althusser's critique of social contract theory, for, as he himself notes, it represents, in many respects, the most progressive political and historical theory of the Enlightenment. But, writes Althusser, its "features of *polemic* and *petition*" against the existing social order are also responsible for its "abstraction and idealism" (p. 27). Despite its critical value, the fundamental

131

concept of all social contract theory, of all theories of the state of nature, is just another transhistorical ideal; such theories root history in an origin or ideal posited outside and above it. Finally, and paradoxically, there is for Althusser what could be called an "empiricist idealism," the result of the idealization of concrete life itself: "Without a *critique* of the immediate concepts in which every epoch thinks the history it lives, one remains on the threshold of a true knowledge of history, . . . a prisoner of the illusions it produces" (p. 99). Like the theologians, moralists, and social contract theorists, these "empiricists" shared "an obsession which masked the real from them" (p. 103).

It is worth noting that Althusser's work on Montesquieu differs in some respects from such later works as *Reading Capital* and *For Marx* in that certain terms figure more prominently in it than in them, and other terms, though prominent in both, are defined somewhat differently in each.[2] As his title suggests, "history" is a central preoccupation in the work on Montesquieu, whereas Marx's "science" is the focus of the later works. This shift in terminology and focus corresponds to a shift in Althusser's definition of science and (scientific) history. Whereas, in "Montesquieu, Politics and History," Althusser stresses "the concrete" and "the real" as the basis for scientific history, in the later works his emphasis on the role of science in constructing its own object is much stronger, and this shift corresponds to a tendency to replace "history" with "science." Or, to put it another way, in these later works, "the real" and "the concrete" in their immediacy are seen as the products of idealism or ideology, and the mark of "science" is precisely a constitutive awareness that it exists as such only when its determining role in the construction of its objects is recognized.[3] The greater importance Althusser attaches

[2] Louis Althusser and Etienne Balibar, *Reading Capital*, translated by Ben Brewster (London: New Left Books, 1970); Louis Althusser, *For Marx*, translated by Ben Brewster (New York: Random House, 1970).

[3] "Contrary to the ideological illusions . . . of empiricism or sensualism, a science never works on an existence whose essence is pure immediacy or sin-

to the critique of empiricism in *For Marx* and *Reading Capital* corresponds to his evolving conception of "science."

While these changes are certainly significant, it is equally important to stress the continuity between Althusser's early and later works. Indeed, instances can be found in both where Althusser uses the term "science" interchangeably with "history." For example, in *For Marx*, he elaborates on what is for him the absolutely crucial "epistemological break" between the work of the young, humanist Marx and that of the Marx of *The German Ideology*: "By founding the theory of history . . . Marx simultaneously broke with his erstwhile ideological philosophy. . . . This 'epistemological break' divides Marx's thought into two long essential periods: the 'ideological period' before, and the scientific period after" (*For Marx*, pp. 33-34). In both "Montesquieu, Politics and History" and *For Marx*, it is not so much the place and definition of "the real" and "the concrete" that organize Althusser's analysis as it is an opposition between history and idealism in the former, and between science and ideology in the latter. One could say that in Althusser's work, the logic of these oppositions or "epistemological breaks" is stable in each case, even if the terms that comprise the oppositions mark a shift in emphasis and a change in Althusser's conception of "the real." In this sense, a critical analysis of the relationship between history and idealism concerns not only Althusser's essay on Montesquieu, but his later works as well.

If he decides to make Montesquieu the central figure in his interpretation of the political philosophy and philosophy of history of the Enlightenment, it is because Althusser considers that unlike his immediate predecessors and many of his contemporaries, Montesquieu refuses to judge what is by what ought to be. But Althusser also argues that Montesquieu avoids traditional forms of idealism only to succumb to still another

gularity ('sensations' or 'individuals'). . . . Its particular labour consists of *elaborating its own scientific facts* through a critique of the *ideological 'facts'* elaborated by earlier ideological theoretical practice" (*For Marx*, pp. 183-184).

form—in his case, unlike Marx's, the "epistemological break" is not absolute. Like Voltaire, whom he quotes, Althusser sees *De l'esprit des lois* as the expression of a conservative *parti pris* that, in the historical context in which Montesquieu was writing, was paradoxically both the condition of the scientificity and the indication of the limits of his work. For if it prevented him from positing a nonexistent ideal, it did not prevent him from implicitly idealizing the "reality" and "concreteness" of the society he studied—his own—by making it *the only possible reality*.

Althusser's interpretation of Montesquieu raises an issue of fundamental importance to the understanding of history. Indeed, any form of historical explanation must ask—as Althusser does of Montesquieu—whether or not the order it perceives or imposes is the mere projection of a structure originating in some individual or collective "subject." In this sense all history is confronted with a choice between two unacceptable alternatives. The first is an idealism or Platonism that refuses history in the name of a transcendent order. The second is some form of empiricism that renounces the quest for patterns of intelligibility without which history ceases to have significance or that pretends to renounce this quest, only to pursue it in the form of underlying assumptions which, because they remain unstated, constitute a covert idealism. All history must reckon with idealism or else be determined by it, and Althusser suggests through his reading of Montesquieu that even in reckoning with idealism, history may still be determined by it.

In Althusser's view, then, Montesquieu is consistently confronted with a choice between two forms of idealism—between social contract theory and the doctrine of natural sociability, between natural and cultural determinism—and he sees Montesquieu consistently rejecting one form of idealism only to embrace another. In my view, however, the interest of Montesquieu lies in his not having made the "choice" Althusser offers him. For *De l'esprit des lois* reveals that the opposition between these terms itself derives from an idealism that regulates all theories of nature and history, and moreover, that this idealism *also* regulates the opposition between history and idealism that provides Althusser with his critical perspective on *De l'esprit des lois*. In other words, the concept of a history beyond or outside idealism would itself be idealist. The task *De l'esprit des lois* sets for itself is to situate all idealisms—whether of nature, culture, or history—in terms of specific contexts. For Montesquieu then, unlike Althusser, history too is determined by its contexts and by some form or other of idealism. The problem then becomes not to escape from idealism, but to confront and undermine the idealist core of history within history itself.

DESPITE a debt to scientific empiricism, Montesquieu, like the majority of Enlightenment historians, is far from defending the worth and dignity of mere facts. *De l'esprit des lois* as a whole reflects a conviction that history cannot be simply narrated because it is not constituted by facts alone. Clearly, in Montesquieu's view, "facts" only become historical when they are presented within a framework of some kind, and thus it is in laying the framework for his history that the historian produces history and at the same time implicitly or explicitly reveals his concept of history. It is all the more important to keep this very basic point in mind where Montesquieu is concerned, inasmuch as in the view of many of his contemporaries as well as of many nineteenth- and twentieth-century readers, Montesquieu's primary contribution to history lies precisely in his command of a vast array of factual material. But Montesquieu himself portrays the wealth of information with which he has to deal as a tide carrying him away (XX, 1) or as an attacking army whose ranks he is struggling to break through (XIX, 1). This attitude is more than the expression of Montesquieu's frustration or determination with respect to the goal of comprehensiveness he had set for himself. Its methodological significance is evident in his preface, where, in a condensed account of the genesis of *De l'esprit des lois*, he describes the hesitation and discouragement that preceded his discovery of what he was to call his principles: "Often have I begun, and as often have I laid aside, this undertaking. I have a thousand times consigned the pages I had written to the winds. . . . I knew neither rules nor exceptions; I would find the truth, only to lose it again. But when I once discovered my principles, everything I had sought came to me."[4] In the composition of the work whose intent is to present a comprehensive view of human institutions, the principles, rather than the material, take precedence.

Montesquieu's declaration concerning the decisive importance of his discovery of his principles highlights the importance of the conceptual as opposed to the empirical aspect of history. Equally important, the term "principle" has a more particular significance which it is the task—it is no exaggeration to say the one and only task—of De l'esprit des lois to uncover; and it is in defining this term that Montesquieu articulates his own concept of history. Montesquieu's "principles" refer neither in a loose way to his own way of going about things, nor to a single general definition or law to which the whole of historical experience could be adduced, but rather, to a very specific aspect of the analysis of the three types of government with which De l'esprit des lois begins. As Montesquieu writes at the end of the chapter entitled "Of Positive Laws": "I shall first examine the relations which laws bear to the nature and principle of each government: and as this principle has a supreme influence on the laws, I shall make it my study to understand it thoroughly; and if I can but once establish it, the laws will soon appear to flow thence as if from their source" (I, 3). This statement puts the chapters on climate and terrain that follow those on the three types of government in a different light from the one in which his contemporaries were to read them. For Montesquieu, the most original aspect of his work (and he is convinced of his work's origi-

4 This passage and all subsequent quotations from De l'esprit des lois in this chapter are taken from The Spirit of the Laws (New York: Hafner Publishing Company, 1949), translated by Thomas Nugent. I have modified the translation where I consider it seriously misleading or distorting.

nality)[5] lies not in those chapters, but rather in a specific element of his typology of governments. Montesquieu's insistence on the capital importance of his principles does in fact distinguish his typology from those coming before it,[6] and this new typology also provides Montesquieu with the cultural and historical contexts in which he situates the other elements of his analyses.

Montesquieu gives a definition of the principle of government in an early chapter of De l'esprit des lois, but while this definition is precise, it is far from simple in its implications. The principle is consistently paired with the nature of a government, and it is from their pairing and opposition that Montesquieu derives his definition of each: "There is this difference between the nature of government and its principle, that the former is that which makes it such, the latter, that which makes it work. One is its particular structure, the other is the human passions which set it in motion" (III, 1). To understand the principle of a government, we must also understand the nature of a government, or, to put it another way, we must understand the relationship between the two terms if we are to understand each individually. One way to

[5] "If this work meets with success, I shall owe it in large measure to the majesty of my subject; however, I do not think that I have been totally deficient in point of genius. When I saw what so many great men . . . had written before me, I was lost in admiration; but I did not lose courage: I said with Correggio 'I too am a painter' " (Preface).

[6] Montesquieu scholars frequently point out two ways in which Montesquieu's typology deviates from the classical (Aristotelian) division of governments. (1) Unlike Montesquieu's typology, that division was made according to the locus of power. Thus classical political philosophers saw two separate categories (democracy and aristocracy) where Montesquieu sees only subdivisions of one category (the republic), and where they saw only one form (tyranny), Montesquieu sees two (monarchy and despotism). (2) Montesquieu posits a principle as an irreducible element of each type of government (see Robert Shackleton, Montesquieu, A Critical Biography [Oxford: Oxford University Press, 1961], pp. 265-269). I would argue that it does not suffice merely to note these differences; there is a relationship between them that must be analyzed if Montesquieu's sense of his originality with respect to classical political philosophy is to be fully understood.

understand that relationship is to view it as a simple opposition. When simply paired with and opposed to the nature of a government, the principle seems to represent the relationship of each government to time—it is what permits a government to reproduce itself, to exist in time, to have a history. Since the nature of a government lies in a form or structure to which the principle gives life and movement, it would follow that the nature of a government is incorruptible, and that any change in a government reflects, in the overwhelming majority of cases, a change in the principle. For Montesquieu, this is indeed the case: "The corruption of each government begins almost always with that of its principles" (VIII, 1).[7]

It is indeed tempting to treat the relationship between nature and principle as an essentially static opposition, and on the whole, that is what Montesquieu scholars have tended to do. More recently, this tendency has been reinforced both by structuralism, which has attempted to isolate a "synchronic" level of analysis in the various fields it has touched, in order to oppose it to a "diachronic" level, and by many of those who have attacked structuralism in the name of "diachrony" and "history." But the critic who adopts either approach ignores Montesquieu's own insistence on the methodological priority of his principles. In this respect too, Althusser's "Montesquieu, Politics and History" stands out, for he argues that the aim of Montesquieu's argument is to establish that *"the nature and the principle are absolutely interdependent in the mobile but pregnant totality of the State"* ("Politics and History," p. 51), thanks, precisely, to the dominance of the principle. Ultimately, however, Althusser takes the position that Montesquieu fails in this aim, because nature comes to dom-

---

[7] The exception to which Montesquieu's "almost always" seems to point is despotism; not so much because the corruption of despotism does not stem from the corruption of its principle, but because that corruption cannot be said to *begin* with the corruption of the principle, since the principle (and hence nature) of the despotism is corruption itself: "The principle of despotic government is subject to a continual corruption, because it is even in its nature corrupt" (VIII, 10).

inate principle, or, in Althusser's terms, because the three forms of government come to dominate history itself conceived as a dynamic totality (p. 60). In making this criticism, Althusser's own aim is to reinvest history with the value Montesquieu's system ultimately fails to give it. But as Althusser progresses in his analysis of *De l'esprit des lois*, it becomes clear that Montesquieu's "failure" is the result of a self-fulfilling prophecy; that is, it is implicit in the very terms Althusser uses to analyze Montesquieu's work and, more broadly speaking, in Althusser's theory of history. Indeed, Althusser conceives of Montesquieu's principles as referring to the "concrete behaviour of men" (p. 56); or again, the principle "has the real life of men as its concrete background" (p. 58). The principle of a government is concrete and thus historical; its nature is by implication formal, abstract, ideal. Althusser may attach a different value to the concrete and the historical than do the moralists, theologians, idealists, and empiricists he criticizes, but the framework of oppositions within which he conceives history is the same. And as long as history is conceived within the framework of this traditional opposition, it remains implicitly secondary and derivative with respect to the form and ideal governing the opposition, even if its priority is proclaimed within the opposition.

When Montesquieu insists on the priority of his principles, he is not merely attaching a new value to the concrete with respect to the ideal, the historical with respect to the formal, or the diachronic with respect to the synchronic; he is not merely reversing a traditional hierarchy. Instead, his insistence on the priority of his principles transforms the definition of both history and idealism, both temporality and structure. If the principle has priority, then it cannot be viewed as merely setting in motion a form that is theoretically or ideally given, but *neither* can it be viewed as producing a form or ideal that remains a foreign body within history, essentially a stranger to the supposed concreteness of history as such. These two complementary views of history equate historicity with what could be called positive history, but the aim of Montesquieu's

139

insistence on the priority of his principles is to establish a distinction between positive history and (a transcendental) historicity.[8] Montesquieu's argument is not that the structure and form of each government are produced by positive history, for positive history cannot "begin" until the principle has been paired with the nature or structure of each government. The historicity designated by the principles is thus "anterior to" or a condition of positive history; it is not *in fact* but rather *by right* prior to the constitution of any ideal or analytical concept of nature. Moreover, the radical form of historicity in question cannot be simply opposed to the ideal, for it is not merely "factual" or "concrete." Because it cannot be simply opposed to the ideal, it cannot be dominated by it either.

By giving a new status to what might otherwise be considered as the mere temporal aspect of each type of government, Montesquieu also transforms the sense of the term "nature" with which the concept of the principle is paired, and, indeed, the transformation of the one term implies a transformation of the other. As has been pointed out, the principle allows a given form of government to exist in time, but it is also the source of the corruption of the different forms of government,

---

[8] "Transcendental historicity" is a term used by Jacques Derrida in his introduction to the French translation of Husserl's *Origine de la géométrie* (Paris: Presses Universitaires de France, 1962) to distinguish Husserl's concept of historicity from a historicist concept. Derrida uses this term to designate a "space" Husserl must delimit in order to consider the origin of geometry, that is to say, of a science that is repeatable and exemplary in its universality. The search for this origin implies that geometry appeared one day, "here and now," and because of this, Derrida argues, Husserl comes to view this eidetic as irreducibly "inhabited" by history. This, in turn, means that phenomenology itself, as the horizon in which the example of geometry can be considered, is itself bound ("engagé") by this historicity. At the same time, Derrida will show Husserl insisting (in particular with respect to Dilthey and to the concept of the *Weltanschauung*) *not* that the intuition of this transcendental historicity would permit us to "dispense with historical investigation," but rather, that "it precedes *by right* all material historical investigation and has no need of facts as such to reveal to the historian the a priori sense of his activity and his objects" (p. 117, my translation).

and thus it is also what makes certain forms of government disappear from history. If the nature of each government is both produced and destroyed by its principle, then the nature of each government, its very essence as an ideal, is complex and contradictory, the matrix of fundamental differences, rather than a form given once and for all time either in or above history or theory.

Montesquieu's use of the term "nature" to describe the form of each government contrasts strikingly with the way in which political philosophers of the seventeenth and eighteenth centuries used the same term, and this contrast further clarifies how Montesquieu's insistence on the priority of his principles changes the way both nature and history are defined. For political philosophers such as Hobbes, Locke, and Rousseau, nature is a state that exists prior to the founding of civil society and prior to history. Nonetheless, they see it as a crucial concept in understanding the existence and form of society, for each considers that man's own nature is most clearly manifest in this natural state, and that all historical societies must ultimately be determined in a more or less direct way by man's fundamental nature. Montesquieu himself uses the term "nature" in this sense in an early section of De l'esprit des lois (I, 2), but unlike Hobbes, Locke, and Rousseau, he devotes only a few lines to it before moving on to his next chapter—"Of Positive Laws." The substance of these lines, as well as their briefness, seems to indicate that for Montesquieu, little or nothing about the existence or form of historical societies is to be explained by referring to a state of nature. Montesquieu's natural man believes in God, is at peace with other men, and is naturally charmed and pleased by the opposite sex. Rousseau was to criticize such representations of natural man on the ground that they project into the state of nature behavior and values that are properly social. But Montesquieu himself implies as much when he gives what he views to be the fourth law of nature: "the desire to live in society."

For Montesquieu, then, a discussion of "nature" in a relative sense—as it pertains to the existence of different types of governments and societies—seems to have all but completely replaced the discussion of "nature" in the sense of either Hobbes, Locke, or Rousseau. Interpreters of Montesquieu have seen this apparent rejection of the concept of the state of nature as decisive in determining Montesquieu's position with respect to the political spectrum of the Enlightenment. For Althusser, "it is *at the time* generally a fairly sure index of discrimination between tendencies to consider that *the doctrine of natural sociability or of the instinct of sociability designates a theory of feudal inspiration, and the doctrine of the social contract, a theory of 'bourgeois' inspiration*, even when it is in the service of absolute monarchy (in Hobbes for example)" ("Politics and History," p. 27). As we have seen, Althusser is quick to point to what he sees as the ambiguities of the choice between the theory of natural sociability and the theory of the social contract. Though the latter permitted its proponents to put into question the existing social order on the ground that it was an artificial, human creation, at the same time it led them to an "abstraction" and an "idealism" that rendered them incapable of producing a concept of history and thus of studying existing institutions in a scientific manner. Althusser sees Montesquieu as choosing the theory of natural sociability for political (ideological) and methodological reasons. On the one hand, his choice was consistent with a conservative *parti pris*. On the other hand, it was consistent with an authentic attempt to deal with history and historical realities—to found a science of politics.

One cannot but agree that, in the form in which it concerned Locke, Hobbes, and Rousseau, the theory of a state of nature does not interest Montesquieu. At the same time, Althusser's contention that Montesquieu must be viewed as subscribing to a theory of natural sociability is open to question on two related grounds. First, *De l'esprit des lois* does not, when read as a whole, constitute a refusal of the problems and concepts of the theory of natural law, even though it modifies considerably the terms in which the entire question is considered. *De l'esprit des lois* should be read as a dialogue with Hobbes and with a position that was to become in many respects that of Rousseau, and the typology of governments in particular should be read as an attempt to situate rather than simply reject theories of the state of nature. Second, *De l'esprit des lois* in general and Montesquieu's debate with Aristotle on the question of slavery in particular argue that the theory of natural sociability is essentially a variant of the theory of the social contract, except that for the former, culture functions as nature or norm. The view that all social forms are equally "natural"—because society is essentially natural—and the view that man's true nature can be determined only independently of any social context are alike in affirming that man has *a* nature.

The common ground upon which social contract theory and the theory of natural sociability rest is pointed to in Montesquieu's discussion of Aristotle's *Politics*, which, along with Plato's *Republic* and *Laws*, must be considered Montesquieu's most important ancient philosophical source. The two features held by Althusser to distinguish the theory of natural sociability and social contract theory are both present in Aristotle's work. On the one hand, the *Politics* argues that man is destined by nature to live in a *polis* or in society. Moreover, it contains a classification of governments (democracy, aristocracy, oligarchy, and monarchy), a common feature of the works affirming man's natural sociability, inasmuch as such works pretend to renounce abstract, universal, or "presocial" ideals of man and study him in the context of existing social forms. On the other hand, the diversity represented by the different types of government coexists with a general level of analysis in terms of which men can be declared "by nature" free or "by nature" unfree independent of any social context, as Montesquieu notes in criticizing Aristotle's explanation of the existence of slavery (IV, 7). However carefully a given typology might reflect the empirical data it is intended to organize and present, then, it does not in and of itself constitute a rejection of the idealism of social contract theory, and may in fact presuppose a single human nature. The notion of the plurality of forms of government must itself be radicalized in some way if the ideal of nature is to be seriously questioned.

Montesquieu's typology represents just such a radicalization, for what Aristotle's *Politics* presupposes as natural is represented by Montesquieu in cultural and historical terms. To the assertion that some men are by nature slaves, Montesquieu responds that men are only slaves as the result of a specific historical situation—that of despotism.[9] Similarly, freedom would not be natural, but rather the product of another specific historical situation—the republic. Even natural sociability, the cornerstone of the *Politics*, is undercut and situated by Montesquieu's typology, for the three forms of government he delineates do not of necessity all constitute societies. A doctrine holding that all forms of society are natural because society itself is viewed as natural to man would be hard pressed to apply this thesis to Montesquieu's theory of despotism, for he takes special pains to make his portrait of it as paradoxical as possible. This social form is in effect a nonsociety, as Montesquieu makes clear when he defines its principle: "The principle of the despotic government is ceaselessly corrupted, because it is corrupt by its very nature" (VIII, 10). This same fundamental point is reiterated in Montesquieu's discussion of education in despotism: "Education, which consists principally in living with others . . . is thus in a manner of speaking nonexistent [under despotism]" (IV, 3). Montesquieu's portrait of despotism thus not only situates slavery in a specific context, it also undercuts the equally or perhaps even more fundamental assertion that men are by nature social creatures in the sense that despotism constitutes a "society" without social life.

It could be argued that even after having situated nature in all of these forms, Montesquieu's typology still presupposes a

[9] "There are countries where the excess of heat enervates the body, and renders men so dispirited, that nothing but the fear of chastisement can oblige them to perform a laborious duty. . . . Aristotle endeavors to prove that there are natural slaves; but what he says is far from proving it. If there be any such, I believe they are those of whom I have been speaking" (XV, 7).

concept of nature that it does not situate—a nature manifest in the typology itself. According to this argument, both Montesquieu and Aristotle's typologies would themselves constitute a second nature that, thanks to its stability and universality, would provide the same sorts of conceptual guarantees and have the same conceptual function as a concept of nature. Each regime would have a "nature," and the sum of these natures would be human nature itself. But on this point too, Montesquieu's typology differs significantly from Aristotle's. Unlike the Greek philosopher, Montesquieu argues that monarchy, in particular, is a form of government known only to modernity and that Aristotle's concept of monarchy is improper, since it does not entail "the distribution of the three powers in the government of a single person" (XI, 9). Thus the regimes Aristotle classifies as monarchies are in fact either republics or despotisms. In Montesquieu's view, Aristotle's understanding of the historicity of all social forms is limited by his own historical situation. The boundaries of his knowledge are those of the ancient world, and yet he takes them as the boundaries of knowledge itself. The moderns, then, are in a privileged position with respect to the ancients, for the disappearance of the ancient world provides the former with a unique opportunity to understand both the historicity of the forms of government of the ancients and the historicity of the form of government peculiar to modernity: monarchy.

It is only when the concept of nature, in both a general sense and the sense it has when it is considered to be specific to a particular regime, is subordinated to the principles, it is only when the historicity of nature, whether that nature is "natural" or social, is affirmed, that Montesquieu's typology of governments can be posed. Montesquieu articulates his own concept of history, then, through a continuous definition and redefinition of his principles. The principles are indications of historicity itself—not as it is manifest in positive history, but rather as it is at work in all ideals and all concepts of nature that might be thought to determine history from a position outside and above history. For Montesquieu, the concept of

145

history cannot be conceived in opposition to any ideal and in particular to the ideal of nature. Instead, the historian's task is to situate the ideal, to analyze the conditions that make the existence of a given ideal possible. Thus, much as Montesquieu argues against Aristotle that slavery is not rooted in nature but in specific historical institutions, so his typology of governments shows that the state of nature as conceived by Hobbes and later by Rousseau is the product of a particular "historical context" that is neither completely ideal nor empirical. In this sense Montesquieu never leaves behind the question of nature, never simply expounds or chooses a doctrine of natural sociability as Althusser affirms he does. The states of nature of Hobbes and Rousseau do figure heavily in *De l'esprit des lois*. Hobbes's violent struggle between men is depicted by Montesquieu as the essence of despotism. In a more complex fashion, the ideal aspects of Rousseau's state of nature already figure in Montesquieu's portrayal of the republic. But by situating each in a specific context rather than simply rejecting them out of hand as idealist, Montesquieu all the more surely undercuts the claims of both Hobbes and Rousseau to have attained a level of analysis beyond history.

Montesquieu openly criticizes Hobbes in his own brief section on the state of nature for describing it in terms of a struggle for domination. "He does not realize that he attributes to mankind before the establishment of society what can happen but in consequence of this establishment" (I, 2). Montesquieu's portrait of despotism carries out the intent of this critique, for it provides a specific context for the state Hobbes views as natural. For Hobbes, the struggle for absolute domination of one man over another characterizes man in the state of nature. Montesquieu equates this struggle with the existence of slavery, and regards slavery as indigenous to despotism. Hobbes repeatedly states that man in the state of nature is motivated by fear, and that all emotions are ultimately reducible to it. For Montesquieu, fear is not "natural" but the principle of *a* government—despotism. The despot, in particular, corresponds to Hobbes's image of natural man, and

Montesquieu himself repeatedly underscores the parallel: "As the peoples who live under a good government are happier than those who without rule or leaders wander about the forests, so monarchs who live under the fundamental laws of their state are far happier than despotic princes who have nothing to regulate their own passions nor those of their subjects" (V, 11).

For Montesquieu, Hobbes's natural man is thus not outside of history but within it; Hobbes's concept of the state of nature is not the basis for historical understanding but rather a projection and idealization of a state that must be understood in historical terms. Of course there is a certain irony in Montesquieu's criticizing Hobbes as an idealist, for Hobbes's state of nature, though it may be ideal in form, hardly seems to be ideal in substance. Hobbes's natural man seems rather to be social man demystified and divested of the conventions— whether politeness or morality—that mask his fear, egotism, and meanness in society. For Montesquieu, Hobbes's "idealism" is indeed complex, for, on the one hand it is speculative and abstract and, on the other, it also represents an attempt to set aside ideals and ideology and to consider man independently of the masks he wears in society: that is to say, it is also a "realism" that deals with actions and facts rather than beliefs and conventions. Considered in this second, "realist" aspect, Hobbes's idealism is the methodological basis of a social or historical empiricism.

Montesquieu's portrayal of despotism, then, not only argues against the view that history is governed from without by an ideal of nature, but also against the (complementary) idea that history can be reduced to a "reality" underlying appearances, to an empiricism that would claim to reject all forms of idealism and to deal only with concrete events, actions, circumstances, and motivations. Indeed, one could say that in a sense, Montesquieu views despotism as having a factual existence without having a historical existence, for while the "life" of despotism is rich in "events," still those events do not constitute a history. Any event or circumstance in despotism—be it a hot climate or the despotism of a vizier, or of the despot himself—is necessarily an accident, for despotism lacks any specific institution or principle of continuity that would permit such events and circumstances to become part of a history. In this light, Montesquieu's treatment of despotism in the section describing in detail the relation between laws and climate is revealing—or rather, what is especially revealing is that in the section in question, Montesquieu deals *almost exclusively* with despotism and with slavery, which he views as indigenous to despotism. According to Montesquieu, climate in the north and in the temperate zones is such that in the end it has little visible effect on political institutions.[10] It is in the zones close to the equator, he argues, that climate has a determining role in a direct sense, rationalizing if not necessitating the institution of slavery and, ultimately, the more pervasive civil and political slavery that is the lot of every subject in Montesquieu's despotism. The "good legislator" institutes laws that compensate for and work against the influence of climate as one nears the equator. The "bad legislator" fails to combat its effects. But it is in the "south" where the particular circumstances of climate have a directly determining effect, and this is one more way in which despotism is subject to accident and circumstance. Circumstantiality marks despotism at all levels, from the relationship between it and its physical setting, to its economic, educational, and political institutions, and ultimately and most heavily, at the level of the despot himself.

Just as all social relationships in despotism are relationships of dominion and servitude, so the despot's relation to his people is that of master to slave. As Montesquieu was not alone among Enlightenment thinkers in pointing out, slavery is det-

[10] This is not to say that, for Montesquieu, climate is determining in the "south" but not in the northern and temperate zones. It is to say that for him, "our" European definition of moral behavior is in fact the norm of the cultures situated in temperate and northern climates, and that, as a result, the determination of behavior by climate remains hidden for us when we consider the peoples living in those latitudes: "If we draw near the south, we fancy ourselves entirely removed from the verge of morality" (XIV, 2).

rimental to the master as well as to the slave. In the case of the despot, the absolute nature of his mastery is the institutional source of his regime's fundamental corruption and instability. In this sense, the despot is the ultimate victim of the circumstantiality that characterizes despotism as a whole. The history of his regime is a nonhistory, a series of absolutely discontinuous moments, or, to use Montesquieu's term, "revolutions."

History in *De l'esprit des lois* does not represent an (unsuccessful) attempt simply to reject idealism, as Althusser argues, for circumstance, the event, and the "concrete" alone do not and cannot constitute history. Idealism does *have a place* in history, and it is in his discussion of the republic, in particular, that Montesquieu indicates what that place is. Whereas his analysis of despotism situates Hobbes's "realist" view of the state of nature within a specific context, his discussion of the republic provides the specific context for an ideal nature. Rousseau was to criticize Montesquieu for his failure to treat political philosophy in terms of an ideal government rather than in terms of existing governments.[11] But whereas for Rousseau the ideal form of government is that which never existed, it is, for Montesquieu, a form that *did exist*—notably in ancient Greece. For Montesquieu, the ideal is a moment in history, and this explains both the striking parallels and the differences between the ideal of nature presented in the work of each writer. As is the case for Rousseau, Montesquieu's ideal of nature takes two forms, one primitive, the other comporting fully elaborated institutions and laws. The difference

[11] "The science of politics is and probably always will be unknown. . . . In modern times the only man who could have created this vast and useless science was the illustrious Montesquieu. But he was not concerned with the principles of political law; he was content to deal with the positive laws of established governments; and nothing could be more different than these two branches of study. Yet he who would judge wisely in matters of actual government is forced to combine the two; he must know what ought to be in order to judge what is" (*Emile* [Paris: Editions Garnier Frères, 1964], p. 584; cited in "Montesquieu, Politics and History," pp. 29-30).

in their treatment of this ideal of nature, however, is already evident in the disparity between their accounts of man's primitive state. For Rousseau, that state is simply ahistorical. For Montesquieu, it corresponds to (a stage of) man's prehistory—that prior to the invention of agriculture. Montesquieu's depiction of "les peuples sauvages" (hunters) and "les peuples barbares" (herdsmen) (XVIII, 10-31) affirms essentially the same values as does Rousseau's state of nature. In Montesquieu's preagricultural society there is a maximum of individual liberty, for there is no civil law, but only political law of the kind that regulates inherently sovereign states. This primitive state, like Rousseau's state of nature, affords a minimum of occasions for the violation of the individual's liberty, for the absence of signs—either written or monetary—makes deception and theft difficult, if not impossible, and furthermore prevents the accumulation of the wealth or knowledge that would lead to inequality and the demise of liberty (V, 3; V, 4). But the similarity between Montesquieu's description of preagricultural society and Rousseau's state of nature only brings out more sharply the fundamental difference between them. Montesquieu's primitive state is still a social state, and thus, though it is prehistorical, is not ahistorical as the state of nature is for Rousseau.

In its fully elaborated institutional and legal form the ideal of nature for Montesquieu, as for Rousseau, is the republic. Clearly for Montesquieu the republic is an ideal, for it reproduces in a cultural and legal setting a state of liberty and equality that existed prior to the institution of law and to the invention of writing and of money. The ideal status of the republic is evident too in Montesquieu's reliance on the utopian models furnished by Plato's *Laws* and his *Republic* in his discussion of this political form. More specifically, the principle of the republic is virtue, and this particular "passion" is the source of a stability that virtually excludes time and change from the republic. For Montesquieu, virtue connotes a love of frugality and equality that maintains the republic in a state of equilibrium and thus precludes the tensions between unequal groups that bring change in other political contexts. Furthermore, virtue implies a respect for tradition and authority that ensures that each generation will resemble the previous one, for the conflict of generations is another important source of tensions and hence of change. In short, the republic tends to exist outside of history, if one defines history as sheer change, and Montesquieu is of the opinion that a republican form of government can only lie in the distant past, never in a future state attained through a process of reform or revolution.[12] It is in this light that he interprets the history of England under the "revolutionary" Cromwell: "A very curious spectacle it was in the last century to behold the impotent efforts of the English towards the establishment of democracy. . . . At length, when the country had undergone the most violent shocks, they were obliged to have recourse to the very government they had proscribed" (III, 3).

At first reading, Montesquieu's designation of "virtue" as the principle of the republic seems to imply the following paradox: the principle gives to each government a properly historical aspect, and yet the principle of the republic seems to place it beyond history. This is Althusser's argument:

> The republic retreats into the distant past: Greece, Rome. No doubt that is why it is so beautiful. Montesquieu, who is quite prepared to call Richelieu crazy for his claim to want an angel for a king, so rare is virtue, accepts that in Greece and Rome there were, at certain periods, enough angels to make up whole cities.
>
> This political angelism makes democracy . . . a regime which attains the *true* sphere of politics: that of stability and universality. ("Politics and History," p. 61)

[12] The only exceptions to this rule are the early European settlement in Pennsylvania ("Mr. Penn is a real Lycurgus") and the Indian community established by the Jesuits in Paraguay (IV, 6). But it seems that it is only because both examples involve the founding of a new community that they escape from the weight of history which in Montesquieu's view prevents the establishment of a republican form of government in Europe.

Just as Althusser sees Montesquieu as turning his back on the concept of a state of nature and on a social contract theory that would encourage political opposition to the *ancien régime* but also lead to idealism and abstraction, so Althusser sees Montesquieu for a second time turning his back on idealism in the form of the republic: "Maybe there are *three species of government*. But one, the republic, does not exist except in historical memory. We are left with monarchy and despotism" (p. 86).

But while one can agree that Montesquieu's republic tends toward a universality and atemporality placing it above history understood as sheer change, circumstance, or event, one must also note that Montesquieu's analysis of the ideal assigns it *a specific place in (a) history*. Montesquieu's stance vis-à-vis the political ideal of the republic is consistent with his stance vis-à-vis the concept of the state of nature, which is the basis of social contract theory: he does not turn his back on idealism in either of these guises; rather he situates it. The republican form of government cannot, for Montesquieu, be recreated in the present or the future, not because it is beyond history but because it has a history, and because the ideals it manifests are determined by a specific historical and cultural setting: that of the ancient world. At the same time, the specificity of the republic as an ideal does not permit Montesquieu to view this age as being simply past when he turns to his discussion of what Althusser considers to be the only regime which for Montesquieu is fully of the present—the monarchy. The past always intervenes in the present, making it impossible for the present to *be* in the full sense of the term: the present of the monarchy is constantly defined and shaped by its relation to this "past" ideal, and it is for precisely this reason that the advent of the ideal, although it is historical, does not have the punctual character of an event as conceived in empiricist terms.

Montesquieu's discussion of the monarchy is thus consistent with his analysis of despotism and the republic in that here too, his aim is to determine the specific historical character of the monarchy without either reducing it to the status of a simple empirical event or turning it into a mere transhistorical ideal. Like all of the historians and political thinkers of his day, Montesquieu is compelled to look to the origin of the monarchy in order to understand it in its modern form and to define its specific character.[13] The overriding question in his discussion of the French monarchy is thus that of its origin; and because Montesquieu's typology reflects the conviction that there is no single nature in which history originates, one might expect an analysis of the origins of the monarchy to lead to *an* origin that is different from either despotism or the republic. In fact, however, one effect of Montesquieu's history of the French monarchy is that it tends to undermine the very specificity of the principles he defends so vigorously elsewhere. But this apparent inconsistency has a critical effect similar to the one Montesquieu seeks when he insists on the priority and plurality of his principles. In investigating the origins of the monarchy, Montesquieu will show that the three types of government are not a static, eternal triad but are rather implicated in each other as part of a complicated history that is not simply progressive.[14] This history can perhaps be under-

[13] The origin of the French monarchy was one of the most, if not the most, politically loaded historical questions of Montesquieu's day. The adherents of the "Romanist" thesis saw the nobility and the institution of chivalry as an instrument of the king and of centralized government. The "Germanist" thesis saw the king as essentially a creation of the nobility. Between these two positions were many gradations and variations. Montesqieu, like other members of the magistracy, occupies an intermediate position, for he sees a clear danger to the monarchy both from the aristocrats who support the Germanist thesis and from the group—composed for the most part of bourgeois and more recently ennobled members of the aristocracy—that supports the king and the central government with more or less enthusiasm. See Elie Carcassone, *Montesquieu et le problème de la constitution française au XVIIIᵉ siècle* (Paris: Presses Universitaires de France, 1926), chap. 4: "Montesquieu et les travaux sur l'histoire de France."

[14] In a similar fashion, the principles of each of these two types of government are also implicated in each other. Honor *replaces, represents*, and *supplements* virtue (III, 6). But honor can do this only because virtue never existed in its purity and unity. Thus Montesquieu says of the republic: "Everything depends, therefore, on establishing this love of the laws and of the country.

stood most clearly if one considers its last chapter—the one that, in Montesquieu's view, has not yet been written, but which Louis XIV tried to write. In its last phase, monarchy degenerates into despotism. This comes about when the monarch tries to gain absolute power—something he can only do at the expense of the nobility. But the essence of monarchy lies in the existence of the nobility as a class; in Montesquieu's view, when the prerogatives of the nobility are ignored, monarchy ceases to be. As Althusser points out, then, Montesquieu's concept of despotism is not only an analytical tool for understanding certain governments, it also warns the monarch—whoever he may be—that his own power will ultimately be seriously threatened (because despotism is as dangerous for the despot as for his subjects) if he tries to seize absolute power at the expense of the nobility. Montesquieu's despotism, then, is a degraded monarchy, and his monarchy, an image of what he considers to be properly exercised royal power.

The monarchy itself, however, is only a phase in a much longer history; in its more modern form (the one described in the section of the typology dealing with monarchy) it may provide an image of properly exercised royal power, but it also provides an image of a degraded nobility.[15] Just as despotism

---

. . . But the surest way of instilling it in children is its being present in their fathers. . . . It is not the young people that degenerate; they are lost only when those of maturer age are already corrupted" (IV, 5). If virtue never existed in its purity and unity, then the process of replacement, representation, and supplementarity is original and not derivative; the difference between honor and virtue is a difference at work within virtue itself and not a distinction external to it. In the context of classical political philosophy, this is an extremely heretical stance, and Montesquieu, in an effort to obscure the scandalous implications of his analysis of the relationship between honor and virtue, covers them up in an elaborate series of footnotes and cross-references (see "Author's Explanatory Note" and also Book III, chap. 5).

[15] Thus Montesquieu scathingly characterizes the court nobility which looked exclusively to the king for favor and recognition: "Ambition in idleness, meanness mixed with pride, a desire of riches without industry; aversion to truth; flattery, perfidy, violation of engagements, contempt of civil duties, fear of the prince's virtue, hope from his weakness, but, above all, a perpetual

follows monarchy in the history of the monarchy, so monarchy follows another form of government—aristocracy. Aristocracy is itself an important concept in Montesquieu's typology of governments, for he classifies it as a subdivision (along with democracy) of the republic, and yet the mere fact that a single type of government can be subdivided in this way seems to undermine the conceptual, let alone historical, stability of the type. Of more immediate importance, Montesquieu's definition of aristocracy also makes his definition of monarchy problematic, for when he describes the origin of the French monarchy, it corresponds in its essential points to his description of this other, presumably distinct form of government. The value exemplified by the French monarchy at its origin turns out to be a relative equality that is for Montesquieu the essence of the aristocratic (and ultimately of the republican) form of government:

> A people who do not cultivate the land have no idea of luxury. We may see, in Tacitus, the admirable simplicity of the German nations; they had no artificial elegances of dress; their ornaments were derived from nature. If the family of their chief was to be distinguished by any sign, it was no other than that which nature might bestow: the kings of the Franks, of the Burgundians, and the Visigoths wore their long hair for a diadem. (XIVIII, 23)

The long hair of the Frankish kings is a purely symbolic distinction, and Montesquieu is recommending to the nobility and king the spirit of moderation that seeks only distinctions of this kind. But when the king and the nobility content themselves with symbolic distinctions, the king comes to resemble the members of his nobility and the nobility, the other members of society. Thus the more the modern monarchy strives to conform to what it was originally, the more it comes to resemble another, distinct form of government—aristocracy.

---

ridicule cast upon virtue, are, I think, the characteristics by which most courtiers in all ages and countries have been constantly distinguished" (III, 5).

For according to Montesquieu's definition, the aristocratic form of government is one in which the nobles must not be allowed to have "personal privileges distinct from those of their body; privileges ought to be for the senate, and simple respect for the senators" (V, 8). Moreover, the principle of the aristocracy is moderation, that is, precisely the virtue that causes the original nobility and the original monarch to content themselves with distinctions of a purely symbolic nature.

Ultimately, however, aristocracy, like despotism and monarchy, is itself a form of government produced by the degradation of a still more original form—democracy. If one considers Montesquieu's description of the democratic republic and the aristocratic republic, one understands why he categorizes them under one heading. Montesquieu's democracy, it has been pointed out, is not Rousseau's. The latter is what one might call a pure democracy in which political sovereignty inheres in each person and cannot be delegated. For Montesquieu, the problem of representation is present in every "moderate" government (democracy, aristocracy, and monarchy). The more democratic the government, the more closely the distinction between those who represent and those who are represented resembles a "natural" distinction. The more monarchic the government, the more arbitrary the distinction, since it tends to be based on birth. But clearly, for Montesquieu, there is no government without distinctions (except despotism), and thus the difference between democracy, aristocracy, and monarchy is not a difference of kind, but of degree. Aristocracy, from which the monarchy is derived, is itself derived from a still more original and more nearly perfect form: "The more an aristocracy borders on democracy, the nearer it approaches perfection" (II, 3).

The typology of governments defines the fundamental difference in terms of which Montesquieu situates all ideals and all concepts of nature. But as is evident in the case of the relationship of the monarchy to the republic and to the despotism, this typology of different forms of government also implies a history in which all seem to have a well-defined place.

The republic is ancient, the monarchy is modern. The republic can be transformed into monarchy or despotism. The monarchy cannot become a republic; it can only degenerate into despotism. Despotism is the point of greatest entropy from which no other form of government can arise. The democratic republic is the point of origin, to which no other form of government can return in any ultimate sense. It seems at this moment, then, that the typology of governments and the fundamental differences it posits may be reducible to *one* history that would narrate the fall from a republican origin to a despotic end, with an optional detour by way of monarchy. This history, then, would supersede the differences founded by the typology of governments, and endow man with a nature, albeit a historical nature, after all. In this way, a concept of history thus tends ultimately in Montesquieu to dominate historicity, to limit or to subordinate the differences and the contradictions within nature or the origin.

As we have seen, Althusser argues that the historical thinkers of Montesquieu's day can all be classified as proponents of either social contract theory or the doctrine of natural sociability, and in his view, Montesquieu belongs to the latter group. Instead, I have argued that Montesquieu's insistence on the priority of his principles makes it impossible to classify him within either group. Montesquieu's principles represent a radical idea of historicity that determines all concepts of nature and all concepts of society as well. Thus for Montesquieu, there is no concept of the state of nature that does not reflect the conditions existing in a particular form of government or society. But the forms of government are themselves not eternal; they are not all present throughout history and thus cannot be considered to constitute, by their presence in the whole of human history, a "second nature." If Althusser is right to say that the historical thinkers of Montesquieu's day consistently failed to produce a concept of history because all interpreted the historical process in terms of an ideal—either nature or society—exterior to history, then Montesquieu's *De l'esprit des lois* would represent the most rigorous attempt by a philosopher of the Enlightenment to produce a proper concept of history—one that would situate all ideals of nature and society and be determined by none of them.

In Althusser's analysis of Montesquieu, it is history that provides the frame in which the interdependence of all concepts of nature and society can be grasped and critically analyzed. But history itself, in Althusser's view, is not implicated in these relations of interdependence whose analysis it makes possible. Whereas they are all the products of a common idealism, history, properly conceived, stands apart from all of them and hence from idealism as well.[16] But Montesquieu's analysis of monarchy reveals that history itself is rooted in an ideal—in the republic, which at the same time is and is not historical—and this involves him in a paradox. For Montesquieu has used history to criticize and to situate all idealisms and all states of nature. And yet, if history itself is rooted in an ideal, then he has in fact situated idealism in terms of itself or another form of itself. As an instrument of criticism, history, then, is double-edged. Although it situates and undercuts all ideals and all idealisms, it also undercuts the critical vigilance to which it gives rise. Montesquieu's idealism, however, is not the idealism of an adherent of the doctrine of natural sociability, as Althusser argues. Instead, it results from his having taken precisely the step that for Althusser is the only safeguard against idealism: the production of a concept of history critical of all ideals.

For Montesquieu, the idealism of all historical thinking is evident in that all history must and does imply the existence of an origin. The origin is the moment that makes history intelligible; all history must be continuous with an origin if it

---

[16] The criticism of history as an ideal has always been denounced by Althusser as historicist, and this denunciation in turn provides the basis of his critique of an entire current of Marxist thought, most notably, that of Gramsci (*Reading Capital*, pp. 119-144). But Althusser can immediately qualify such a position as historicist only because he himself, like the historicist he denounces, believes that any context in which one might situate history (science) would of necessity be purely empirical.

is to be history and not some unintelligible process of random change. But though it makes history intelligible, the origin also makes it redundant—the mere illustration of what was already implicitly present at the beginning. In criticizing the concept of the state of nature, Montesquieu substitutes a historical origin for an ideal, conceptual, fictional origin. To argue that all states of nature are historically determined, however, is both to criticize the origin in the form of the concept of nature and at the same time to use another, historical concept of the origin. Montesquieu is thus in the paradoxical position of criticizing the concept of the origin when he makes his critique of the concept of nature and of using the concept of the origin when he situates all states of nature in history. Montesquieu's principles condense this paradox in a single term. Though he uses it only in the plural, and though it is synonymous with the historicity that situates all ideals and all origins, the principle is itself a concept of the origin. In the end, then, the principles, which in a first moment imply a critique of the concept of a unique origin for history and an assertion that there can be only multiple origins, in a second moment themselves imply a single history with a transhistorical, and hence extrahistorical, ideal origin.

De l'esprit des lois makes clear, regardless of what Althusser asserts, that it is not possible to break with idealism simply by producing a concept of history.[17] In Montesquieu's text his-

---

[17] The idealism of all concepts of history lies in the fact that they all imply a concept of the origin, and Althusser's own theory of history is no exception. For in his view, "true" history, which he calls "science," originates with Marx. "Does *Capital*," he writes, "represent . . . the absolute beginning of the history of a science?" (*Reading Capital*, p. 15). Althusser's work as a whole responds that it does. For though he considers that under certain conditions knowledge that is produced by ideology may, after the fact of its production, attain scientific status, science never "descends" or "reverts" to ideology; and thus if *Capital* is the first truly scientific study of society, it is also the absolute origin of a history of science. Although Althusser does not acknowledge it, the science he posits as absolute is marked by the idealism to which it is opposed, for it too depends on the concept of an origin that Althusser himself claims is absolute.

tory is divided against itself, at the same time critical of all extrahistorical ideals and dependent on such ideals for its own concept. What *De l'esprit des lois* shows is that the flight from history into idealism, the assignment of an origin or end to history is not merely imposed on it either by an extraneous ideology or idealism, or by an empiricism that refuses to develop a critical concept of itself and of the origin. Rather, idealism is an integral part of history itself, implicit in the necessity to assume or produce a concept of history in order to write (produce) history. There is no history, then, without a concept of history, no writing of history without a theory of history. But as Montesquieu also shows, no history is truly "historical" that ignores or simply accepts its own idealist origins and does not confront, situate, and attempt to undermine the idealist assumptions that make its concepts and ideals—its theory of itself—trans- or metahistorical.

FIVE

(*Condillac, Diderot*)
The Limits and Conditions
of Empirical Knowledge or
The Theaters of Perception

INSOFAR as the concept of perception demands there be an empirical eyewitness to events, it seems to play a restricted role in virtually all theories of history, and this is certainly true for the eighteenth century. Voltaire insists that the historian make use of eyewitness accounts when they are available but also that they alone cannot constitute history. The historian must determine if the eyewitness account is authentic or not, if the character of the eyewitness is such that he should be believed. The historian must also piece together more than one such account, for any single account is bound to be seriously limited. Finally, he must determine which eyewitness accounts are worthy of being incorporated into history, since everything that has been perceived and recorded is not necessarily of historical value. In *De l'esprit des lois* there is a similar emphasis on the necessity to go beyond the data furnished by perception—to discover general laws, types, and principles which, though not themselves perceivable, nonetheless make intelligible the phenomenal world. Even in the "empiricist" eighteenth century, when philosophers are preoccupied with the analysis of perception and sensation and their role as the basis of all forms of knowledge, history cannot be equated with perception. The collation of accounts representing different points of view, their criticism, and their interpretation are all of as great or even greater concern to the historian than the simple perception and recording of what happened.

In his "History and Fiction as Modes of Comprehension," Louis O. Mink argues that philosophers have assigned history a secondary position in the field of knowledge in general, because they have judged it to be difficult or impossible to root the theory of history in perception.

> Since the seventeenth century, philosophy has been dominated by the problems of the cognitive status of perception on the one hand and the interpretation of natural science on the other. The great controversies of rationalism and empiricism now appear to have been complementary phases of the enterprise, extending over three centuries, to construct a comprehensive account of the relation between our direct perception of the world and our inferential knowledge of that world through the discoveries of natural science. In this epistemological enterprise there was no room for either imaginative worlds or the inaccessible world of the past. The latter, in particular, appeared significant only as something not perceptible, not as something past.[1]

Mink's assessment of the central role of perception in the philosophy of the seventeenth and eighteenth centuries raises a question as to how the theory of perception is related to the critique of empiricism and of the eyewitness account that is found in the works of historical thinkers such as Montesquieu and Voltaire. According to the logic of the "epistemological enterprise" Mink describes, their critique of perception would have to be seen as imposed upon them by the constraints of history itself, and thus that critique would be pertinent only in the field of history and not in the other fields—particularly not in the sciences—where perception would be the ultimate basis of knowledge.

The overview Mink gives of the modern history of philosophy and epistemology indicates that, even if history and fiction are not directly and immediately implicated in the ques-

---

[1] Louis O. Mink, "History and Fiction as Modes of Comprehension," in *New Literary History*, vol. 1 (1979), p. 541.

tion of the cognitive status of perception, that question is nonetheless of crucial relevance in determining the nature of the boundary between them. For one way of treating that boundary is to abandon it altogether, to "concede" that history is an art, or that it has infinitely more in common with literature than with science, since neither a theory of history nor a theory of literature can be comprehensively accounted for by our "direct" perception of the world. But in making this concession, a new and powerful line of defense is drawn between history and literature on the one hand and science on the other, and what is at stake in the defense of this "new" boundary is essentially what was at stake in the defense of the previous one.

One can only agree with Mink that the concept of perception plays a central role in the philosophy, epistemology, and science of the Enlightenment and that it continues to play an important role today. The Enlightenment, however, views perception not only as the source of many certitudes underlying all fields of knowledge, but also as a process requiring thorough examination in order to be fully understood. Through their careful analysis of the place and function of perception, certain Enlightenment figures are even led to challenge the closed nature of the boundary between the fields of inquiry related to perception and those related to "imaginative worlds or the inaccessible world of the past." From the perspective of the complex model that emerges when philosophers such as Condillac and Diderot attempt to analyze perception in detail, one can say that the critique of perception implied or stated in the historical theories of the Enlightenment is not marginal, but rather central, even with respect to eighteenth-century science and the theory of perception on which it is based. For in this complexly structured model of perception, certain historical factors—but principally memory and what we would now call ideology—can be shown to be already at work in perception from the start, even though they are explicitly treated by Condillac and Diderot as secondary distortions of perception. If their postulates concerning the unified character of perception and its unifying role in knowledge implicitly relegate history to the margins of knowledge and place science at its center, their analyses of memory, imagination, and a fundamental sociality inherent in perception in effect acknowledge the "original historicity" of perception and show that all knowledge based in any way on perception (even science), rather than being totally rooted in the immediacy of the present, is complicated by the historical contradictions constituting any act of perception.

For the philosophers of the Enlightenment, an investigation of perception and its relationship to all other mental faculties implies first of all a critique of all previous theories of knowledge that argue that ideas are innate in the mind. The concept of perception is a tool with which they seek to undo the mystifications of scholastic philosophy, for, in their view, perception implies the existence of a single, unified system capable of registering sense impressions and organizing, remembering, and transforming them into abstract thoughts, all without any direct intervention from a soul whose ideas originate with God. At the same time, by showing that all ideas, no matter how fantastic or apparently metaphysical, are in fact distorted or transformed sensations or perceptions, they provide a critical analysis of perception itself and very frequently present rules designed to prevent distorted perceptions from becoming the source of equally distorted philosophical and scientific systems divorced from any relation to perceived reality.

But the philosophers of the Enlightenment who critically examine perception also base their critique on a crucial chain of assumptions: that all mental faculties derive from sensation or perception, that perception is itself immediate and unified, that is to say a punctual and localizable event, and that the mind, however complex its functioning, is ultimately reducible to a unity based on the derivation of all the faculties from perception. One could argue that the conflict between the idealism of Berkeley, for whom the perceiving system can only know of the existence of its own perceptions and not of any "external" matter, and the materialism of d'Holbach, for whom sensation necessarily stems from an "external" matter that acts as the first cause of perception, is secondary with respect to their tacit agreement concerning the unity of perception and the integrity of the perceiving subject.[2] In particular, the French philosophers concerned with the problem of perception frequently acknowledge Locke as the founder of their tradition, but they consistently criticize him for failing to demonstrate adequately the *unity* of the mind. They implicitly or explicitly argue that Locke preserves what they see as an essentially theological dualism when he distinguishes between purely mental processes (characteristic of human intelligence) and those processes he interprets as stemming directly from sensation.[3] Thus Diderot takes what he calls sensitivity ("la sensibilité"), which for him is the common denominator of matter, sensation, and "higher" mental processes such as memory, to be the single unifying principle that makes possible a scientific (as opposed to a metaphysical or theological) understanding of the universe: "Because you don't accept a simple supposition that explains everything, that is, sensitivity, a general property of matter, or a product of the organization of matter, you renounce common sense, and you throw yourself into an

[2] Lenin, on the contrary, in his *Materialism and Empiriocriticism* (Moscow: Foreign Language Publishing House, 1947) views this conflict as fundamental, not only for the intellectual history of the Enlightenment but for that of the twentieth century as well. He thus argues, in a surprisingly ahistorical fashion, that the twentieth-century debate between Machians and authentic dialectical materialists is identical to that between Berkeley and the eighteenth-century materialists (see "How Certain 'Marxists' in 1908 and Certain Idealists in 1710 Refuted Materialism").

[3] In his introduction to the *Essai, sur l'origine des connaissances humaines* (Paris: Editions Galilée, 1973) Condillac gives Locke credit for being the first modern philosopher to have fully understood the fundamental role of sensation in the life of the mind, but he faults the *Essay on Human Understanding* for failing to show how the "higher" mental processes grow out of sensation: "it is established that in infancy we experience sensations long before knowing how to draw ideas from them. Thus the soul, not having, from the first, the use of all its operations, it was essential, in order to elucidate better the origin of our knowledge, to show how it [the soul] acquires this use, and how it progresses. It does not appear that Locke gave this matter any thought."

abyss of mysteries, contradictions, and absurdities."[4] Even the abbé de Condillac considers it necessary to preclude contradiction and dualism by relegating the notion of innate ideas and inherently mental processes to a Garden of Eden totally beyond the scope of his philosophical analysis of the mind.[5]

While the notion of the unity of perception and of the mind plays a critical role in relation to all previous theories of knowledge, it is itself an *assumption* of eighteenth-century philosophy. In *The Philosophy of the Enlightenment*, Ernst Cassirer points to the thesis of the unity of phenomena in general as the unproven first axiom of the science and scientifically derived philosophy of the Enlightenment taken as a whole. In this respect, he sees d'Alembert's philosophy as embodying a problem common to all the philosophers and scientists of the Enlightenment:

> D'Alembert's philosophy gives up all claim to establish a metaphysical formula which could reveal to us the nature of things in themselves; its aim is to remain within the realm of phenomena and simply to reveal the system, the coherent and general order of these phenomena. But . . . where is the guarantee, the decisive proof, that at least this general system of phenomena is completely self-contained, homogeneous and uniform? . . . Is not this postulate simply faith in disguise? Does it not contain an unproven and undemonstrable metaphysical presupposition?[6]

[4] *Entretien entre d'Alembert et Diderot, Oeuvres* (Paris: Editions Gallimard, 1951), p. 881. In this chapter, all references to Diderot's work are to this edition and will be given hereafter in the text.

[5] "Prior to original sin [the soul] was in a situation altogether different from the one in which it finds itself today. Free of ignorance and concupiscence, it gave orders to the senses, suspended their action, and modified it at will. [The soul] thus had ideas anterior to the use of the senses. But things have indeed changed as a result of its disobedience. God has taken all this empire away from the soul: it has become as dependent on the senses as if they were the physical cause of what in fact they are only the occasional cause" (*Essai sur l'origine des connaissances humaines*, Part One, section I, chap. i, 8).

[6] Ernst Cassirer, *The Philosophy of the Enlightenment* (Boston: Beacon Press, 1965), pp. 56-57.

The presupposition of unity is apparent for Cassirer in the specialized studies undertaken by the Enlightenment—in biology, in epistemology and psychology, in history, political theory, and aesthetics—and it is, moreover, the general horizon of all these specialized objects and fields.

The presupposition of the unity of the mind common to the theory of perception of the two thinkers under consideration here, Condillac and Diderot, thus constitutes a bond linking them to each other and to the Enlightenment as a whole. Though Diderot's materialism and Condillac's sensationalism are clearly distinct, they have a common function in the sense that each thinker sees his doctrine as the most solid basis for the demonstration of this unity. In Condillac's view, the unity of the mind stems from the primacy of sensation in all experience and mental activity, and according to him, the unifying role of sensation can only be clearly described and understood once essentially metaphysical concepts such as "substance," "matter," and "being" have been debunked. For Diderot, that unity is guaranteed by matter and the material basis of perception, for without these postulates (and the complementary thesis of the inherent sensitivity of all matter), the world is once again split between the material and the spiritual; man is once again divided between his body and mind, and his mind, in turn, between sensation and the "higher" mental faculties.

Condillac's and Diderot's investigations of the workings of perception are thus designed to bear out an initial postulate: that the mind is a unity because all mental life can be traced to a simple origin in sensation. And yet, though these philosophers scrupulously seek to avoid all dualisms, their own presentations of the workings of perception frequently imply a model that seriously threatens the essential postulate of unity and thereby points to the abstract, ideal nature of the concept of perception itself. In establishing the unity of perception, Condillac's *Essai sur l'origine des connaissances humaines* and Diderot's three dialogues, the *Entretien entre d'Alembert et Diderot*, the *Rêve de d'Alembert* and the *Suite de l'entretien*, at the same time all raise fundamental questions concerning this unity:

167

how can perception be reconciled with memory? How can *one* system account for these two functions? The answers proposed by Condillac and Diderot to these questions imply a model so complex and differentiated that it cannot be reduced to a unity, even if Condillac and Diderot never renounce unity as a postulate. This fundamental lack of unity will in turn imply a radical revision in the epistemological status of perception.

Condillac begins his *Essai sur l'origine des connaissances humaines* with the assertion that "whatever our knowledge, if we want to go back to its origin, we will ultimately arrive at a first, simple idea."[7] All mental life thus has a simple origin for Condillac. Experience can be reduced to a series of mental operations with sensation, the simplest, at the beginning of the chain, so that the "first" sensation that comes to "a man at the first moment of his existence" is the origin of all ensuing knowledge. Sensation is the simple foundation on which Condillac hopes to build in the following chapter dealing with perception, consciousness, attention, and reminiscence.

Condillac writes in his *Traité des sensations* that he is dissatisfied with his earlier *Essai* for having "given too much importance to signs," that is, for having placed too heavy an emphasis on the role of language in developing "the germ of all our ideas," to the detriment of his thesis that all mental life stems from sensation.[8] But a close reading of the *Essai* belies Condillac's own subsequent interpretation of it, for Condillac himself begins to undercut sensation as the unique origin of mental processes in the chapter immediately following the one on sensation,[9] and thus well before the issue of the sign has

[7] Condillac, *Essai sur l'origine des connaissances humaines*, Part One, I, i, 1.

[8] *Traité des sensations, Oeuvres complètes*, vol. 3 (Geneva: Slatkine Reprints, 1970), Introduction.

[9] The chapter on sensation (Part One, I, ii), contains no discussion of the workings of sensation but instead merely affirms that all sensation is "clear and distinct" and blames language for creating false impressions and confusion in our apprehension of these simplest ideas. Condillac cannot even begin to explore the workings of sensation independently of the "secondary" processes he describes in the following chapter.

been raised "for the first time."[10] The chapter on perception, consciousness, attention, and reminiscence runs counter to the affirmations of the chapter on sensation, for it shows that sensation in and of itself is not and cannot be the simple origin of all knowledge. Sensation itself can only take place when it is accompanied (or supplemented) by these "secondary" mental operations. This is clear in Condillac's discussion of each of the concepts dealt with in the chapter in question, but most explicitly in his discussion of reminiscence:

> Once objects attract our attention, the perceptions they occasion in us link themselves with the sense of our being and with everything that has some relation to it. . . . Consciousness, considered in relation to these new effects, is a new operation which serves us at every instant and which is the basis of experience. Without it each moment of life seems to be the first in our existence, and our knowledge would never extend beyond a first perception: I will call this [operation or faculty] *reminiscence*. (Part One, II, i, 15)

Contrary to his opening argument that sensation is the basis of all experience, here reminiscence plays that role. Without reminiscence, the perceiving or sensing substance would have no way of distinguishing successive sense impressions one from another. Experience would consist of one uninterrupted per-

---

[10] In "L'Archéologie du frivole," *Essai sur l'origine des connaissances humaines* (Paris: Editions Galilée, 1973), Jacques Derrida gives an interpretation of Condillac's *Essai* that focuses on the role played by the sign or by language in general in relation to its "simple" origin in sensation. For Derrida, the concept of the sign coincides with a "detour" from the simple analytical course Condillac had set for himself—a detour that is already present at the origin of experience (pp. 62, 66), and it is in this light that he analyzes Condillac's statement that he has "given too much importance to signs." The functioning of the notion of the theater in Condillac's text is, I believe, consistent with the functioning of the concept of the sign as Derrida analyzes it. If I have chosen the theater rather than the sign as the focus of my interpretation, it is because of the special emphasis I would like to place on the social and historical aspects of the problem of the sign.

ception or sensation which, because the subject would have nothing to compare it to, could not be identified in even the most rudimentary way as a sensation. For Condillac, reminiscence permits the subject to link and at the same time to distinguish between different impressions, and, thereby, makes sensation itself possible.

In Condillac's view, reminiscence is to be distinguished from memory. The latter faculty is "higher" in the hierarchy or chain linking the various faculties to each other, and thus is held by Condillac to be more active, more general, and less concrete than reminiscence. But reminiscence itself prevents sensation from being a purely passive faculty, inasmuch as the subject must recall a past sensation in order to experience a present one. Reminiscence also prevents sensation from being purely specific and concrete, inasmuch as it links the attention we bestow on an object to "the sensation of our being" and to "everything that might have a relationship" to the sensation of our being. Thus the sensation of a "concrete" object is always abstracted from a complex of relationships that are the condition of the sensation of the object. Moreover, the concept of reminiscence implies that sensation takes place where a relationship, however rudimentary, is established between the object and its background or between the object and the perceptual system itself, and this distinction could not exist were the system purely passive.[11] Finally, reminiscence not only implies a relative degree of activity and abstraction in sensation itself, it also implies that sensation is to a degree like memory in that neither takes place in the full presence of the object. For the necessity that reminiscence already be at work in order for the *first* sensation to take place means that no object is fully present in its integrity to the perceiving system;

[11] A major, if not the major argument of the *Traité des sensations* is that the distinction between the perceptual system and the object cannot be passive. For this distinction is only discovered by the statue Condillac employs to illustrate his theory of sensation once the philosopher allows it use of the sense of touch, and touch is the only sense that Condillac considers to be active rather than passive.

instead, sensation takes place only when *more than one* object competes for the attention of the sensory apparatus. Memory, then, can be said to grow out of reminiscence, but, for that very reason, the distinction between memory and sensation cannot be hard and fast. Reminiscence is a protomemory—it is memory *as* sensation.

Simple sensation, then, cannot be the origin of mental life, since sensation itself implies difference and complexity. Indeed, there could be no such thing as sensation if there were only *one* sensation or perception. There are three other faculties—consciousness, perception, and attention—that, like reminiscence, must be operative in sensation itself if there is to be any such thing as sensation. These faculties all imply each other, and thus Condillac's descriptions of them overlap significantly. Each bears the same relationship to memory as does reminiscence; each implies that memory is already at work in sensation; and each, like reminiscence, can be considered a form of sensation *as* memory.

In his analysis of perception, Condillac emphasizes a point already implicit in his definition of reminiscence. In sensation, there must be differentiation, not only between various sensations, but also between sensation and the perceptual apparatus itself: "Objects would act to no avail on the senses, and the soul would never have knowledge of them, if it did not perceive them. Thus the first and least degree of knowledge is to perceive" (Part One, II, i, 2). Perception is a redoubling or consciousness of sensation, and without it, there would be no sensation. Furthermore, because perception implies an awareness or consciousness for Condillac, it also implies (as does the notion of reminiscence) that there must be *more than one* sensation in order for *even one* sensation to be recorded: perception takes both the perceiving system itself and the sensation as its objects, and it is produced by the difference between the two. Condillac's definition of perception clearly implies a third operation or faculty—consciousness—that functions as a resistance to sensation, for it does not allow the perceiving subject to be totally invaded by sensation, and thus it maintains his sense of his existence independent of his sensations.

Condillac's discussion of reminiscence, perception, and consciousness not only undercuts sensation as the simple origin of all mental processes, it also serves to introduce a crucial problem and set the stage for that problem's solution. For, Condillac acknowledges, consciousness is not full, consistent, and neutral, but partial and inconsistent, full . . . of gaps. Condillac's description of sensation and the secondary faculties is intended to explain how the subject remembers and perceives, but it does not yet explain why and how the subject forgets. Condillac's task, then, is to interpret reminiscence, perception, and consciousness in such a way that they can explain the partial nature of consciousness and, ultimately, the incomplete nature of memory. It is at this point in his argument that the unity of the perceiving subject is most seriously threatened. The ability of consciousness to resist external impressions and, ultimately, to forget seems to be leading the philosopher to produce a concept of an unconscious, where the impressions that are put into the background by reminiscence and ultimately lost to consciousness altogether would be stored in some way. But, intent on preserving the unity of his model of the mind, Condillac explicitly rejects the notion of an unconscious when he denies the possibility of perceptions of which the subject might not be aware. For Condillac, the notion of unconscious perception is ruled out because it involves a logical inconsistency:

> At this point one could hold two views different from mine. . . . The second view would be that there is no impression upon the senses that does not communicate itself to the brain. . . . But one would have to add that it [the impression] is without consciousness, or that the soul does not become conscious of it. Here I declare myself to be with Locke; for I cannot conceive of such a perception: I would just as willingly have it said that I perceive without perceiving. (Part One, II, i, 7-8)

According to Condillac, then, there is no such thing as an unperceived perception.

Having rejected the notion of an unconscious, however, it still remains for Condillac to explain how, if all perception is *conscious*, the subject does not retain all of his perceptions, and how what was present in or to consciousness can be lost. According to the logic by which Condillac distinguishes sensation and perception or consciousness, there must be some analogous mechanism that resists perception and thus is responsible for the distinction between perception and memory. Having rejected the notion of an unconscious, it remains for Condillac to explain the workings of memory in relation to perception without violating the unity of the perceiving subject. The concept to which Condillac turns to resolve his difficulty is that of attention, but the metaphor he uses to "illustrate" this concept will only cause the same difficulty to be resuscitated in another form.

According to Condillac, the perceptions that attract our attention make the greatest impression on us and are thus remembered. Others are perceived but without our being attentive to them, and as a result they are immediately forgotten. Attention is thus responsible for endowing the different sense impressions with the different value or quantity of force without which there could be no memory (and no forgetting), and thus, no perception. Condillac "illustrates" the concept of attention by citing the experience of a spectator in a theater. It should be stressed that this use of the theater as a model for perception occurs several chapters before Condillac explicitly discusses the whole question of the sociohistorical origins of the theater in connection with the development of language. And this recourse to the theater as an example is neither innocent nor neutral, no more so than is perception itself. While the example used to "illustrate" a philosophical argument is, in principle, replaceable and inessential, the common denominator of all the examples Condillac uses to explain his concept of attention is that they imply society.[12] In this respect, at

---

[12] The two other examples proposed by Condillac to illustrate attention are

least, the metaphor of the theater appears to be irreplaceable and essential for Condillac. Just as it is necessary to supplement sensation and perception by memory and attention, so it is necessary to supplement the individual mind, *before it is even fully constituted as such*, by a "sociality" even more fundamental than the society to which the fully constituted subject gains access through perception.

Memory is both possible *and* partial because, according to Condillac, the more our consciousness of certain impressions increases, the more our ability to remember contiguous impressions decreases:

> The illusion that is created in the theater is proof of this. There are moments when consciousness does not appear to divide itself between the actions taking place on stage and the rest of the spectacle. It would seem at first that the illusion ought to be all the more vivid when there are fewer objects capable of distracting from it. However, everyone has had occasion to remark that one is never more apt to believe oneself the only witness of an interesting scene, than when the theater is filled to capacity. This is perhaps because the number, the variety, and the magnificence of the objects stir the senses, heat up and lift up the imagination, and thereby make us more susceptible to the impressions the poet wants to arouse. Perhaps too the spectators mutually prompt each other, through the examples they give each other, to fix their gaze on the stage. (Part One, II, i, 5)

Condillac's metaphor is intended to explain how it is that attention bestows not only greater value on the object of our attention but also a lesser value on related perceptions that are not objects of attention and that, as a result, "disappear" from

---

that of a reader before a printed page (he will be attentive to the content conveyed by the text and inattentive to the letters conveying it) (Part One, II, i, 9) and that of an individual who considers a painting (he will be more conscious of the general effect produced than of the details of the picture) (Part One, II, i, 12).

memory and consciousness. But the logic of this passage undermines his argument, for, as he himself notes, it is precisely when the theater is packed, that is, when there are the most "objects" present to distract the spectator from the spectacle, that it fixes his attention most firmly. Our attention for the stage may even be a result of our emulation of the other, attentive spectators. If this is so, then in an "attentive" audience, all the spectators in fact must be at once attentive to and forgetful of the other spectators. Condillac has rejected the notion of an unperceived perception only to create the notion of an inattentive attention.

According to the theatrical model proposed in his discussion of attention, perception is possible not because the perceiving system is originally simple and passive, but because it is originally differentiated and active. For the model for attention is not the individual spectator in the theater, but rather the theater itself, including the individual spectator, the other spectators, and the stage. If the stage represents the object of attention, and if the individual spectator represents the perceiving consciousness, it still remains to be seen what the other spectators represent *within* the perceiving subject. For they are neither the perceiving subject nor the perceived sensation; they are an essential background *within* the subject, a condition of consciousness without being an object of consciousness. If Condillac refuses to see the division between the individual consciousness and the other spectators as constituting an "unconscious," his use of the theatrical metaphor nonetheless threatens the fundamental postulate of the unity of the perceiving system conceived as a conscious subject.

Condillac's use of the image of the theater reveals a paradox at the heart of the concept of attention. But lest it be thought that this paradox is introduced into Condillac's explanation of the workings of the mind accidentally, by a metaphor that is only casually invoked, it should be noted that the theatrical model can serve to illustrate not only attention but also the other mental operations that "precede" it. The stage, by creating or implying a frame that sets it off from the audience, makes it possible to differentiate and thus to perceive both the stage itself and the audience, just as consciousness differentiates itself from its object. The theatrical model also underscores the active nature of perception and memory, for our attentiveness to the events on the stage is in direct proportion to our resistance to those impressions coming from the direction of the audience. We cannot perceive anything without at the same time resisting other sensations or perceptions. Finally, the theater is a reminiscence of "life" or "reality" in the same way that a perception is more or less a replica of an "earlier" perception with which it must be compared to be perceived. But the theater, as a "representation" or "figure" of reality, must be present *from the beginning* in order that "life" or "reality" may define themselves in opposition to the stage, just as a "second" perception must be present at the origin for the "first" perception to be registered. The differentiation and, ultimately, the alienation characterizing the theatrical situation are present at every level of perception—reminiscence, consciousness, and attention—and this means that the social and theatrical situation that illustrates attention is implicit in perception itself. Before I can perceive the theater as an object, or any object, a structure of differentiation that implies an apparatus analogous in form to the theater has already become the necessary condition of my being able to perceive at all. Before I can see others as objects or even as constituting a society, others are the necessary structural condition of perception. Moreover, it should not be forgotten that the metaphor of the theater is called forth by the problem of the selective nature of memory. "The theater" is Condillac's answer to the question, What apparatus can account for *both* memory and perception? It accounts for both by showing, as Condillac implies in his earlier discussion of reminiscence, that memory is already at work in the "first" sensation.

At this point, one could expect that Condillac might seriously revise his postulate of the unity of the perceiving subject and of the simple nature of perception in a manner consistent with the complexity and differentiation implied by these "secondary" processes. Instead, he returns to a simple model for sensation in the chapter on imagination, contemplation, and memory. There, sensation serves as the guarantee of the distinction, judged by Condillac to be capital, between imagination and memory: "It is important to distinguish clearly the point that separates imagination from memory. . . . Until now what philosophers have said on this subject is so confused that one can often apply to memory what they say about imagination, and to imagination what they say about memory" (Part One, II, ii, 20). The distinction between imagination and memory is based, for Condillac, on their different relation to sensation. Imagination, he asserts, is a retracing of perception "as if one . . . had before one's eyes" the object that caused the original perception. Memory is more "abstract" than imagination. It does not produce a reexperiencing of the perception, but a (partial) representation of it, such as a name, a set of circumstances, and a general notion of the nature of the sensation (an odor, a color, etc.). The distinction between imagination and memory is threatened, however, by the fact that it rests on a question of degree. As Condillac himself remarks, there is nothing *in principle* to distinguish imagination from sensation itself. The inability to distinguish the two is characteristic of certain forms of madness, he writes, and, moreover, it is an experience accessible to the "normal" subject in sleep: "Sometimes, even, our ideas retrace themselves without our participation, and present themselves with such liveliness that we are duped, and we believe that we have the objects before our eyes. This is what happens to madmen and to all men, when they dream" (Part One, II, ii, 24).

At the other end of the spectrum from this vivid form of imagination indistinguishable from sensation is an imagination without force that functions much as memory does. We can imagine a triangle, says Condillac, because of its simplicity and regularity. We cannot imagine forms with one thousand or with nine hundred and ninety-nine sides. Such complex figures can only be grasped through language and thus, through memory. But at what precise point do figures become uni-

177

maginable and only memorable? How many sides does the most complex figure we can still imagine have? Condillac's definitions of imagination and memory are ultimately based on their *degree* of proximity to an original sensation. But the difficulty of determining the *exact* degree reflects the underlying complexity of sensation itself. The problems raised by sleep and by imagination are not "new" in Condillac's exploration of the chain of mental faculties; rather they are inherent in the discussion of sensation itself. For though, in the chapter on memory and imagination, sensation is the state of having the object "before one's eyes"—a state that imagination and memory can only approximate in their ways—the earlier chapters reveal that sensation does not take place in the full presence of *an* object and that it already requires the participation of memory in order that the "first" sensation might take place. The difficulty of distinguishing between imagination and memory, then, is already implicit in sensation itself.

Many readers of Condillac have argued that his *Traité des sensations* and his *Logique* differ significantly from the early *Essai*. Nonetheless, all of Condillac's work does in a sense return to these early chapters and to the conflict in them between memory and sensation. In the *Traité des sensations*, the complexity of sensation is evident in Condillac's assertion that *interest* is an essential component of all sensation. He argues that the perceiving subject registers sensations because they are all either pleasurable or painful: a sensation that would be neither does not exist or, what is the same thing, would not be registered by the perceiving subject. Sensation occurs, then, because it is in the interest of the subject to seek pleasurable sensations and avoid painful ones and because the subject discriminates sensation according to the pain or pleasure it causes. Pleasure and pain, however, are not themselves inherent in objects. According to Condillac, they are only qualities of sensation and as such have no meaning except in opposition to each other. But if all sensation must have a quality in order to register, and if, at the same time, the quality of one sensation is always relative to the quality of another, then this is further confirmation of the argument that there must be more than one sensation for even one sensation to occur. In the *Traité*, as in the *Essai*, sensation implies memory.[13]

The *Logique* too confronts anew the problem of the relationship between memory and sensation when Condillac criticizes those who have conceived of the brain as a "substance molle" for not having recognized the difficulty of reconciling these two faculties: "Others say that the brain is a soft substance, in which animal spirits make traces. These traces are conserved; the animal spirits pass through the traces again and again; the animal is thus endowed with sense and memory. They don't take note of the fact that if the substance of the brain is soft enough to receive traces, it will not have enough consistency to conserve them."[14] In the *Logique*, Condillac proposes a new model to resolve and account for the conflict between memory and sensation—the harpsichord:

> The brain, like all the other sensory organs, has the capacity to affect itself according to its habitual determinations. We experience sensations more or less the way a harpsichord makes sounds. The exterior organs of the human body are like keys, the objects that strike them are

[13] The concept of interest thus introduces a fundamental complexity into Condillac's treatment of sensation in the *Traité des sensations*, but just as in the *Essai* Condillac constantly returns to a simple theory of sensation, so in the *Traité* the complexity introduced into sensation by the concepts of interest, pleasure, and pain is ultimately reduced in the name of the *conservation* of the perceiving subject. By defining pleasure as that which contributes to his conservation, Condillac gives an absolute meaning to a term that he previously acknowledges can be only relative. Though there is nothing in Condillac's initial definition of pleasure and pain that would make it impossible for the subject to find death relatively pleasurable in relation to some other, even more painful sensation, Condillac will decide that the subject spontaneously avoids death no matter how great the pain from which it would rescue him. The conservation of the subject, then, is the reality principle of the *Traité des sensations* just as the postulate of a simple sensation is the reality principle of the *Essai*.

[14] *Logique*, in *Oeuvres complètes*, vol. 15 (Geneva: Slatkine Reprints, 1970), chap. 9.

like the fingers on the keyboard, the interior organs are like the body of the harpsichordist, sensations and ideas are like sounds; and memory takes place when ideas that have been produced by the effect of objects on the senses are reproduced by motions that have become habitual to the brain. (chap. 9)

In sensation, it is the harpsichordist who acts as the agent of sensation, and the harpsichord as the sensory apparatus. But it is less clear how the harpsichord model illustrates memory. What is it that touches the keys of the harpsichord and produces memory or sound if it is not the harpsichordist or the "external" cause of sensation? Is it the harpsichord itself? How does a harpsichord play itself? If it is the harpsichord, how can it know when it is being played and when it is playing itself? If it is not the harpsichord, if it is, once again, the harpsichordist doing the playing, how can the harpsichord distinguish between memory and sensation? When raised in terms of this model, such questions are unanswerable. The unity assumed to be the foundation necessary to provide definitive answers to such questions has been complicated to such a degree in this and the other models used by Condillac that they no longer illustrate that unity but instead put it into question.

The fact that the boundary between sensation, imagination, and memory is never conclusively drawn and is even actively questioned by Condillac, in his later works as well as in the *Essai*, has far-reaching implications when one considers the role of perception in the theory of knowledge. Just as, in Condillac's *Essai*, perception is at times invoked as the criteria by which each ought to be defined, so rationalism and empiricism define literature and history according to their proximity to a science considered to be more directly rooted in perception. But if memory and imagination are both potentially active in all perception, then the distinction between science, history, and fiction, like the distinction between perception, memory, and imagination is at most one of degree and not of kind. As Condillac notes in his *Essai*, the most vivid observation is at times indistinguishable from a fiction or dream, and Condillac himself provides no test by which to ascertain whether the subject is awake or asleep at any given moment. Ultimately, the complex model of perception that emerges from the *Essai* shows that memory is the condition of all perception or sensation, and thus in an important sense all acts of observation are historical in character. The historicity of perception is not simple however; rather, it is complicated by the relationship of memory to imagination. Indeed, the logic that implicates memory in all acts of perception also implicates imagination in all acts of remembering. Just as perception is complicated, historicized by memory, so memory is complicated and historicized, that is, fictionalized, by imagination.

IN THE TRILOGY that includes the *Entretien entre d'Alembert et Diderot*, the *Rêve de d'Alembert*, and the *Suite de l'entretien*, Diderot, like Condillac in his *Logique*, uses the harpsichord as a model for the perceiving subject, and this shared metaphor is indicative of assumptions and questions concerning sensation they also share. Despite their differences, the goal of Diderot's materialism is in a crucial respect the same as Condillac's sensationalism, for both seek to produce a scientific, rational account of the perceiving subject based on sensation as the simple origin of all experience. But, as is the case in Condillac's *Essai*, Diderot's texts simultaneously propose a second theory of perception, evident in the conflicting positions taken by various characters in the dialogues, in the staging of the dialogues themselves, and finally in the contradictions inherent in each of the conflicting models of perception proposed by two characters in particular—Diderot in the *Entretien* and Doctor Bordeu in the *Suite* and in the *Rêve*. As in Condillac's *Essai*, these contradictions stem from a fundamental tension *within* the perceiving system between sensation on the one hand and memory (and imagination) on the other.

In the "Entretien," d'Alembert is portrayed as a skeptic who draws—in devil's advocate style—upon a dualist conception of the mind to justify his unwillingness to accept his friend's system. His questions, however, pose difficulties not only for the materialist doctrine defended by Diderot, but for the Lockean (or even Cartesian) doctrine from which d'Alembert draws many of his arguments. D'Alembert asks how thought can derive from sensation when thought implies a prolongation of sensation after the physical "event" that brought about the sensation is past. Clearly in d'Alembert's view this objection speaks in favor of some sort of distinction between perception and "purely mental" activity. But the question itself raises what becomes a central issue in the *Rêve de d'Alembert*: the relationship between memory and sensation. Is the full presence of an object the true basis of sensation? If not, can sensation be said to precede and be the sole condition of memory? In terms of the harpsichord model Diderot takes over from Condillac, the question is, does the harpsichord have the ability to play itself? Diderot clearly states what Condillac only implies in the *Logique*—that for the harpsichord to serve as complete model for the perceiving system, it must be thought of as capable of doing so. But once this question has been answered in the affirmative, the more fundamental question remains: how can the harpsichord distinguish between being played by another (sensation) and being played by itself (memory)?

The conflict between sensation and memory is also central to the discussion of language in these dialogues. D'Alembert asks how conventions between various harpsichords (perceiving subjects) are established, and Diderot makes a standard reply, again essentially that of Condillac. Sensory systems (harpsichords), because their principles of construction are essentially the same, will produce the same sounds given what must of necessity be similar sense experiences:[15] "So you will

---

[15] The *Rêve de d'Alembert* provides ample material for putting this response into question however. In 1769, the probable date of composition of this three-part work, the scientific community was in the process of dismantling the theory according to which all "new" life was the product of a "germ" that preformed it and that had been created by God at the beginning of time.

find that interjections are more or less the same in all languages dead or living. Need and proximity must be taken as
the origin of conventional sounds" (*Entretien*, p. 883). Syllo-
gism and analogy are similarly derived from perception for
Diderot, for in his view the relationship they describe is a
natural one—except in certain cases:

> Analogy . . . is a fourth cord, harmonious with and pro-
> portional to three others, to whose resonance the animal
> is always attentive, a resonance that always occurs in him-
> self but not always in nature. This matters little to the
> poet, who considers it true nonetheless. For the philos-
> opher it's something else again; he must subsequently cross-
> examine nature, which, by often giving him a phenome-
> non altogether different from the one he had presumed,
> makes him see that he had been seduced by the analogy.
> (p. 884)

Language is like memory in that it has two contradictory
functions in the *Entretien* and the texts that follow. On the
one hand, it acts as the instrument of sensation, registering,
storing, and making sensations available for use in mental
processes thought to take place "after" the "initial" sensation.
On the other hand, the dialogues also note that language
functions in the absence of the object. This relative autonomy
from reality is characteristic for Diderot of poetic language,
and throughout the three texts, Diderot's meditation on the

Certain thinkers most actively engaged in this dismantling continued to believe, however, that the species had existed in the same form since the beginning of time even if the individual had not. Others, like Diderot, felt that
there was no ultimate guarantee of the uniformity of the species and cited
"monsters" in particular to support their contention. Though this is not the
place to pursue fully the relationship between Diderot's discussion of the
biological origins of both the species and the individual and his theory of
perception, in general that discussion serves to undermine the notion that all
sense apparatuses in a given species are identical and thus to further undermine simple sensation as the origin of language. For a discussion of Diderot's
biology, see Jacques Roger, *Les Sciences de la vie dans la pensée française du
XVIIIᵉ siècle* (Paris: A. Colin, 1963), pt. 2, chap. 3, pp. 585-682.

relationship between language and perception is formulated in terms of the following question: is language in essence poetic or philosophical?

Diderot's remarks on language raise a third closely related question, not asked by d'Alembert, but nonetheless of critical importance for all that follows: what is the status of pleasure and sexuality in relation to "perceived reality"? This issue is introduced by Diderot's characterization of the poet (in the passage just quoted) as being motivated in his use of analogy by a pleasure principle not necessarily accounted for by the referential function of language—hence Diderot's remark that the poet is "seduced" by the analogy or metaphor. In his *Traité des sensations*, pleasure and pain, because they produce *interest*, are considered by Condillac to be conditions of sensation itself; they function as the origin of the origin. Diderot's characterization of the poet also raises the question of the role of pleasure, as opposed to "pure" sensation, in the origin of language, and the *Rêve de d'Alembert* portion of the trilogy raises the same question at the primary level of sensation itself through the explicitly sexual content of d'Alembert's dream and his autoeroticism. D'Alembert in his sleeping state is the harpsichord that plays itself. But in this case, the harpsichord/d'Alembert is no longer under the sway of reality and of objects or even of their mere images as retraced in memory: the erotic character of d'Alembert's dream makes evident the importance of the *quality* of sensation and of memory and the way in which pleasure is a dominant aim of the subject who has sensations or remembers.[16]

---

[16] Throughout his work, Diderot can often be seen to subordinate the pleasure drive to the need of the human species to reproduce itself. In the *Supplément au voyage de Bougainville*, he presents the image of a society in which sexual desire is liberated from the constraints of a false, European morality. But despite their apparent freedom to pursue their own pleasure, the sexual behavior of Diderot's Tahitians is ruled by a "natural" morality in some ways even stricter than the "artificial" European morality. Sexuality is rigorously subordinated to the end of procreation, and thus is altogether forbidden to those too young, too old, or otherwise incapable of producing children. In the *Suite de l'entretien*, Bordeu takes the position that masturbation is an

The parallel issues raised by memory, language, and pleasure in relation to sensation all converge in the figure of the sleeping d'Alembert. In him, memory (imagination), language, and sexuality, all more or less divorced from the reality principle governing them when the subject is awake, are released to pursue their own ends. For Diderot, then, the specific question of the role of memory in sensation is related to the question of the role of these other factors, which, like memory, seem to interfere to some extent with "pure" sensation. In the *Rêve de d'Alembert*, memory is one aspect of a general resistance offered by the perceptual system to external stimuli. All sensation involves a modification in the pattern of resistance offered by the perceiving system, and thus all sensation or perception is active; no sensation or perception is ever passive or pure.

The notion of resistance in relation to perception is heavily thematized in Diderot's dramatization of the *Rêve de d'Alembert*. To begin with, Diderot writes the dialogue as though the dream state overcomes or lifts d'Alembert's resistance to Diderot's theories, so that he now accepts what he refused when awake.[17] This acceptance can serve as a model for per-

---

evil necessitated by the perversity of conventional morality which prevents sexuality from attaining its proper end—the production of offspring. But in the *Rêve de d'Alembert*, Diderot seems to comment ironically on both of these positions when he puts a form of them in the mouth of the sleeping d'Alembert, who has just reached the climax of his dream: "Nothing must be lost that might be useful" (p. 894).

[17] Though to some readers there may seem to be a great disparity between a "simple object" and a complex idea such as Diderot's theory of sensitivity, it should be kept in mind that for the eighteenth-century materialists and sensationalists, all mental acts are fundamentally acts of perception, and all thought is an image of reality, as is evident in Diderot and d'Alembert's discussion of analogy. The materialists argue that even ideals such as "the good" and "virtue" are objects of perception. In *De l'esprit*, Helvétius states that moral judgment is a form of sensation: "What art should the poet or orator employ to make his listener more vividly perceive that justice, which, in a king, is to be preferred to generosity, conserves more citizens and thus is of greater benefit to the state? The orator will present three tableaux to the imagination of this same man: in one, he will present the just king who

ception, but, ironically, not the classical model of perception propounded by Diderot, the character in the dialogue. For Diderot's theories of perception and sensibility have not changed. Awake or asleep, the "object" is the same for the perceiver, d'Alembert. What has changed is d'Alembert's resistance to the object; it has been "lifted" by sleep.

The *Rêve* and the *Suite* abound in situations such as this. Throughout the dialogues, perception, that is the knowledge of an object, be that object empirical or intellectual, is always a function of resistance that is either active or suspended. In the case of Mlle de l'Espinasse, resistance is thematized as sexual prudishness and feminine modesty. These at least initially prevent her from entertaining certain of Bordeu's more "daring" ideas. As the conversation with Bordeu continues, however, her initial resistance dissolves under his charm and encouragement, so that when he suggests that they use her as an example to investigate the question of the origin of the nervous system, she readily consents: "If it were the custom to go about naked in the streets, I would be neither the first nor the last to do it. So do with me whatever you please, as long as it's educational" (*Rêve*, p. 906). Thus her increasing lack of inhibition goes hand in hand with her increasing desire to learn. Or, to put it another way, her awakening interest in Bordeu overcomes or suspends her resistance to his theories, so that his ideas, which several lines before she had held to be mad and extravagant, now appear clear and distinct.

Mlle de l'Espinasse's behavior may serve as a model for perception not only in relation to Bordeu, but also in relation to the sleeping d'Alembert. Much of the dialogue between her and Bordeu is based on her transcription of d'Alembert's dream;

---

condemns the criminal and has him executed; in the second, the generous king, who has the cell of the same criminal opened and takes off his chains; in the third, he will represent this same criminal, who, arming himself with his dagger upon leaving his cell, runs and massacres fifty citizens. Now, what man, having seen these three tableaux, would not sense that justice . . . is preferable to generosity? Nonetheless this judgment is really only a sensation" (Discourse 1, chap. 1).

she has sought merely to record his words and gestures while asleep. However, Diderot suggests, for these words and gestures to become objects of perception for Mlle de l'Espinasse, they must first arouse her *interest*, and though their bizarre character might be considered to explain that interest to some extent, Diderot clearly suggests that its ultimate source is a dim, one could properly say repressed, awareness that her lover's dream concerns sex and thus, more or less directly, herself: "Then his face flushed. I wanted to take his pulse, but I don't know where he had hidden his hand. . . . His mouth was partly open, his breathing, labored. . . . I looked at him attentively, and I was myself moved without knowing why, my heart was beating, and it wasn't from fear" (p. 894). Mlle de l'Espinasse's interest in or (to use her own word) "attention" to the content of d'Alembert's dream is linked to a pleasure principle, but that principle functions in a complex way, similar to the faculty of attention in Condillac's *Essai*. For the sexual character of her interest causes certain perceptions to be repressed (she does not explicitly acknowledge the sexual character of d'Alembert's dream) while at the same time it makes possible and even intensifies others (the gestures that are the signs of the sexual character of his dream) to the point of fascination.

Like the *Traité des sensations*, the *Rêve de d'Alembert* shows that pleasure is frequently, if not always, involved in perception. And the more pronounced the dominance of the pleasure drive over the subject, the more blurred the distinction between memory and imagination, between memory and sensation. D'Alembert's monologue suggests that in the dream state he no longer distinguishes the presence of his interlocutors from their absence, their real status from their remembered or imagined status, or, what amounts to the same thing, the distinction is no longer significant to the dreaming subject, who seeks as much his own pleasure as he does a clear and precise grasp of the scientific question he debates with himself while asleep. But if pleasure is potentially involved in all perception, then what is true for the sleeping d'Alembert

187

must to some extent be true for the subject considered to be awake and conscious. There would be no clear-cut basis for distinguishing between Mlle de l'Espinasse, Bordeu, and the character Diderot on the one hand and their sleeping friend on the other. Indeed, Mlle de l'Espinasse asks Bordeu more than once if he is not asleep or as mad as d'Alembert. In the waking as in the sleeping subject, the potential involvement of pleasure in all sensation would undermine the distinction between sensation and memory and between memory and imagination.

Like Condillac, Diderot points to a resistance that is always at work in perception. This resistance is located both "within" the subject—in memory, in imagination, and in a pleasure drive—and "outside" the perceiving subject in society. Or rather, as Condillac's use of the theater as a model for the perceiving subject suggests, this resistance is a sign that the "outside" is already "inside" and vice versa.[18] Mlle de l'Espinasse illustrates this latter aspect of resistance as well. As has already been noted, her initial reluctance to discuss Bordeu's theories has a specifically feminine component, and thus is not unique to her but represented as typical of her sex. This "feminine" resistance to science also points to the resistance of an even larger public to scientific ideas in conflict with conventional education and mores—one that would include men as well as women. For Diderot, true scientific theory is essentially clear and distinct and can be expressed with the greatest economy and sim-

---

[18] In "Freud and the Scene of Writing," *Writing and Difference*, translated by Alan Bass (Chicago: University of Chicago Press, 1978), Jacques Derrida analyzes the "original" role of memory in Freud's model of perception and argues that because memory is already at work in perception, the latter has an inherently "social" character: " 'Perception,' the first relation of life to its other, the origin of life, had always already prepared representation. We must be several in order to write and even to 'perceive.' . . . The subject . . . is a *system* of relations between strata: . . . the psyche, society, the world. Within that scene, the punctual simplicity of the classical subject is not to be found. In order to describe this structure, it is not enough to recall that one always writes for someone; and the oppositions sender-receiver, code-message, etc., remain extremely coarse instruments" (pp. 226-227).

plicity. Thus what makes scientific knowledge difficult to acquire for an educated but lay public and virtually inaccessible
to the common man is not the inherent complexity and oc-
cultness of science, but a resistance to a self-evident reality. In
the light of Mlle de l'Espinasse's initially prudish reaction to
Bordeu's ideas and the calculated obscenity of d'Alembert's
oneiric speculation, it becomes clear that, for Diderot, the most
general form of this resistance is conventional morality.

Though Diderot, like Condillac, points to a resistance always at work in perception, he is also like Condillac in that
he never simply renounces the hypothesis of a pure perception. Nonetheless, it should now be clear that perception is
the result of a struggle rather than the simple recording of
experience by a passive system. If there is to be such a thing
as pure perception, then it can come about only for an exceptional subject, capable of overcoming the resistance that language, his own memory, and his own sexuality place in his
path. But because neither language nor sexuality, nor perhaps
even memory is strictly private, the subject's struggle to perceive clearly also involves him in a struggle with convention
and society as well as with himself. Correct perception is not
just spontaneous, it is rather a norm that is very difficult if
not impossible to attain.

Bordeu represents the perceiving subject in his relation to
convention and society and in relation to his own, unconcious
desires. As a physician, he possesses the intimate, detailed
knowledge of empirical nature that for Diderot is the basis of
true science. He is ready to call things by their technical name,
even when that name is obscene by the standards of polite
society. He is also ready to speculate on such "forbidden" subjects as bestiality and autoeroticism, because he is convinced
of their scientific and theoretical importance. In short, Bordeu
perceives "clearly" and is presumably sufficiently judicious and
courageous to convey his perceptions to others. Bordeu, then,
in almost all ways exemplifies the *philosophe* who, as we shall
see, serves in his own theory of perception as a model of lucidity and "correct" perception. Moreover, Bordeu's theory of

perception not only approximates the theory presented by the character Diderot in the *Entretien entre d'Alembert et Diderot*, it also adumbrates in a number of ways the theory of perception or of sensibility exposed in *Le Paradoxe sur le comédien*, where the great actor and also the philosopher and the political man of genius are defined as observers who perceive clearly what other, sensitive people experience too vividly to understand: "Hot-tempered, violent, sensitive men are on the stage; they provide the spectacle, but they don't enjoy it. They are the originals of the copy made by the man of genius. . . . As for us, we feel; as for them, they observe, study, and paint."[19] In the *Paradoxe*, the just man or political genius and the great actor are alike in that, for both, all political and aesthetic action or experience is defined with reference to a "frame" that determines that experience is neither spontaneous nor passive. In the case of the actor, the "frame" is the theatrical stage itself, and the great actor, in the view of the principal speaker of the *Paradoxe*, is the one who remains at all times conscious of the stage qua stage—who, unlike the sensitive actor, never gives in to the illusion that he *is* the character he is playing. Diderot is less explicit as to what constitutes the "frame" of experience in the case of the poet, the philosopher, and the political man. However, his use of the great comedian as a model for these other exceptional types implies that the process of framing, which is the condition of the outstanding theatrical performance, is not confined exclusively to the theater or to an aesthetic realm, but is rather an element of experience in general. This element is unrecognized by the "sensitive man," but the genius remains cognizant of it at all times. The many points of contact between the *Rêve de d'Alembert* and the *Paradoxe sur le comédien* make it clear that Diderot's model of perception, like Condillac's, implies a stage and an aesthetics of representation.[20] Perception is always framed by interest or

[19] *Le Paradoxe sur le comédien, Oeuvres* (Paris: Editions Gallimard, 1951), pp. 1008-1009.

[20] The question of the place of the *Paradoxe* in Diderot's aesthetics and particularly in relation to his earlier aesthetic text, the *Entretiens sur le fils*

attention, and the clearest perception occurs when the consciousness of the process of framing is most acute—or when the spectator in the theater of perception is most conscious of the other, attentive spectators, whose presence reminds each spectator that he is indeed in a theater.

When viewed from the perspective of the *Paradoxe sur le comédien*, Bordeu appears as a great observer who, as such, occupies the same position as the great actor and thus judges and observes the manifestations of the sensitivity of others without himself being sensitive. Nonetheless, Bordeu has real difficulties expressing his scientific theories to his own satisfaction throughout the *Rêve* as well as in the *Suite*. These difficulties raise serious questions as to the capacity of even this exceptional individual to perceive clearly. I have noted that her interest in Bordeu provides Mlle de l'Espinasse with the

---

naturel, has been much debated, and many critics have gone so far as to argue that this work is incompatible with the rest of Diderot's aesthetic theory. In contrast, Yvon Belaval, in his *L'Esthétique sans Paradoxe de Diderot* (Paris: Editions Gallimard, 1950), concludes that there is a "consistent basis" to all of Diderot's aesthetic writings: reason and judgment are always given a place in the aesthetic process by Diderot, not just in the *Paradoxe*, but elsewhere. Conversely, enthusiasm has a role to play, even in the *Paradoxe*. In *Absorption and Theatricality: Painting and the Beholder in the Age of Diderot* (Berkeley: University of California Press, 1980), Michael Fried places the concept of "absorption"—defined as the creation of the illusion that the beholder of a given painting does not exist—at the center of Diderot's aesthetics. For Fried, "absorption" is the antithesis of what he calls "theatricality," and he argues that this latter concept is consistently devalorized by Diderot. Fried stresses (p. 220, n. 142) that though Diderot's *Paradoxe* might appear to contradict his reading, such is not the case. In addition to the reasons he gives in support of this contention, one would want to add that though Fried's reading stresses the *content* of art, that is, the way absorption is thematized in eighteenth-century painting, he also notes that the beholder's absorption and ultimately his "disappearance" are the result of an *illusion*. One could say, using Fried's terms, that it is the *conditions* of this illusion that preoccupy Diderot in the *Paradoxe*, and it is in terms of them that Diderot develops a second concept of theatricality, more fundamental to his aesthetic than the concept of theatricality to which Fried, quite rightly, opposes absorption. Only the great artist, who is himself aware of the frame structuring the aesthetic process, can create the illusion of absorption.

incentive to overcome at least some of her conventional distaste for scientific learning. But Bordeu is no more immune to Mlle de l'Espinasse's charms than she is to his, as is indicated by the state of disarray in which he frequently finds himself in the course of their conversation (*Rêve*, notably, pp. 920-921). Bordeu is strangely weak and excitable in his exchange with Mlle de l'Espinasse, and this weakness cannot but reflect on his character as scientist, since the very definition of science and of scientific lucidity, according to Bordeu, is a firmness with respect to both the social conventions and the temptations that Mlle de l'Espinasse represents. The question is: Does Bordeu's weakness fundamentally compromise either science or perception, or is his attraction for Mlle de l'Espinasse a mere decorative element of the dialogues, unrelated to their scientific "core"?

The importance the stage itself assumes in relation to perception and observation in the *Paradoxe sur le comédien* already argues against the latter interpretation. In a sense the *Paradoxe* directs the reader of Diderot's work (and not just the actor) to avoid becoming submerged in the flow of the action or, in the case of the *Rêve de d'Alembert*, in the exposition of the theory, and forces him to consider seriously the stage framing that theory and determining the characters of Diderot, d'Alembert, Bordeu, and Mlle de l'Espinasse as *roles*. If we make an a priori decision to take them, their actions, and their speeches literally, Diderot suggests, we, as spectators, are in a situation analogous to that of the bad actor who takes his own role literally. Diderot, however, does not ultimately force us to choose between a theory of perception implicit in the dramatic elements of his three dialogues and another theory manifest in the lines spoken by Diderot and Bordeu. Instead the theory of perception exposed by Bordeu in the course of the *Rêve de d'Alembert* raises the same issues that are apparent in Diderot's dramatization of the dialogues. Just as Bordeu as a scientist seems caught between contending forces, both within himself and within society, so the perceiving system he describes is beset by contention among its various functions. In the case of the scientist as in the case of the apparatus he describes, it is not clear that the contending forces or functions can be reduced to a unity or referred back to a simple origin in sensation.

Bordeu's discussion of perception with Mlle de l'Espinasse recapitulates Condillac's and Diderot's theories, but instead of the analytical terminology employed by them to describe a chain of faculties extending from sensation at one end to complex thinking and action at the other, Bordeu uses a topographical model in which the different elements of perception are localized in different parts of the nervous system. While sensation originates on the periphery of the system, it can be said to take place only when the stimulus occurring on the periphery is conveyed to a center, the "origin of the bundle" of nerve filaments. This center identifies a specific location on the periphery as the site of the sensation. The center, to perform its function, must possess not only a sense of the periphery, but a specific sense of itself as center, and this specific sense Bordeu calls *memory*. Thus perception, according to Bordeu's model, is by definition a complex process involving at once a periphery and a center, memory and sensation, and because of this complexity, perception is not always uniform and consistent. For Bordeu, the most convincing proof of his theory of perception lies in its capacity to illuminate precisely those cases in which perception is "abnormal." It is the quality of the relationship between the center and periphery that according to Bordeu, explains differences in perception and sensibility. "Is the principal element or stem too vigorous relative to the branches? The result is a poet, an artist, people with imagination, fearful men, enthusiasts, madmen. Too weak? The result is what we call the brute, the ferocious beast. The entire system loose, soft, without energy? You have an imbecile. The entire system energetic, well adjusted, well organized? You have a solid thinker, a philosopher, a sage" (*Rêve*, p. 924). The system can function in a number of different ways, and clearly, for Bordeu, only the system of the philosopher perceives reality correctly and successfully imitates it in thought.

193

Perception requires more than that an object and a sense system be immediately present to one another. It requires a balance between different elements within the sensory apparatus itself.

The balance characteristic of the sage or the philosopher exists only when the imbalance that produces the poet and the madman (this same imbalance is characteristic of sleep as well) is corrected. Bordeu, however, never succeeds in finding a consistent definition of what balance and imbalance are, and this reflects the fundamental paradox of sensation itself as Diderot defines it. In a long passage adumbrating the *Paradoxe sur le comédien* in a particularly vivid way, Bordeu defines the disordered system as one dominated by "pure sensitivity," understood as the totality of the nervous system *minus* both the "original" object, which provided the occasion for the stimulus, and the "center" of the system, which establishes hierarchy among different perceptions: "In the waking state the nervous system is subject to impressions made by the exterior object. In sleep, everything that happens to it [the nervous system] emanates from the workings of its own sensitivity" (*Rêve*, p. 927). This form of imbalance is highly problematic, for, as Condillac too remarks, such a mutilated sensitivity can produce a synthetic "reality" as perfect a reflection of "external" reality as that produced in the mind by experience:

> BORDEU: There is no distraction when one dreams. . . . Concepts are sometimes as consequent, as distinct as in the animal exposed to the actual spectacle of nature. [The dream] is only the tableau of this spectacle reanimated: hence its truth, hence the impossibility of discerning the dream from the waking state: in this state, the probability of one's being awake or asleep is equal; there is no way to recognize one's error except experience.
> MLLE DE L'ESPINASSE: And can experience always do so?
> BORDEU: No. (*Rêve*, pp. 927-928)

This definition of imbalance is disquieting in itself, for, as Bordeu admits, experience may not provide the necessary criteria for distinguishing the "synthetic" from the "true" reality, and if this is so, then the view that the sleeping subject is "imbalanced" compared to the wide-awake, philosophical subject becomes unjustifiable. This point is essential, and it is reiterated every time the sleeping d'Alembert sets forth a new argument in favor of the material nature of sensibility and is corroborated by the wide-awake Bordeu. The scientist may be a man who mistakes the fictions he produced in his sleep for experience itself, or, to put it another way, science depends on the exercise of a faculty of imagination that cannot be derived wholly from sensation.

The second definition of imbalance is that it is the result of a domination of the sensory apparatus by the external object or of a lack of resistance which renders experience excessively vivid or even traumatic: "The ear is struck by a touching phrase, the eye, by a singular phenomenon, and there, all at once, an interior tumult is raised, all the filaments of the bundle become agitated, a shiver spreads" (p. 925). As is the case with the first definition of imbalance, the domination of the system by the object functions equally well as a definition of balance or of imbalance. For in the previous example it is precisely the absence of the object that makes the sleeper "mad," whereas the lucidity of those who, like the philosopher, are considered to be truly awake is guaranteed by the fidelity to or domination of the system by the external object. Finally, there is a third definition of imbalance contained in the previously quoted passage on the poet, the philosopher, and the brute, according to which the "imbalance" that produces not philosophy and reason but poetry and imagination results from a "too vigorous" *center* of the system: "Is the principal element or stem too vigorous relative to the branches? The result is a poet, an aritst, people with imagination."

Bordeu concludes his discussion of sensibility by affirming the unity of the system that perceives, acts, and thinks: "the least of our actions is the necessary effect of one cause and

only one cause: ourself—very complicated, but unitary nonetheless" (p. 929). But his affirmation is seriously challenged
by his own description of the perceiving system, by the contradiction between his various definitions of the poorly ordered perceptual system, and by the underlying tension between sensation and memory to which those contradictions
point. The perceiving system is such that there is no definition
of a balanced system that is not also a definition of an imbalanced system. If this is so, it is because sensation cannot be
located at a single point in the system. The periphery (sensation) is always involved in events "taking place" at the center
(memory), but, more important, the center is already involved
in a sensation "taking place" on the periphery—memory is
already involved in sensation. Balance cannot be achieved by
subordinating the periphery to the center or vice versa, precisely because the periphery is already involved in the center
and vice versa. It is only by accepting the role of memory in
sensation that Diderot, like Condillac, can preserve the unity
of the perceiving subject, for memory is the link uniting sensation and perception to the "higher" mental processes. But
by acknowledging that memory is already at work in sensation, Diderot also acknowledges that the unity of the perceiving subject is never demonstrable. For he has thereby undercut the basis of that unity—the primacy of sensation over
memory. If memory is already at work in sensation, then the
distinction between the waking and sleeping (dreaming) state,
between memory or imagination and sensation cannot be rigorously drawn. The weakness and sensitivity apparent in Bordeu's dealings with Mlle de l'Espinasse are not accidental, but
already implicit in his firm, philosophical character. The similarity between d'Alembert's dream and Bordeu's theories is
not a mere coincidence, but a predictable occurrence.

The complexity of the mind described by Condillac and Diderot is great, for it embraces many separate faculties or operations of which sensation, reminiscence, perception, consciousness, and attention are only a few. And yet that complexity
is ultimately only relative for both, insofar as they refer it back

to what they consider to be a localizable, punctual event: sensation. The heterogeneity they describe is ultimately rooted in the unity of sensation and the perceiving subject. In their actual description of the workings of the mind, however, the fundamental unity they posit is radically threatened, not by a split between sensation and the higher mental faculties, but by a split *within sensation itself* between sensation and memory. The "unity" of perception is the "unity" of a theater, so highly differentiated that it becomes questionable that it can be considered a unity at all. The "object" as it appears both in Condillac's *Essai* and in Bordeu's topographical model, is an object for perception only insofar as it has become an object of attention, only insofar as it is framed or placed on a stage by the system itself. That attention, in turn, implies that the system itself is not passive and undifferentiated, for attention is produced by the repression of certain sensations and the intensification of others, by a distinction between the sensation (or stage), the perceiving subject (or spectator), and a background (the other spectators) that is both present and absent in perception itself. Or, as Bordeu puts it, the sensation of an "object" is produced by a *relationship* between different locations in the perceiving system, each of which, when deprived of the other, produces a distinct form of "madness." The "object," then, is only revealed fully to an (ideal) observer/philosopher/actor in whom a consciousness of the relationships of the system is most fully realized, so that the object of sensation is perceived as being on stage, the subject as being in the audience. The theories of perception of Condillac and Diderot, with the crucial importance both attach to the "framing" of the object, as well as to the role of pleasure and pain in sensation, are thus dominated by the "theatricality" of representation. But by showing the role "theatricality" plays in perception itself, Diderot and Condillac undercut all classical theories that assume the theater can only be an object of perception rather than the condition of it.

The ("theatrical") subject described by Condillac and Diderot bears little resemblance to the perceiving subject whose direct observations provide science with the basis of many of its certitudes. Even if it is acknowledged that perception may be distorted by a number of factors, the critical measures taken to restore perception to a pristine state before memory and ideology have affected it are to no avail if memory is an active participant in and a condition of all perception and if the perceptual apparatus resembles not a pure undifferentiated surface, but a theater. The notion of a perception that would not be contaminated in its essence by memory and alterity implies an ideal perceiving subject located not in society but in a "state of nature." An empiricism that rejects thought as the foundation of being holds that perception is by right if not in fact the most primitive attribute of subjectivity. But in the models provided by Condillac and Diderot, the perceiving subject is already implicated in history and society at the moment of perception itself; a fundamental sociality is already implicit in the constitutive differentiation of the perceptual apparatus.

The theater illustrates perception in the theories of Diderot and Condillac, but it is no *mere* illustration. Once it has been offered as a model of the perceptual apparatus, the step outside the state of nature has already been taken. The structure of alterity implied by this internal theater cannot be conceived as constituting a single individual; it does not correspond to the limits of *a consciousness*, no matter how complex. The perceiving subject is already a social subject in a radical, fundamental sense, because the possibility of a social existence is already "within" him in the theater that structures perception and makes it seem as if perception, memory, and attention were results of an emulation of other perceiving subjects. It should not be forgotten that when memory and theater are placed at the origin of perception, imagination becomes central to perception as well. The differentiation and, ultimately, alienation of the subject structured like a theater are so fundamental and radical that it cannot always be determined whether he is awake or asleep, mad or sane. Once memory has been shown to be at work in sensation or perception, there are no longer any absolute criteria to distinguish between imagination and memory, for such a distinction is based on the relative proximity of each to a sensation thought to be distinct from both. If the perceptual apparatus itself is conceived of as a theater, the criteria for distinguishing between "reality" and the representation of reality, between the faculties that produce fiction and those that produce perception, memory, history, and science, can no longer be accepted as simply given.

Instead of a perceiving subject abstracted from history and society and witnessing them from a safe, objective distance, the subject Diderot and Condillac describe has already been brought into history and society by perception itself. According to their description and contrary to the stated goals of their analyses and of eighteenth-century empiricism in general, there are no ultimate criteria for distinguishing between a science based on direct observation and a history based on a reconstruction of the past: science, like history, is based as much on memory and representation as on "pure perception." Condillac's *Essai* and Diderot's *Rêve de d'Alembert* reveal the complex "theatricality," that is, the fundamental sociality and historicity, that deprives perception of its place as the simple origin of experience, memory, history, and fiction.

SIX

(*Diderot*)
The Boundaries of Narrative:
Determinism and Narrative Theory

THE ROLE of narrative in both history and literature is much debated today. The current emphasis on narrative is certainly not, however, the result of the discovery of a "new" object, for those who acknowledge that the theory of narrative has a central role to play in history and literature also readily admit that narrative is as old as the history of thought itself. Instead, one could say that this emphasis stems from a common attempt to understand the specificity of narrative, that is, to understand what exactly determines the form and function of any given narrative. It is this emphasis on the *specificity* of narrative that is new, even if narrative itself and the analysis of narrative are not. In most cases, theorists who assert the necessity of focusing on the specificity of narrative argue that the problem has been neglected in traditional theories of history and literature, where consideration of narrative is subordinated to questions concerning a variety of causes thought to determine narrative from without: namely, the intentions of the narrator, the events being narrated, or the history thought to be represented in the narrative. Opposing these traditional views, the narrativist holds that the form taken by a given narrative is always in some measure arbitrary if one considers it from the standpoint of these external causes, and that what must be understood is the way in which narrative itself implies a system providing individual narratives and narrative-in-general with an internal logic and necessity.

One of the most striking features of this investigation of

the specificity of narrative is that it is being carried out in such different philosophical and cultural contexts, and these differences in context no doubt account for important differences in the aims and conclusions of the various theorists.[1] The question of narrative has figured prominently in recent debates in Anglo-American philosophy of history, with Arthur C. Danto and W. B. Gallie in particular representing the narrativist position. In the view of both, the theory of history has until very recently emphasized aspects of historical research such as the analysis and evaluation of data and the formulation of general laws of historical causation at the expense of a consideration of the construction of historical narratives. And yet, they argue, this latter activity is what gives history its specific character, setting it off from not only the natural sciences but the social sciences as well. According to Danto, the specific character of narrative is evident in narrative sentences, which he defines as referring "to at least two, time-separated events though they only *describe* (are only *about*) the earliest event to which they refer."[2] The narrative sentence never refers exclusively to the past event whose occurrence it narrates, but also always to a later moment from the perspective of which the (a) significance of the past event becomes evident. The narrative sentence thus could not have been uttered by a witness of the event but refers, not only to the event, but to narration itself.

For W. B. Gallie, history is characterized by its narrative structure, and, like Danto, he argues that narratives or stories explain through a retrospective illumination. According to

[1] In "Pour une théorie du discours narratif," in *La Narrativité* (Paris: Centre National de la Recherche Scientifique, 1980), Paul Ricoeur summarizes the contributions of Anglo-American philosophy of history and of structuralist analysis of narrative to narrative theory in general. He concludes by incorporating what he takes to be the most positive features of each of these narrative schools into his own general theory of narrative discourse, according to which history and fiction represent two distinct but complementary modes in which "our historicity is inscribed in language" (p. 65).

[2] Arthur C. Danto, *Analytical Philosophy of History* (Cambridge: Cambridge University Press, 1965), p. 143.

Gallie, the importance and significance of events narrated in the story are evident from the standpoint of the end of the story. Gallie accepts Collingwood's three requirements for the construction of a coherent, historical "picture." First, it "must be located in space and time." Second, "all history must be consistent with itself." And third, "the historian's picture 'stands in a peculiar relation to something called evidence.' "[3] But he also distinguishes the thrust of his analysis from that of Collingwood, by asserting that the latter is primarily concerned with the first and third requirements, whereas he, Gallie, is concerned with the second. Gallie thus argues that what should be stressed is the degree to which the truth-value of narrative is in some sense internal to it—it must be consistent both with itself and with other narratives. In a similar fashion, he argues that the ability of narratives to explain events does not lie in the events themselves, precisely because history is concerned specifically with events of a contingent nature. Thus the narrator does not—indeed, he cannot—uncover laws immanent in the phenomena he describes. Rather he forges an explanation through narration itself, by showing that the events that lead up to the end of the narrative are part of a pattern that makes sense in the light of that end. Though the historical narrative conforms to what Gallie calls evidence, its shape and the type of explanation it gives are determined by rules or by a logic inherent in narrative itself and in this sense arbitrary with respect to the evidence.

The question of narrative has played an equally prominent role in the history of structuralism and particularly in the structuralist theory of literature. The situation giving rise to the structuralist interest in narrative is, of course, very different from the situation in Anglo-American philosophy of history. The philosopher of history sees the narrative character of history as a feature distinguishing history from other social sciences. The structuralist literary critic sees narrative as prac-

---

[3] W. B. Gallie, *Philosophy and the Historical Understanding* (New York: Schocken Books, 1964), p. 57.

tically synonymous with discourse itself, and his concern with narrative reflects his interest in the fundamental role played by language in all of the human sciences as well as in literature. Though one can say that, like Gallie and Danto, structuralist literary critics such as Gérard Genette, Roland Barthes, and Tzvetan Todorov focus on the problem of the specificity of narrative, it is important to note that their work amounts to an implicit critique of the concept of narrative as defined by these philosophers of history. The distinction between "evidence" and "narrative" that Gallie takes over from Collingwood is naive from their point of view. This can be seen in the following passage, in which Tzvetan Todorov argues that *l'histoire*, whether conceived as history or story, is always a convention:

> *L'historie* is thus a convention, it does not exist at the level of events themselves. The report of a policeman concerning an incident follows precisely the norms of this convention; it sets forth the events as clearly as possible. . . . This convention is so pervasive that the particular deformation made by the writer in his presentation of events is confronted with it [the convention] and not with the chronological order. *L'historie* is an abstraction because it is always perceived and narrated by someone; it does not exist "in itself."[4]

In this passage, *l'historie* can thus be translated either as *story* (in the sense of plot) or as *history* (in the sense of events in themselves), because, for Todorov, neither exists outside of language, both constitute a specific form or aspect of discourse. Thus while he distinguishes between the coventional narrative produced by the policeman and that produced by Proust or Laclos, Todorov argues they are opposed as one type of narrative to another and not as narrative to nonnarrative or "true history" to fiction.

[4] Tzvetan Todorov, "Les Catégories du récit littéraire," *L'Analyse structurale du récit, Communications*, no. 8 (1966), p. 127.

Anglo-American critics of Danto and Gallie have argued that while the emphasis on the narrative nature of history may enable the philosopher to distinguish it from the sciences and social sciences, it does so at the cost of making history into a form of art or literature.[5] For the structuralist literary critic, this is indeed the case, and he considers it one of the strengths and not a weakness of narrative analysis to have demonstrated as much. In "Historical Discourse," Roland Barthes argues that fictional discourse has an arbitrary relationship to historical reality, but, even more, that historical narratives are also arbitrary in this sense.[6] The difference between historical narratives and most fictional narratives is that the former tend to disguise their arbitrary nature by the use of certain linguistic devices judged most apt to create an illusion of objectivity or a "reality effect." Nonetheless, Barthes argues that illusion or effect is fundamentally linguistic and hence arbitrary in character.

While the structuralist literary critic broadens the notion of narrative considerably, so that it comes to include all discourse and to override traditional distinctions between history and fiction, his primary concern, like that of Danto and especially Gallie, is to study narrative itself and to discover the intrinsic rules governing it. Gallie points to the French historian Cournot as the first to have understood that the historian typically comprehends history the way a spectator comprehends a game of chess: particular moves may create contingent situations, but these situations are nonetheless intelligible in terms of the rules of the game and its outcome as well as in terms of the skill of the players. The game-of-chess analogy figures importantly in the origins of the structural analysis of narrative as well, for in the theory of Ferdinand de Saussure language is defined as a closed system, governed by rules immanent to it in the way the rules governing the game of chess are imma-

[5] See W. H. Dray, "On the Nature and Role of Narrative in Historiography," *History and Theory*, vol. 10 (1971), p. 153.

[6] Roland Barthes, "Historical Discourse," *Introduction to Structuralism*, edited by Michael Lane (New York: Basic Books, 1970).

nent in each game. A move by one player or another may not be caused by the rules of the game, but it is still intelligible according to the rules. The proper study of the linguist is not, Saussure argues, the individual events making up the game, but the system of rules according to which any game is played.

The structural analysis of narrative is based first on the assumption that Saussure's definition of language is valid, and second on the assumption that it can serve as a model for the definition of narrative inasmuch as narrative is itself essentially language. In "An Introduction to the Structural Analysis of Narrative" Barthes argues that narrative cannot be studied inductively.[7] Just as the linguist must posit *la langue* or language as a system, so the narratologist must work from the assumption that there exists something that could be called narrative-in-general and that all narratives thus share certain characteristics. These characteristics cannot and should not be discerned by looking at all narratives—an impossible task—but rather by looking at a limited number of examples. The narrative totality posited at the beginning of the narratologist's research is also its end point. The theorist, according to Barthes, can and must integrate individual narratives into the larger, hypothetical narrative-in-general, and, analogously, the different subunities or levels of analysis (such as functions and actions) can and must be integrated into narration itself as it defines the limits and the coherence of each individual narrative. The *integration* of all subunits of narrative into the larger, narrative totality is the aim of all structural analysis of narrative. As Todorov puts it, the goal of the structural literary critic is less to understand the *parole* of literature, that is, the individual literary work, than the *langue*—the system formed by all of literature and the rules of integration governing it as a system. The structural critic seeks to uncover and articulate the rules of this system through his analysis of individual narratives, each of which he also views as constituting a system.

[7] Roland Barthes, "An Introduction to the Structural Analysis of Narrative," *New Literary History*, vol. 6, no. 2 (Winter 1975).

The more the narrative theorist stresses the specificity of narrative, the more he stresses its arbitrary character in relation to any "external" factors. As Gérard Genette puts it, the *first* task of the narratologist is to combat the illusion that narrative is "natural" and to heighten awareness of its artificiality:

> To define narrative in a positive manner is to accept, perhaps dangerously, the idea or the feeling that narrative is self-evident, that nothing is more natural than to tell a story or to arrange a group of actions. . . . The evolution of literature and of literary consciousness in the last half-century will have had, among other fortunate developments, that of drawing our attention to the singular, artificial and problematic aspect of the narrative act. . . . The falsely naive question—Why narrative?—should at least be able to incite us to seek or more simply to recognize the negative limits of narrative, to consider the principal plays of oppositions through which narrative defines and constitutes itself in the face of various nonnarrative forms.[8]

Like Saussure, when he argues that the sign, because it is neither a natural nor a logical consequence of the object to which it is supposed to refer, is arbitrary, Genette argues that the first step in understanding narrative is to grasp its artificial or arbitrary character. The limits of narrative are not imposed on it from without: narrative constitutes its own limits, from within, through "plays of oppositions."

In this way, the narratologist espouses his own kind of determinism: the narrative system may not be governed from without, but it is governed from within. It is arbitrary in relation to what is external to it, but the relations between its elements are necessary. In his "Nature du signe linguistique," Emile Benveniste seeks to clarify Saussure's teaching concerning the arbitrary nature of the sign by stressing that the sign

---

[8] Gérard Genette, "Boundaries of Narrative," *New Literary History*, vol. 8, no. 1 (Autumn 1976), p. 1.

is only arbitrary in relation to a referent.[9] Benveniste argues that inasmuch as Saussure maintains that the sign or signifier in fact represents a concept or signified, and inasmuch as he also affirms that the signifier and signified are as inseparable as two sides of one sheet of paper, Saussure in fact implies what for Benveniste is indeed the case: that the sign is necessary. The relationship between the signifier and its concept is never arbitrary, for there is no thought and no concept without language of some kind. When language and thought are considered as a system, there is, then, a necessity inherent in both. Like Benveniste, the narratologist, when he analyses the elements of a narrative, proceeds as if there were a necessity internal to narrative. In his view, any individual narrative and its elements are necessarily susceptible of being integrated into a larger narrative unity, and the rules governing this larger unity both constitute the "negative boundaries of narrative," as Genette calls them, and govern the functioning of all individual narratives.

If for Gallie and Danto narrative is to be distinguished from evidence, facts, or events, Todorov, Barthes, and Genette, on the other hand, would emphasize that evidence and facts are already part of narrative—they must already be narrated to achieve their historical status. But though the structuralist literary critic considerably broadens the sense of the term, there remains one type of discourse he does not clearly label as "narrative": the narratologist's own theoretical discourse. To posit narrative as a totality is *also* to delimit it, and by delimiting narrative, the narratologist also implicitly constitutes his own theoretical discourse as metanarrational, with the result that the distinction between narrative and the theory of narrative becomes one of those "negative boundaries" of narrative to which Genette refers.

One would want, then, to contrast the narratologist's position with that of the philosopher of history or literary critic for whom the question of the specificity of narrative is sec-

[9] Emile Benveniste, "Nature du signe linguistique," *Problèmes de linguistique générale* (Paris: Editions Gallimard, 1966).

ondary or irrelevant. At the same time, it should be emphasized that theorists who treat narrative from either the more traditional or the narratological point of view are faced with a common problem: they must delimit narrative. If it is arbitrary, it must be arbitrary in relation to something else lying beyond its "negative boundaries." If it is determined, it must be determined in relation to something else. The drawing of the boundaries of narrative is thus the basis for any theory seeking to understand its specific character, whether the theory argues that narrative is arbitrary in relation to any external reality or determined by it, that narrative is caused or is its own cause.

DIDEROT'S *Jacques le Fataliste* has increasingly come to be read by critics as a self-reflexive novel whose principal subject is the conventions of narrative. There are two major phases in the narrative analysis of *Jacques le Fataliste*, and they correspond roughly to the views of narrative that have just been outlined. In both phases, critics have acknowledged the necessity of analyzing the way the rules governing narrative organize the novel. For some critics, however, those rules are only one of the factors determining the novel; others are the intentions of the author and an extranarrative reality, which the novel seeks to capture. For example, in his "La Parodie romanesque dans *Jacques le Fataliste*," Robert Mauzi argues that Diderot's immediate aim in *Jacques le Fataliste* is to reveal the arbitrary or conventional nature of the realism of the novel as a genre. But his ultimate aim is to write a novel that transcends the arbitrary character it ascribes to all the others: "Such is, we believe, the ultimate intention of the author: . . . destroy the traditional forms of the literary work and this traditional illusion of truth, which is, in reality, falsehood. The author thereby thinks he will attain a more authentic truth, one built on the ruins of the novel, the rout of the characters, and the vestiges of broken illusion."[10] Though toward the end of his

[10] Robert Mauzi, "La Parodie romanesque dans *Jacques le Fataliste*," *Diderot Studies*, vol. 6 (1964).

essay Mauzi hints that Diderot's novel may not conform to his intentions and may thus remain to an important degree arbitrary and conventional like the novels it satirizes, still it is not entirely arbitrary. For, according to Mauzi, it is nonetheless determined to an important extent by those intentions and by the underlying reality Diderot seeks to express.

Mauzi's view of the status of narrative in *Jacques le Fataliste* is widely shared, and perhaps one reason for this is that it seems such a view can be reconciled with the philosophical position of Diderot—what critics call his determinism. The implication is that there is an inadmissable contradiction between, on the one hand, the view that narrative in *Jacques le Fataliste* is arbitrary and, on the other, the importance Diderot and more particularly his character Jacques, attribute to necessity and the laws of causation. When *Jacques le Fataliste* is read as a defense and illustration of determinism, Mauzi's analysis of its narrative form can be seen as roughly consistent with the philosophical position of the hero. For Mauzi, narrative, like history in *Jacques le Fataliste*, is determined, not perhaps by a great scroll, but at least by the author and by the nature of an underlying reality the author seeks to capture through his narrative.

In a second phase, *Jacques le Fataliste* has been interpreted as an affirmation of the arbitrary character of narrative. Moreover, it is argued that the novel, far from pointing beyond convention to an ultimate reality or truth in which the novel would be grounded, instead reveals the fundamentally self-referential character not only of *Jacques le Fataliste* but of the traditional novel as well—and, ultimately, of all narrative. In *The Vacant Mirror*, Thomas Kavanagh defines the novel this way:

> Jacques le Fataliste is . . . a text, a manipulation of language ordered to the apparent goal of telling a story. . . . My goal will be to show how the literary use of the word distinguishes itself by a refusal to seek its own disappearance, by a refusal to be but a transitive means assuring the perception of some mythic reality which it is pre-

sumed to represent. The literary message takes as its subject the very code in virtue of which it is able to exist. Literary discourse becomes, as a thing of language, both its own reality and its own self-defining object.[11]

Kavanagh sees the novel as an integrated totality irreducible to any exterior reality, be it that of its historical period or the life of its author; and in this sense he considers it arbitrary. There are certain respects, however, in which he implicitly views Diderot's novel as determined and necessary. Arbitrary with respect to an external reality, it is still ruled by an *internal* necessity that gives the work its meaning and at the same time makes the work "creative of its own interpretative grill" (p. 14). The task of the critic is to respect the work's "immanence as a self-defining act of language" (p. 15). The immanence and unity of the work are themselves necessary: they determine that the work is always equal to itself and thus, that the supreme authority for the interpretation of a work is always the work itself. Kavanagh insists that the unity of the work only becomes apparent when the work is viewed as a linguistic object, and this leads him to argue that ultimately, despite its self-contained nature, the work must be integrated into a larger totality in order to be understood—the totality of literary discourse, of the "code," or of language-in-general. The background for Kavanagh's reading of Diderot then, is a poetics, a theory of narrative, and a linguistics that view literature, narrative, and language respectively as totalities each governed by their own necessity and their own rules of immanence, but each arbitrary in relation to any "external" nonnarrative element.

Given this view of the narrative status of *Jacques le Fataliste*, it seems inevitable that such a critic should either ignore the problem of determinism or deny it as a valid theory pertaining either to history or to the novel, not only because that prob-

[11] Thomas Kavanagh, *The Vacant Mirror: A Study of Mimesis through Diderot's Jacques le Fataliste* (Banbury, Oxfordshire: Voltaire Foundation, 1973), pp. 11, 14.

lem seems to lead away from the more formal issues of narrative and language, but also because the doctrine of determinism appears to contradict directly the view that language and narrative are in essence arbitrary. Indeed, Kavanagh treats determinism as equivalent to the mimetic theory of the novel, and he rejects both on the same grounds:

> This same mimetic contradiction manifests itself on the second level, as regards the philosophical question of determinism. . . . On the levels of both the narrative form and the thematic intent, mimesis is a lie. . . . The transformation of authorical discourse into mimetic history is characterized by a substitution of a false present (one effectively relegated to the past by its subordination to an already anticipated future state) for *the true present of an inaugural act of language freely elaborating itself.* (pp. 63-64, my emphasis)

Kavanagh is not alone, of course, in interpreting *Jacques le Fataliste* as a critique or satire of fatalism rather than a defense of it,[12] but in his case, such a position seems inevitable. For

[12] Though Aram Vartanian's principal aim in his *Diderot and Descartes* (Princeton, N.J.: Princeton University Press, 1953) is to understand the contribution of Diderot's "scientific naturalism" to the history of science, he argues that where man himself is concerned, Diderot's scientific determinism gave way to a "set of values, both in art and in morals, which transcended . . . the principles on which the *philosophe*'s system of nature was erected" (p. 315). Vartanian concludes then that *Jacques le Fataliste*, far from representing an application of his scientific theories to the human sphere, is a "satire on the kind of fatalism which, fusing scientific pretentiousness with a disenchanted reading of Spinoza's chapter on 'Human Bondage,' might seek entirely to identify human values and purposes with the inexorable chain of physical events" (p. 315). Similarly, Herbert Dieckmann, in his *Cinq Leçons sur Diderot* (Paris: Minard, 1959), argues that, in *Jacques le Fataliste*, Diderot's determinism remained "as an aspiration and an exigency," but that the novel's purpose is also to articulate a conflict between his materialist theses and his "humanism" and that, in this sense, it represents an important qualification of his determinism. From a position much closer to that of Kavanagh, Simone Lecointre and Jean Le Galliot argue that *Jacques le Fataliste* defends a freedom, not so much of the human subject, but of narrative itself: *"Jacques*

it alone can save the unity he ascribes to the novel, that is, prevent the novel from being split between a philosophical determinism and a formal theory of the arbitrariness of narration.

Though they are polemically opposed, these two interpretations of Diderot's novel converge on a crucial point, just as do the more broadly focused theories of narrative discussed earlier. Though Mauzi stresses the role of "nonnarrative" factors in determining narrative form while Kavanagh stresses the arbitrary and systematic nature of narrative as well as the immanence of the rules governing it, both theories assume that it is possible to delimit narrative. For Mauzi, it must be possible to distinguish between narrative and the intentions of the author or an extranarrative reality. For Kavanagh, like the structuralist literary critics he cites, narrative is self-delimiting, narrative itself establishes the boundaries between itself and the nonlinguistic, and the task of the critic is to respect this self-delimitation and to remain faithful to the definition of itself already contained within the narrative.

I would argue that the conflict between these two views of narrative and the readings of *Jacques le Fataliste* they imply cannot be decided by referring for support to the novel itself (both views, of course, claim to be rooted in the novel), precisely because *Jacques le Fataliste* does not, in my view, defend and illustrate either view. Instead, it puts narrative itself into question. The novel shows the way in which concepts of necessity and the arbitrary depend on a common delimitation of narrative and reveals that particular, discrete narratives and narrative-in-general *do not exist* as distinct objects. On the contrary, narrative in the novel constantly transgresses the boundaries delimiting it and defining its objective status. Diderot's

---

le Fataliste . . . affirms that no novel has yet been written that would not be in conformity with the principles of narration. This is to claim a double liberty: vis-à-vis 'literature' and vis-à-vis the social formation literature reflects and is determined by. It is to claim the freedom of writing" (Introduction, in Denis Diderot, *Jacques le Fataliste et son maître* [Geneva: Librairie Droz, 1976], p. cxxiii).

philosophical and historical position can be fully understood only in the light of his critique of any and all of the boundaries that could be claimed to make possible the delimitation either of a narrative or of narrative-in-general. His determinism is neither a theory of the existence of rational causes and laws regulating all phenomena, nor merely a discredited world view that his novel proclaims only in order to satirize. Instead, *Jacques le Fataliste* argues against the notion of a *transcendent* law, a universal reason, or even a closed, narrative system that would be all-determining without being determined by anything but itself. Understood in this way, Diderot's determinism is entirely consistent with the theories of language, "narrative," and the novel presented in *Jacques le Fataliste*.

To UNDERSTAND Diderot's determinism, it is important not to assume a definition of law and apply it to *Jacques le Fataliste*, but rather to consider the way in which Diderot uses the novel to provide its own definition of necessity and law. The concept of law undergoes an important transformation in the course of the eighteenth century, largely thanks to Montesquieu's *De l'esprit des lois*, and it is useful to compare Montesquieu's definition with that of Diderot in order to understand the special significance of the latter. In large measure, the novelty of *De l'esprit des lois* itself stems from the "new" meaning (at least in the context of political philosophy) Montesquieu gives to law. He defines it as the necessary relationship between things, and, in doing so, breaks with a long tradition in political philosophy that defines the law as a rule imposed on one subject by another. Certainly a major basis for the criticism that Montesquieu's work was Spinozist or atheist was his "depersonalization" of the law. According to his definition, law no longer implies an enforcer (a prince or ultimately a God), and, as a result, it takes on a new secular and scientific meaning. In *Jacques le Fataliste*, Diderot too criticizes a traditional concept of law, but the tactic he adopts to undercut the authority it implies is significantly different from that of Montesquieu. For Diderot, law retains much of the moral and political character dispelled, at least on the surface, by Montesquieu's scientific definition. Law is presented by Diderot as the constraint imposed by a master on a servant. The question of determinism is thus directly related to the status of the relationship between masters and servants in *Jacques le Fataliste*, and the explication of Diderot's definition of the law hinges in large measure on the character of their relationship.

Even the most casual reading reveals that the master-servant relationship in *Jacques le Fataliste* is not simple. As both the narrator and Jacques point out, Jacques is in most if not all ways the master of his master (*"Jacques leads his master"*).[13] Jacques's master is not in every way a Hegelian master, however, who is dependent on the work and the recognition of his slave for his existence as master. He also depends on the recognition of a broader social organization comprising all the masters and servants taken together. By the same token, Jacques himself does not correspond to the Hegelian slave, who himself becomes free as a result of his master's dependence on him on the one hand and his relationship to the products of his work on the other. Jacques's master's position is radically undercut by his dependence on Jacques, for as the servant argues, he, Jacques, is the one with the actual authority: "It has been decided that you will have the title and that I will have the thing" (p. 229). But Jacques's own autonomy is also limited by the constraints of a society that, whatever Jacques's power, still gives the master the title. In gaining mastery over his master Jacques becomes like his master, and thus he comes to share his views and values, which are also those of the society as a whole. As Jacques remarks, he is like the horse that will no longer do agricultural work once it has carried and been owned by a gentleman (p. 353). In gaining a measure of authority over his master, Jacques has become like his master, and therefore, like him, he cannot be free.

The convergence of the concept of mastery and the concept

---

[13] Diderot, *Jacques le Fataliste* (Geneva: Librairie Droz, 1976), p. 230. All references to *Jacques le Fataliste* are to this edition.

of law or cause is illustrated by Jacques toward the end of the novel when he arranges a series of events, foreseeing at every step what his master's reactions and subsequent actions will be. His master, who keeps insisting that he is a free agent, is forced to recognize at the end of the sequence that everything has been planned, foreseen, and determined by his servant. The true master, it seems, is the one who brings about the actions of the other, and, in this instance, Jacques appears to reign supreme. Jacques's assertion of his master's dependence on him is at the same time an implicit assertion of his own freedom, and such an assertion contradicts his determinist principles. But while his implicit assertion contradicts his determinism, Jacques's actual situation does not. For he has put himself in the position of proving something and thus is effectively in the same position as the man who throws himself from his horse and breaks his neck to prove that he is free. Jacques's captain's reaction to the latter incident could easily be applied to Jacques: "My captain would say: What! you don't see that without my contradicting you, you would never have had the fantastical idea of breaking your neck? It is I, then, who have taken you by the foot and thrown you off your saddle" (p. 350). While Jacques has clearly shown that his master's actions are not free, he also shows that he himself is not the ultimate cause of his master's actions. For his own actions are determined by his master, inasmuch as they are prompted by a desire to prove the master wrong. By espousing determinism, Jacques does not become himself free. There is always another master, for every master has a master (p. 63); and, for this reason, there is no absolute Master. By the same token, there is no action that is free, for every action that is a cause is also caused. Because there is always a cause— because events are *always* determined—there is no unique Cause, that is, no original cause which would itself have no cause. Or, to put it another way, it is because there is no Law that events are determined.

There is relative mastery in *Jaques le Fataliste* but no absolute master. In this respect, too, Diderot's master-servant relationship differs from the dialectical relationship of Hegel's master-slave pair. In the latter, there is a fundamental dissimilarity between the two antagonists, evident in the fact that the slave is initially utterly dependent on the master, and later free with respect to a master who has become himself the slave. The master-servant relationship in *Jacques le Fataliste* could be called specular rather than dialectical, for underlying all the relationships depicted in the novel is a fundamental similarity between individuals who are all someone's master and someone's servant—who are all each other's doubles. The thematic prominence of doubles and dueling in the various stories that make up *Jacques le Fataliste* (there are duels between Jacques's captain and his friend, Desglands and his rival, Jacques's master and the chevalier de St. Ouin, etc.) reflects Diderot's critique of the concept of mastery. Dueling, the narrator remarks, is not only caused by the adherence of certain individuals to the aristocratic code, it is a figure for a multitude, if not all, social relationships: "Duels repeat themselves in society in all sorts of forms . . . every estate has its lance and its knights-errant" (p. 89). Mme de la Pommeraye uses her wits, her unfaithful lover's own desires, and Mme and Mlle d'Aisnon as her weapons in a "duel" with her lover. The story of Mme de la Pommeraye combines the themes of determinism and dueling in that Mme de la Pommeraye seeks to best her unfaithful lover by creating a world that she can manipulate perfectly. Once the marquis has entered it, she can predict and control his actions with a frightening accuracy. Equally "diabolical," to use Jacques's adjective, is the way in which she completely reifies the two women who serve as her instruments. Their pleas, their protestations, their sense of humiliation and degradation as the fraud Mme de la Pommeraye is willing to perpetrate to avenge herself becomes apparent to them mean absolutely nothing to Mme de la Pommeraye. Jacques frequently claims that destiny is amoral if not immoral, and thus Mme de la Pommeraye's ruthlessness along with her quasi-absolute power are both signs of the degree to which she has become a destiny, a master, and a first cause for Mlle and Mme d'Aisnon and the marquis. However, the end of the story of Mme de la Pommeraye reveals that her mastery is only relative. The marriage of the marquis and Mlle d'Aisnon takes place exactly as she had foreseen, as does the revelation of the new bride's sordid past. But that the marquis's new wife should, by her behavior, show herself to be worthy of him in every respect and that the marquis should acknowledge and return her esteem and love are developments that negate the sense of all Mme de la Pommeraye has brought to pass. Destiny has determined all the events, but those events prove to have an ironic meaning for destiny itself. This irony is built into the law; one could even say that it is the law. The source of the law—be it a lawgiver, a destiny, or a principle of reason—is always itself subject to the law; the law always doubles back on itself, undercutting the authority at its source, revealing that every master has a master.

If one turns now to the problem of narration, the consistency of the narrative aspect of the novel with Diderot's determinism is clear. In *Jacques le Fataliste* narration is always situated in terms of a struggle for mastery between the different narrators and their listeners or readers—that is, a struggle over who will be Narrator. The specular relationship between Jacques and his master is identical in form to the relationship between the general narrator and the reader he addresses throughout the novel, and, moreover, the relationship between Jacques and his master is in itself a relationship between a narrator and a reader (or listener). As it is presented in the novel, the act of narration is never free or neutral. In the case of Jacques and his master, storytelling is a part of the struggle for recognition that binds them together. Telling a story can be an assertion of self, a task performed to entertain a master, or, most often, both of these things at once. The teller of the tale may assert his mastery over the listener, or the listener may demonstrate that the narrator depends on him (as when Jacques enrages his master by falling asleep at the "high point" of his master's story of his relations with Agathe).

This inconclusive tug of war describes not just the relationship between Jacques and his master as they alternately listen and narrate, but also between the "general" narrator and the reader who is always virtually present and who is occasionally represented more directly by the language the narrator puts in his mouth. Like the struggle between Jacques and his master, the struggle between the narrator and the reader has two phases. In a first phase, the freedom and autonomy of the narrator are emphasized. When narration is presented in this light, *Jacques le Fataliste* reads very much like an illustration of the structuralist theory of narrative, for the ultimate source of the narrator's freedom seems to be the arbitrary character of narrative itself. When he asserts his own authority over the development of the narrative, the narrator constantly reminds the reader of its artificial, constructed nature. The very first interruption in the story line is accompanied by the narrator's reflection that "I am well on my way, and I have a good mind to make you wait a year, two years, three years for the story of Jacques's loves, by separating him from his master and by making each of them suffer all the dangers I want" (p. 5). If the narrative were subject to the constraint of mimetically representing a given reality then the narrator's grounds for making such claims would be seriously limited. But the freedom of narrative clearly supersedes such a constraint. For if the narrator's claim to be writing a history is taken literally (but how can it be?), nonetheless, Diderot's narrator remains *in principle* free to disregard "reality," and if he respects a reality principle, it is by choice (p. 18). The narrator's threats to his reader imply that a concession to anything other than his own will is *mere* concession and, as such, a further affirmation of his will. Thus the narrator does leave the reader a measure of freedom in the composition of the story when he gives him the right to make a trivial decision as to whether Jacques slept in a chair out of choice or necessity (p. 214) and also an apparently more important decision as to whether or not Jacques's captain is dead (p. 315). But these "choices" are calculated to point up the reader's dependence and the narrator's freedom, and, ultimately, the underlying arbitrariness of narrative itself.

The narrator's freedom, however, is as circumscribed as is that of Jacques or his master. Like them, he and his reader are both liberated and constrained by the specular relationship uniting them. The ultimate form of the novel is a compromise between the narrator's desire to digress and his reader's desire to get to the story of Jacques's first love (p. 87). Moreover, the narrator, who constantly seeks to prove and to flaunt his own freedom, ends up in the position of Jacques, his master, and the man who deliberately falls off his horse and breaks his neck in order to disprove Jacques's captain's fatalism. This is evident when the narrator at one point entertains the idea of interrupting the story narrated by Jacques's master, "if only to infuriate Jacques by proving to him that it was not written above, as he thought, that he would always be interrupted and that his master would never be" (p. 330). The narrator's freedom is thus a form of mastery subject to the same qualifications as the authority of Jacques's master or even of Jacques himself. Like them, he is effectively the servant of the reader before whose eyes he parades his freedom.

Perhaps the ultimate sign of the limitation of the narrator's authority, however, is that he, like the master, is always in principle replaceable by the reader or servant. At the end of the novel, the narrator is supplanted by an editor who comments on what has explicitly become a manuscript. The editor is a reader turned narrator who is now in a position to write an appropriate conclusion to the novel. The reader/editor will offer the virtual reader a choice as to which ending he prefers (as the "general" narrator has done more than once), and what was always implicit now becomes explicit: the virtual reader can now assume the narrator's place and write a conclusion to the novel. Just as it is always in principle possible for the servant to take the place of the master, so it is in principle always possible for the narrator to be replaced by a reader. In *Jacques le Fataliste*, narrative is always situated by a conflict among narrators and never in relation to a single, masterful

Narrator.[14] Mauzi's interpretation implies that Diderot is free to respect or break with the traditional novel, but Diderot's description of the master-servant relationship as it bears on the novel contradicts this view. The narrator is never free, according to that description, and as a result, he never has the power to determine his work—he never is or becomes its primal cause.

Because the narrator is always, in principle, replaceable by the reader, one can say that he is never just a narrator, but also potentially a character in another narrative. The structure of *Jacques le Fataliste* makes this point clear, inasmuch as all of the many narrators whose stories are incorporated into the novel are themselves also characters in a story. The hostess who narrates the story of Mme de la Pommeraye is a character in the story of Jacques and his master, as is Richard, who narrates the story of Father Hudson to Jacques. Jacques and his master are also both characters and narrators. That all of these particular narrators are characters in another, metanarrative still leaves open the question of whether or not the "general" narrator in *Jacques le Fataliste* is not himself an ultimate narrator who cannot be considered to be a character in any "metanarration" and who, as a result, determines *Jacques le Fataliste* as a unity containing other narratives but itself closed off from other narratives. The answer is clearly that he is not. Like all the other narrators, he too becomes a character in the last pages of the novel, when another narrative voice is heard (that of the "editor") commenting on a manuscript before him. Because there is no narrator who is not potentially a character in another narration, there is, strictly speaking, no general narrator and no general narrative line in *Jacques le Fataliste*. In

[14] Diderot would thus be a "postmodern" writer in the sense in which Jean-François Lyotard defines the postmodern, as "an incredulity with respect to metanarratives" (*La Condition postmoderne* [Paris: Editions de Minuit, 1979], p. 7). Indeed, each time a "metanarrative" level is pointed to in *Jacques le Fataliste*, it always proves to be a mere narrative from the standpoint of still another metanarrative. Diderot thereby undermines the notion of a metanarrative that would not be subject to this (infinite) process of reversal.

this sense too, then, the narrator's freedom is far from absolute. Whatever his assertions, his freedom is nonetheless always limited by the logic of the (meta)narrative in which he figures as a character.

It might be claimed that the lack of freedom and autonomy of the narrator is the condition of the freedom or of the arbitrary character of narrative itself. In *Jacques le Fataliste*, however, the law governing the narrator and the law governing narrative are one and the same. Narrative is not "an inaugural act of language freely elaborating itself" (Kavanagh, *Vacant Mirror*, p. 64), but what limits its autonomy is not an external reality, nor the intentions of a narrator, nor even a set of immanent linguistic laws. Instead, narrative is limited by the fact that *no narrative can totally situate itself*, for just as a given narrator is always potentially a character in another story, so a given narrative is always potentially set within the context of still another narrative, and so on. It is significant that the appearance of the figure of the editor is the last pages of the novel not only transforms the "general" narrator into a character, but also situates *Jacques le Fataliste* in terms of another narrative—*Tristram Shandy*.

Indeed, *Jacques le Fataliste* cannot be viewed as arbitrary or "inaugural" in large measure because of the way it borrows from *Tristram Shandy* and the way Diderot's narrator borrows from Sterne's. In *Jacques le Fataliste*, the figure of the editor, commenting on what is now described as a manuscript of that novel, gives two possible interpretations of the narrator's borrowing from Sterne, neither of which proves adequate in describing the relationship between the two. One is that *Jacques le Fataliste* is plagiarized, at least in part. The other is that it is an original work, at least in part. According to the editor, Sterne would at times be the master of the general narrator and, ultimately, of Diderot himself, and at times a servant from whom Diderot borrows in order to assert his own mastery and originality. Diderot's borrowing from Sterne is not, however, limited to the one instance noted by the editor. The narrator's delay in recounting the story of Jacques's first love echoes Tristram Shandy's delay in recounting the story of his Uncle Toby's love for the widow Wadman. The philosophy of Jacques's captain—"everything good or bad that happens to us here below was written above"—is a "translation" of lines that are attributed to William of Orange by Sterne's narrator. The wound in the knee received by Jacques at the battle of Fontenoy supplies the beginning of his story, just as the wound Uncle Toby receives in the groin at the siege of Namur is the beginning of his. Jacques himself is clearly in certain respects a copy of Uncle Toby's servant, Corporal Trim, who was wounded in the knee at the battle of Landen and who has an insatiable desire to talk. Readers of the two works have consistently exonerated Diderot of copying Sterne in a servile manner by insisting that the French novelist uses these borrowed thematic elements to develop an original thesis—a philosophy of fatalism or determinism. Wayne Booth's brief reference to *Jacques le Fataliste* sums up volumes of criticism on this point: "In general the successful imitations [of *Tristram Shandy*] have been based on a discovery of new uses for this kind of narrator. Diderot, in *Jacques le Fataliste*, . . . created a narrator who illustrated, in the fatalistic principles that governed his writing, the fatalistic principles which govern the book and life itself."[15] Jacques's captain's motto has been consistently interpreted as a "philosophical" statement whose systematic development sets *Jacques le Fataliste* apart from *Tristram Shandy*. Such an interpretation assumes that the narrator of each work (whether the narrator is defined as the author or as a linguistic function) is a Narrator—an ultimate master of his work and an ultimate source of the internal law determining his work's specific character. In the light of Diderot's critique of the concept of a master narrator, however, Jacques's captain's motto takes on a second meaning that instead underscores the fundamental lack of specificity of *Jacques le Fataliste*: Everything good or bad that happens in this novel (here

---

[15] Wayne Booth, *The Rhetoric of Fiction* (Chicago: University of Chicago Press, 1961), p. 235.

below) has already been written above—in *Tristram Shandy*
and elsewhere. Diderot's borrowing from Sterne cannot be
conceptualized by the opposition between "copy" and "original" used by the editor, because that borrowing is calculated
to make it impossible to determine rigorously the boundaries
of his narrative. It cannot be determined whether the passages
borrowed from Sterne are part of or extraneous to *Jacques le
Fataliste*, and thus the novel cannot be considered a closed
narrative totality, or its own self-defining context. Rather, its
context is still another narrative—*Tristram Shandy*—or, more
precisely, a series of narratives.

It should be stressed that the process by which a "specific"
narrative points to "still another" narrative that serves as its
context does not lead of necessity to a narrative-in-general that
would be the total context for all specific narratives. For the
totality can exist, that is, its limits can be defined, only when
the boundaries of each entity constituting the totality have
been fixed; and yet, in Diderot's interpretation, the boundaries defining each individual narrative never are. In this respect, his "quotation" of Montaigne has a similar effect to his
borrowing from Sterne. In a famous passage justifying his use
of a so-called obscene word, the narrator first presents the
freely paraphrased text from Montaigne as his own and then
reveals that its "author" is Montaigne. This process of quotation—which the narrator calls, significantly, translation—raises
important questions. When does the passage cease to be Montaigne's and become that of someone else? How "free" must
the "translation" be to be regarded no longer as the "creation"
of Montaigne, but rather of Diderot's narrator or of Diderot?
Does this "translation" itself really have *a single* author? It is
significant that this passage raises the problem of quotation
with respect to Montaigne in particular, for Montaigne's own
work is constructed from quotations that he claims are as much
at home in his text as in their "original" text. Even if it were
determined that the passage "translated" by Diderot's narrator
were "originally" written by Montaigne, the source of the
statement would still, ultimately, be unclear, for Montaigne's

text itself is calculated to undercut both authority and originality.[16] According to Diderot's interpretation there is no narrative immune in principle to quotation. Any narrative (or
even, any narrative theory), no matter how general, is always
quotable, just as the texts of Montaigne, Sterne, and Diderot
are. This quotability is the sign of the impossibility that any
level of narrative analysis, no matter how general, should ever
be its own ultimate context.[17] Moreover, it means that the
"transformations" that take place when a narrative is borrowed, translated, even traduced are already in some sense
constitutive of the "original" narrative.[18] For the process that
opens any narrative up to "alien" contexts has already begun
in the narrative itself—no context, even that of narrative or
language-in-general, is ever original or ultimate.

[16] For an analysis of Montaigne's work from this perspective, see Richard
Regosin's "Sources and Resources: The 'Pretexts' of Originality in Montaigne's *Essais*," *Substance*, no. 21 (1978).

[17] In "Signature Event Context," *Margins of Philosophy*, translated by Alan
Bass (Chicago: University of Chicago Press, 1982), Jacques Derrida argues
that the quotability of not just narrative but of all signs, linguistic or other,
determines that there is no ultimate context, for any sign "can break with
every given context and engender infinitely new contexts in an absolutely
nonsaturable fashion. This does not suppose that the mark is valid outside its
context, but on the contrary that there are only contexts without any center
of absolute anchoring. This citationality, duplication or duplicity, this itera-
bility of the mark is not an accident or an anomaly, but is that (normal/
abnormal) without which a mark could no longer even have a so-called 'normal' functioning" (pp. 320-321).

[18] M. M. Bakhtin sees the novel as being born in translation, and this
"other-languagedness" continues to inform the novel throughout its history:
"Translation, reworking, re-conceptualization, re-accenting—manifold de-
grees of mutual inter-orientation with alien discourse, alien intentions—these
were the activities shaping the literary consciousness that created the chivalric
romance. . . . The first prose novels were in an analogous situation with regard to language. The element of translation and reworking is foregrounded
in them even more sharply and bluntly. It could even be said that *European
novel prose is born and shaped in the process of a free (that is, reformulating)
translation of others' works*" (*The Dialogic Imagination*, translated by Caryl
Emerson and Michael Holquist [Austin: University of Texas Press, 1981],
pp. 377-378).

Jacques le Fataliste is neither the symptom of a wavering of Diderot's belief in his materialism and determinism nor a satirical rejection of determinism, because rather than conflicting with the determinist thesis as it is thematized in Jacques's relation to his master, the narrative form of the novel is entirely consistent with its philosophical content. From the standpoint of both, it is possible to speak of "necessity" and "determination" only because there is no transcendent (or general) Necessity, that is to say, no transcendent (general) Narrator (or Narrative) and no transcendent (or general) Master or Cause. It is inevitable that the master (narrator) be replaced by the servant (reader), that the master be a potential servant, and the servant a potential master. At the same time, the fact that there is always, of necessity, one more master and one more narrator means that there is no totality (no Master, no Narrative) upon which to base an ultimate judgment as to the arbitrary or necessary character of the process of substitution.

Diderot's determinism is at once a historical and a formal theory in which both action and narration are always derivative of a "prior" action or narration, and because neither is ever original, neither can be said to serve as a model for the other. *Jacques le Fataliste* does not support the view that the historical process is modeled after a narrative or textual order; it does not constitute a theory of the primacy and autonomy of the text, of literature, or of language. Nor does it provide grounds for arguing that the narrative process is modeled after a historical process and that the text is an effect caused by a master Narrator. In Diderot's determinism, history has no unique or ultimate origin—there is no subject who is the author either of his work or of his actions, though he *is* their narrator in the sense that *Jacques le Fataliste* defines that function. Narration and action are predetermined, already inscribed "above," but even that inscription must lack originality, for the author of the "great scroll" is in the position of the narrator of *Jacques le Fataliste*—of *any* narrator of *Jacques le Fataliste* (i.e., the hostess, the master, Jacques, the narrator, the reader, etc.). If Jacques considers that the question of *who* writes the scroll is ultimately unimportant, it is, no doubt, because it changes nothing to know this, but also, as the novel as a whole implies, because the identity of the narrator does not determine narrative. Destiny, like the narrator and, in particular, like Mme de la Pommeraye when she manipulates the marquis and Mlle and Mme d'Aisnon, does not and cannot control the ultimate sense of what it nonetheless preordains. In the allegorical language Jacques uses to describe destiny, it is represented as playing tricks on men, not only because destiny treats men ironically (p. 99), but also because destiny itself may not know what it wants: "One never knows what heaven wants or doesn't want, and perhaps it doesn't know either" (p. 125).

Destiny is in the position of what Booth would call the "unreliable narrator," but whereas Booth argues that such narrators are the exception, *Jacques le Fataliste* indicates that their situation is the condition of all narrators, including destiny itself. Thus when destiny speaks to men, the message is like the text of *Jacques le Fataliste*; its meaning is always potentially duplicitous. This is especially evident when Jacques's horse on more than one occasion bolts toward nearby gallows. Jacques's master can only interpret this as a message from on high foretelling an ignominious death for Jacques. The message, however, turns out to be ironic when Jacques and his master discover that the attraction of the gallows for Jacques's horse stems from the fact that its previous owner was an executioner. Jacque's remark that destiny may not know what it wants suggests that the irony of destiny cannot be reduced to an original intention. Instead it is a more radical irony based on a lack of an intention, end, or ultimate destination. The great scroll does not bear a determinable meaning or serve as the model of a rational history. Rather, it is "plagiarized," quoted, translated, and traduced. According to this view of destiny and the great scroll, what men call history itself would represent still another form of "plagiarism," quotation, or translation, not an original source for narrative.

The law of the unreliable narrator and of the traducer is not the law of reason. Diderot's determinism is incompatible with the view that history is logical and rational, or that, at least, it develops according to logical, rational laws. Such laws have as their unstated assumption a theory of narrative and a theory of history that reinforce each other. According to such theories, history is like a text produced by a reliable narrator: it does not contradict itself (that is, it obeys the rules of logic), and it has a beginning and an end (or mediate beginnings and endings), because its mode of being is uniform, linear temporality. Such assumptions are not confined to philosophies of history that posit an entelechy or a (reliable) providence in history. They are the basis of the most "empirical" theories insofar as the latter posit a logic and rationality, a principle of noncontradiction inherent in history (and in nature or the physical world).

In the philosophy of history of the eighteenth century, the view that rationality and logic inhere in nature and history is particularly evident in the treatment of the concept of time. Understood as a linear chronology, time has a special place in Enlightenment and perhaps all theories of history, because it is often thought both to have an objective existence and at the same time to supply a rudimentary structuring principle around which all historical laws or interpretations can be organized. If it is indeed the mode of existence of all reality, then time can supply history with an order that cannot be suspected of having been superimposed on it by some stated or unstated philosophical system.[19] The concept of linear time is also vital to theories of historical causation insofar as the cause is assumed to be prior to its effect or effects. If time is not linear, then the priority of the cause cannot be clearly established, and it ceases to be a cause in a rational, deterministic sense.

[19] Voltaire, for example, is convinced that chronology is the first step in the development of a rational historiography, and this conviction explains his admiration for those historical cultures in which astronomy was an advanced science. It is not that Voltaire admires astronomy per se so much; rather he sees it as the secure foundation of chronology, and chronology, of history.

In *Jacques le Fataliste*, however, the linear, "logical" structure of time is not taken to be self-evident, for the view that history and nature spontaneously conform to laws of logic and reason is put into question through a critique of the concept of the event, which Diderot sees as the foundation upon which the concept of linear temporality rests. Indeed, the peculiar temporal structure of *Jacques le Fataliste* hinges entirely on a crucial "event": the death of Jacques's captain. Diderot uses it to locate other events within the temporal structure of the story (and ultimately within the history of the eighteenth century).[20] In the episode concerning the "death" of Jacques's captain, Diderot asks what it is that makes an event an event. Jacques believes his captain is dead because he encounters a funeral procession with a coach bearing his captain's arms and containing a coffin. A priest accompanies the coffin, and a domestic informs Jacques that his captain is dead (p. 62). These signs are all accepted by Jacques at face value. A few pages later, however, everything that served as evidence in these lines is put into question when the same procession is described as retracing its steps, this time under the escort of either the mounted constabulary or the tax-farm guard, with the priest in front, his hands tied behind his back (p. 69)—the entire funeral procession may be a fraud, and Jacques's captain may not "really" be dead at all. The funeral procession can be interpreted in two, very different ways, and Jacques is left to speculate on which meaning is appropriate. Jacques's captain's "death" is emblematic of all "events" narrated in *Jacques le Fataliste* and, Diderot implies, of events in general. For all knowledge of the event is based on a representation of it. To assert that an event has or has not taken place is to adopt one

---

[20] Indeed, the novel alludes to such historical events as the Battle of Fontenoy, the illness of the infante de Parme, and the illness of the duc de Chevreuse, but by implicating these events in the chronology of the novel, Diderot implies that they can themselves contribute to a chronological order only insofar as they can be shown to fall "before" or "after" other events. In this sense, it is not just the temporal order of the novel, but chronology itself that depends on a concept of the "event."

interpretation of the representation of the event over another, to believe more strongly in one set of conventions (those of the church, for example) than another (those of the civil authorities). In *Jacques le Fataliste* as in the *Rêve de d'Alembert*, the perceiving subject is in the position of the historian—always working from representations which are not natural but conventional and which, as a result, can be considered to be true or false only within an already established context. Before the event can become the basis of chronology and history, the conventional nature of the representation of the event will have already undermined the distinction between history as a record of events as they actually occurred and fiction as a reflection of the "possible," the various ways events could occur.

The possibility of determining a linear temporal structure "internal" to the novel and, eventually, the possibility of integrating that temporal structure into the larger chronology of "history" hinges on the status of this crucial "event"—the "death" of Jacques's captain. Because of its questionable nature, however, the temporality it supports becomes one in which "before" and "after" no longer have a clear meaning and in which, as a result, the cause is no longer certain to predetermine its effects. Jacques dates a story concerning his captain's friend as taking place after the death of his captain, but the story is impossible to situate in terms of any consistent chronological framework, for at the point in the novel at which Jacques tells the story, it is "still" unclear whether Jacques's captain is "actually" dead. And to make it clear that this ambiguity is not owing to any mistake on the part of the narrator (or, ultimately, on the part of Diderot), the narrator again brings up the subject of Jacques's captain's death toward the end of the novel in an exchange between himself and his reader, which begins with the reader asserting "but Jacques's captain is dead," to which the narrator replies:"—you think so?" (p. 315). Thus according to the peculiar logic of a chronology based on the death (?) of Jacques's captain, the story Jacques is about to narrate concerning what his captain's friend did "after" that death may take place "after" Jacques narrates it, since the death of his captain may not have yet occurred.[21] Though such an argument may seem frivolous and absurd, Diderot implies that it is at least necessary to entertain it as being itself a "logical" possibility once the notion of the linearity of time is no longer unquestioningly accepted.

It would seem that such an absurdity is only possible in the fictional world of the novel, but by inverting the relationship between event and narration, cause and effect, Diderot is also making an argument about the way narrative structures not only the novel but all historical experience. In narrative, Diderot appears to argue, all temporality is constructed by the narrative, and because of this, the event is always located in at least two temporal moments: first, in a linear temporal structure "normally" projected by the narrative but refused to us by Diderot, who undercuts this projection in order to show the discrepancy between it and the narrative sequence itself; and second, in a narrative sequence or structure distinct from the projected, linear temporality. The nature of any "event" is continually modified by the relationship between these two structures, or, to put it another way, the "event" is continually modified in and by its narration. To use Danto's terms, one could say that narrative always implies a temporal distance from the event, but this distance permits a description of the event not possible at the "moment" the event "takes place"

[21] In his *Analytical Philosophy of History*, Danto critically analyzes what he calls the "logical determinism" of Jacques. In his view, this determinism "rests upon certain allegedly timeless properties of sentences, namely their truth values" (p. 186). Though Danto's critique is too intricate to reproduce here, it is based on two questionable hypotheses where Diderot is concerned: (1) that language is either true or false (how are we to apply such an assertion to the novel?) and (2) that the future, unlike the present and past, is neither true or false (whereas, for Diderot, the future, in this respect, is no different from the present and past). In general, Danto does not consider the problem fiction poses for history, except in the form of a "general skepticism" which he dismisses too quickly because it puts into question the notions of presence and of truth and falsehood on which Danto's discussion of the narrative sentence is based. In other respects, however, Diderot's view of narrative is close to Danto's, particularly as concerns the temporal status of narrative.

(*Analytical Philosophy*, p. 155). In this sense, Danto argues, narrative is a *sufficient condition* for the event's having taken place *as described*, even if it is not a *cause* of the event. Diderot's determinism, I would argue, is a determinism of *sufficient conditions* in Danto's sense,[22] in which the linearity of temporality is no longer taken for granted, but in which temporality is instead viewed as complex and dependent on narrative. According to such a model of temporality, any "event" takes place more than once, and each narration of an event is a condition of the event, or, to put it another way, in Diderot's determinism the "great scroll" narrating the "whole" of history is a condition of history itself. At the same time, it is important to note that the view that the "great scroll" is an ultimate narrative event, embracing and subsuming all other narratives and events, is subject to the same critique as any theory that denies that narrative is constitutive of events. The great scroll, like all other events and like all other narratives, cannot be punctually located in time or space. It must always be located in *at least* two sites: in the narrative it plagiarizes and in its repetition of the plagiarized narrative; in the narrative that "precedes" (or "follows") it, and in its own, retrospectively constituted present.

Jacques le Fataliste, then, does not answer the question of whether language, narrative, and history are determined or arbitrary, and it is precisely in refusing this alternative that the novel articulates a new, "monstrous" determinism governing both history and narrative. The concepts of the arbitrary and the necessary do not present narrative or historical theory with a choice, for they are interdependent, and, as a result, frequently overlap. The theory of the arbitrary nature of narrative posits narrative unity as a necessity. The theory that narrative is determined posits a nonnarrative cause which is itself accepted as original and arbitrary or without cause. Diderot's

[22] Where *Jacques le Fataliste* implicitly diverges from the *Analytical Philosophy of History* is on the question of whether or not what Danto calls a *cause* can be ultimately distinguished from what he calls a *sufficient condition*.

determinism does not combat either view through simple rejection, but rather through a radicalization of both. Where structuralist critics have postulated both the arbitrary nature of narrative and its necessary unity and homogeneity, Diderot's novel shows that this second postulate is *also* arbitrary. The unity of narrative and language is always conventional, as Diderot points out through allusion, quotation, "plagiarism," and translation—all of which he uses to undercut the status of the novel as a closed narrative unity and ultimately to undermine even the closure constitutive of narrative-in-general as an object of a science or theory of narrative. The theorist who claims to take narrative as an "object" deludes himself if he believes that his situation is in principle different from that of the narrator in *Jacques le Fataliste*. His "theory" is of necessity another form of narrative, in one sense distinct from the narratives he analyses, but in another sense implicated in them; it can in no way be claimed to dominate the totality of narrative from a "scientific" perspective totally outside (or inside) narrative.[23]

At the same time, in contrast to the views of historians and traditional critics of the novel, *Jacques le Fataliste* indicates that when theorists see fiction and history as determined by a law, a cause, or some abstract notion of rationality, they implicitly accept these elements as in some sense "natural" and, hence, without cause: they take them to be there, much as the structuralist posits language and narrative as simply there. Determinism in this sense is always rooted in an arbitrary concept of law or reason. Philosophers of history who see reason and logic as inherent in history, who view time as linear and the "event" as "given," bestow on "history itself" the essential qualities bestowed on narrative by the narratologist. There is thus a complicity between traditional historical determinism and any theory of narrative based on the delimitation of nar-

[23] In a similar vein, Jean-François Lyotard argues in *Instructions païennes* (Paris: Editions Galilée, 1977) that "theories are themselves narratives, but dissimulated narratives; one should not be fooled by their pretension to omnitemporality" (p. 28).

rative. Both implicitly or explicitly reduce history to a closed, rational, and logical process, and both reduce the complexity of narrative by viewing it as produced by a narrator who, whether he is present or absent, is presumed to be reliable or at least located within a closed narrative system.

A critical reading of *Jacques le Fataliste* reveals, however, that narrative is not an object in any simple sense, because it always overreaches the boundaries delimiting it by invading the spaces—whether they be natural or theoretical—that are thought to lie beyond narrative. Diderot's narrative determinism is a critique of all theories of the "event," "law," "reason," and "language" that place these entities beyond or outside narrative. Such a determinism should not be confused with skepticism, however. Rather, it is those theories that continue to posit beginnings and ends, causes or laws, reason or narrative, on a priori formal or "practical" grounds that are forms of skepticism; for they refuse the possibility of a knowledge of their own conditions of existence. *Jacques le Fataliste* implies that narrative is the condition of the concepts of reason, law, event, or language, that all of these concepts are always situated in and by narrative. At the same time, the novel also offers a critique of the view that narrative itself constitutes a totality or an ultimate context for the entities it situates. A critical analysis of the role of narrative in history and fiction, then, reveals not only how each is "determined" by its own narrativity, but also how narrative itself cannot be determined or delimited by any narrative or historical concept or context.

SEVEN

(*Rousseau*)
The Theatricality of Nature and History:
de Man, Derrida, and the
Historicity of Language

NO CRITIC'S WORK more forcefully analyzes and illustrates the interdependence of the practical task of reading specific texts and the theoretical task of reflecting on the status of the language of criticism than Paul de Man's extensive interpretation of the writings of Jean-Jacques Rousseau. Whether one's interests lie in eighteenth-century scholarship or in critical theory in general, de Man's work must be reckoned with, because it maintains a critical perspective on each field that is rooted in a scrupulous analysis of both. De Man's work also implicitly argues that the interests of the critic never lie exclusively in one domain or the other: criticism and literary theory cannot free themselves from what he calls "the humble act of reading." At the same time, the literary critic who attempts to restrict himself to a historically or textually "immanent" reading invariably presupposes notions of history, of the aesthetic, the literary, and so on, of which he may be unaware, but which are still very much operative in his reading. Thus if one's interests lie in both a specific field—such as the interpretation of Rousseau—and also the more general field of literary theory (and de Man suggests that this is the case for all readers, since all literary specialists are in fact literary theorists and vice versa), then de Man's work is all the more important as a model of what an explicit analysis of the interrelationship between the two fields can produce.

There is, however, an additional reason for closely examining de Man's work, if, as is the case here, the question being considered is that of the relevance of Rousseau's work to the problem of the relation between history and fiction in the discourse of the French Enlightenment. For de Man's reading of Rousseau criticizes precisely the aspect of interpretations of Rousseau that has been the basis for the view that Rousseau is a thinker who rejects history. "Rousseau," asserts de Man, "is one of the group of writers who are always being systematically misread."[1] A central aspect of that misreading, according to de Man, is a misconstruction of Rousseau's theory of the state of nature. Whereas it has traditionally been seen as the expression of a nostalgic longing for wholeness, innocence, and transparency, de Man stresses that Rousseau assigns a fictional status to the state of nature and that, in doing so, Rousseau clearly alerts the reader that the "elegaic" tone of the passages in which he describes it "is associated with a deluded primitivism unequivocally condemned in the text as a whole" ("The Rhetoric of Blindness," p. 133). By reading Rousseau as a writer who rejects the search or even nostalgia for an ahistorical or prehistorical state, de Man clears the way for a reexamination and rethinking of Rousseau's work in relation to the problem of history.[2] At the same time, de Man, more than any other interpreter of Rousseau, insists that the reader of Rousseau must confront the problem posed by the *fictional* status Rousseau ascribes to the state of nature:

> Consider . . . the status of what seems to be the inescapable *a priori* of the text itself, what Rousseau calls the "state of nature." . . . It is a fiction; but . . . the question remains why this radical fiction . . . continues to be in-

[1] Paul de Man, "The Rhetoric of Blindness: Jacques Derrida's Reading of Rousseau," *Blindness and Insight* (New York: Oxford University Press, 1971), p. 111.

[2] Lionel Gossman's analysis of Rousseau as a historical thinker starts from a similar critique of the view that Rousseau is a "nostalgic" writer whose work can be reduced to a quest for a kind of personal state of nature outside of time. See "Time and History in Rousseau," *Studies on Voltaire*, vol. 30 (1964), p. 311.

dispensable for any understanding of the present. . . . How can a pure fiction and a narrative involving such concrete political realities as property, contractual law, and modes of government coalesce into a genetic history that pretends to lay bare the foundations of human society?[3]

The focus of de Man's reading of much of Rousseau and of the *Second Discourse* in particular is a relationship between what de Man calls the fiction of the state of nature and the genetic history that Rousseau claims to account for by the construction of this fiction.

If de Man thus opens up the field of Rousseau interpretation to a critical examination of the significance of Rousseau's work in relation to history, his interpretation of Rousseau almost immediately cuts short such an examination in the name of a concept of language that de Man claims overrides any concept of historicity, not only in the work of Rousseau but in all texts. Ultimately, de Man joins those traditional scholars who take the view that the importance of Rousseau's work is not evident when considered from the standpoint of a theory of history. The reasons de Man takes this position on Rousseau and the concept of language upon which such a position rests are highly significant in terms of both the interpretation of Rousseau and the problem of the status of the languages of theory and criticism in general, and it is from these interrelated perspectives that I analyze both de Man's reading of Rousseau and Rousseau's work itself—in particular three texts, the *Second Discourse*, the *Lettre à d'Alembert*, and *Emile*.

To understand the concept of language that stands at the center of de Man's work and his interpretation of Rousseau, it is useful to compare de Man, as he compares himself, to such structuralists as Benveniste, Barthes, Todorov, and Genette. Like them, de Man makes language the central issue in his work and takes the position that the determining role of language itself in shaping all forms of discourse—science, phi-

[3] Paul de Man, *Allegories of Reading* (New Haven: Yale University Press, 1979), p. 137.

losophy, history, and literature—argues against the claims of these types of discourse to refer to anything "outside" themselves. Language, de Man argues, is in essence neither neutral nor "reliable"; it always undercuts the effort of the speaker or writer, whether he is a philosopher, historian, or literary theorist, to intend or name objects beyond language. De Man's view of language differs from a structuralist view in an important respect, however, for the questioning of the substantiality of the linguistic referent and of the subject (speaker or writer) of discourse coexists in structuralist theory and analysis with a kind of naive faith that language itself is an object that can be described (or referred to) by the linguist or poetician. De Man rejects any linguistics or poetics that pretends to reduce language to the status of an object and that thereby attempts to elevate its own language to the status of a metalanguage or science. The impossibility of such a reduction is most evident for de Man when the "object" confronted by the linguist is a literary text:

> Since it is assumedly scientific, the language of a structuralist poetics would itself be definitely "outside" literature, extrinsic to its object, but it would prescribe (in deliberate opposition to describe) a generalized and ideal model of discourse that defines itself without having to refer to anything beyond its own boundaries; the method postulates an immanent literariness of literature that it undertakes to prescribe. The question remains whether the logical difficulties inherent in the act of interpretation can be avoided by thus moving from an actual, particular text to an ideal one. ("The Rhetoric of Blindness," p. 107)

The question de Man asks here is clearly rhetorical. According to him, the ideal model of literature postulated by a structuralist poetics depends on two interrelated distinctions, one between literature and language, the other between literature and poetics, and in his view, both of them are "delusive." On the one hand, de Man argues that literature represents a potentially of all language; on the other, he sees the poetician or structuralist literary critic as unable to grasp (literary) language from an exterior, scientific perspective. Linguistics or poetics is itself a language, and thus the discourse of the poetician is implicated in the linguistic "reality" he falsely claims to be able to treat as an object. For de Man, there is no science, but only pseudoscience.

De Man, then, is like structuralist literary critics in that he analyzes discourse in general and literature in particular from the standpoint of a theory of language, but unlike them he does not consider language to be an entity that can be treated scientifically or objectively. De Man's position is one situated "within" language, and as such, critical of any theory that seeks to describe language as a closed system in order to make it possible to distinguish between an inside and an outside of language. In "Semiology and Rhetoric" de Man criticizes literary semiology for its "use of grammatical (especially syntactical) structures conjointly with rhetorical structures, without apparent awareness of a possible discrepancy between them" (*Allegories*, p. 6). For de Man, grammar and rhetoric are not continuous, and the discrepancy between them is what gives language its open-ended character. We cannot move beyond or dominate from the outside a language in which meaning is radically suspended between grammar and rhetoric. Such a language has no inside and no outside; it is a kind of abyss into which we of necessity fall. In an analysis of the rhetorical versus grammatical character of the question, What's the difference? de Man asserts: "The grammatical model of the question becomes rhetorical not when we have, on the one hand, a literal meaning and on the other hand a figural meaning, but when it is impossible to decide by grammatical or linguistic devices which of the two meanings (that can be entirely incompatible) prevails. Rhetoric radically suspends logic and opens up vertiginous possibilities of referential aberration" (*Allegories*, p. 10). The rhetorical potential of all language is what makes it impossible to give language a determinable meaning, whether referential or intentional, and if language is radically indeterminate, then it becomes impossible to close it off and make it the object of a science.

It might seem that de Man's definition and interpretation of language lead to a confusion or anarchy of discourses so radical that it cannot be overcome—no linguistic analysis can restore distinctions between types of discourse if all meaning is radically suspended by the rhetorical nature of language and if the position of the linguist is radically undercut. In fact, however, de Man's rhetoric does imply division and hierarchy within discourse, for all forms of language do not have the same relationship to the fundamentally rhetorical nature of language. "I would not hesitate to equate the rhetorical, figural potentiality of language with literature itself" (*Allegories*, p. 10). "Literature as well as criticism—the difference between them being delusive—is condemned (or privileged) to be forever the most rigorous and, consequently, the most unreliable language in terms of which man names and transforms himself" (*Allegories*, p. 19). According to de Man, it is not linguistics or poetics that supplies the ultimate insight into the functioning of language, but rather literature. And because literature is the supreme authority for the interpretation of all linguistic phenomena, literary criticism can strive only in vain to distinguish itself from literature. Language, then, comprises two categories for de Man: "pure" language and impure language, or rigorous language and delusive language. Philosophy, history, science, and criticism are all deluded or delusive languages, he implies insofar as they deny their own "literariness" or "rhetoricity."

De Man's theory of language thus contains a resolution to the crisis it appears to create. The linguistic anarchy that would seemingly result if types of discourse can no longer be distinguished according to their objects is avoided, but not by making language itself an object and privileging the position of the linguist or poetician. Instead, literature emerges as the privileged mode of language, "accounting for" or "signifying" at all times its fundamental rhetoricity and unreliability ("The Rhetoric of Blindness," p. 137). This privilege, de Man stresses, should be viewed as a condemnation, but, I would stress, it is a privilege nonetheless. De Man's theory of language amounts to a powerful defense of literature according to which all other forms of discourse are judged as inherently "blind" to their own rhetoricity, although certain forms of discourse are viewed as capable of becoming rhetorically consistent insofar as they come to do what literature does inherently. Such is apparently the case for philosophy: "A discursive, critical, or philosophical text that does this [i.e., 'signifies its own rhetorical mode'] by means of statements is . . . not more or less literary than a poetic text that would avoid direct statement. . . . The criterion of literary specificity does not depend on the greater or lesser discursiveness of the mode but on the degree of consistent 'rhetoricity' of the language" ("The Rhetoric of Blindness," pp. 136-137 n.).

The privilege de Man gives literature seems in certain respects to be no privilege at all if other forms of discourse such as philosophy and criticism can be considered literary provided the rhetoricity of their language is consistent. But there is one form of discourse that cannot become literary in this sense, that is condemned to make direct statements inconsistent with the rhetorical nature of language. That form of discourse is the historical, and whereas the privilege of literature seems relatively benign with respect to philosophy and criticism, it becomes a privilege in a more traditional, discriminatory sense with respect to history. Thus when historical discourse figures in the work of an exemplary figure such as de Man takes Rousseau to be, it does so only to provide a negative moment that is overcome in and by the literary text as a whole. When Rousseau writes that "the times I will speak of are very distant," he is making a statement in order to undo it, for, de Man argues, such "passages are associated with a deluded primitivism condemned in the text as a whole" ("The Rhetoric of Blindness," p. 133 n.). According to de Man, "Rousseau gave tension and suspense to the story of language and of society by making them pseudo-historical," but, he goes on to assert, Rousseau tells us "obliquely, but consistently, that we are reading a fiction and not a history" ("The Rhetoric of Blindness," p. 137). History, then, is condemned as a deluded, albeit inevitable, moment of language itself. In its historical phase, language "blindly" affirms its referentiality, and this phase exists only to be revealed as illusory. It is against this referential, historical moment that language points to and defines its literary, rhetorical, or metaphorical nature. For de Man, then, history stands condemned by the nature of language itself.

De Man's statements concerning literature and its relationship to language have an undeniably peremptory quality.[4] It should be remembered, however, that they are not rooted in a concept of literature or language that de Man holds to be incontrovertible in a purely theoretical fashion. Literary criticism, he argues, cannot "free" itself of literature and, more specifically, of the pragmatic act of reading, and de Man frequently reiterates that it is ultimately from his readings that his own theory of literature takes whatever authority it might have. Those who contest his view of literature and language are always open to what is, in de Man's terms, a decisive criticism: "Opponents of the approach have been more eager to attack what they assume to be its ideological motives . . . than the technicalities of its procedure" (*Allegories*, pp. ix-x). The "technicalities" of his readings are thus central to his statements concerning language or literature, and any challenge to those theories must challenge his reading if it is to be an authentic challenge in de Man's terms. De Man's theory of literature places his readings of "literary" texts at its center, but, beyond this, one could say de Man places his readings of Rousseau's texts at the center of all of his other readings. For de Man, the interpretation of Rousseau is no mere testing ground among others for his theory of literature. Instead, as

---

[4] In a chapter of *After the New Criticism* (Chicago: University of Chicago Press, 1980), entitled "Paul de Man: The Rhetoric of Authority," Frank Lentricchia analyzes the significance of this quality in an interpretation of de Man's work extending from some of his earliest essays to "Semiology and Rhetoric."

de Man rather directly acknowledges, his whole enterprise stands or falls with his reading of Rousseau, for Rousseau's work is not an example, but in a sense *the* example of literature. "Rousseau's text," de Man tells us, "has no blind spots: it accounts at all moments for its own rhetorical mode" ("The Rhetoric of Blindness," p. 139). According to de Man's definition of the "literary" as "any text that implicitly or explicitly signifies its own rhetorical mode and prefigures its own misunderstanding" ("The Rhetoric of Blindness," p. 136), Rousseau's text is clearly held by de Man to be literary in an ultimate, exemplary sense.[5]

Because of the very special status de Man gives Rousseau, no disagreement about the interpretation of his texts can be contained within the mere confines of literary history, but rather of necessity becomes a debate about the status of language and literature themselves and, indirectly, about philosophy and history as well. The relationship between the privilege de Man gives Rousseau and the privilege he gives to literary language undoubtedly accounts for the importance he attaches to rectifying what he sees as the misrepresentation of Rousseau contained in Jacques Derrida's *Of Grammatology*. Though in his article "The Rhetoric of Blindness" de Man professes to agree with what he interprets as Derrida's general position on language, literature, and metaphysics, that Derrida should "misapply" his general theory to Rousseau is a serious matter for de Man when one considers the examplary, central status he

---

[5] The special status de Man gives Rousseau is particularly striking in de Man's influential essay, "The Rhetoric of Temporality," in *Interpretation: Theory and Practice*, edited by C. S. Singleton (Baltimore: Johns Hopkins University Press, 1969), in which he analyzes the two-century-old debate, central both to romanticism itself and to the interpretation of romanticism, concerning the relationship between symbol and allegory. In de Man's interpretation, Rousseau's *La Nouvelle Héloïse* provides not only the key to an authentic understanding of that debate but also represents the "true voice" of early romantic literature. In language that clearly anticipates "The Rhetoric of Blindness," de Man writes: "Whereas the symbol postulates the possibility of an identity or identification, allegory designates primarily a distance in relation to its own origin, and, renouncing the nostalgia and the desire to coincide, it establishes its language in the void of this temporal difference" (p. 191).

gives Rousseau. But one could also say *in de Man's own terms* that no disagreement about the interpretation of Rousseau's text can be purely local. If it has the exemplary status de Man claims for it, then a disagreement concerning its interpretation of necessity involves the larger issues it in some sense exemplifies, de Man's professions of agreement with Derrida notwithstanding. Indeed, I would argue that de Man first equates Derrida's general position with his own theory of the fundamentally rhetorical nature of language and the privilege of literature in order to then criticize him for misapplying that theory to Rousseau, when in fact Derrida's reading of Rousseau and his general position are *both* at odds in certain crucial respects with those of de Man.

A central element of de Man's argument that Derrida's general position coincides with his own is his assertion that Derrida ultimately shares his view that history is a negative moment, a mere "dramatization" of the essentially rhetorical nature of language. Like Rousseau's, Derrida's historical language is a rhetorical device according to de Man. Like Rousseau's work, *Of Grammatology*

> also tells a story: the repression of written language by what is here called the "logocentric" fallacy of favoring voice over writing is narrated as a consecutive, historical process. Throughout, Derrida uses Heidegger's and Nietzsche's *fiction* of metaphysics as a *period* in Western thought in order to dramatize, to give tension and suspense to the argument, exactly as Rousseau gave tension and suspense to the story of language and of society by making them *pseudo-historical*. Neither is Derrida taken in by the theatricality of his gesture or the fiction of his narrative: exactly as Rousseau tells us obliquely, but consistently, that we are reading a fiction and not a history. Derrida's Nietzschean theory of language as "play" warns us not to take him literally, especially when his statements seem to refer to concrete historical situations such as the present. ("The Rhetoric of Blindness," p. 137, my emphasis)

243

Despite his claim to agree with Derrida's position, de Man finds it necessary to distinguish among the elements of Derrida's text. We should not take Derrida literally, but *especially* when his statements "seem to refer to concrete historical situations such as the present." Other statements, which would presumably refer to the rhetoricity of language, can be taken "more literally."

De Man's discounting of Derrida's use of historical language or of concepts such as "period" strictly parallels his discounting of Rousseau's historical language. De Man asserts that whether it is Derrida's or Rousseau's, historical language is either naively or deliberately misleading, for "chronology is the structural correlative of the necessarily figural nature of literary language" ("The Rhetoric of Blindness," p. 133); it is the figuration of "the pattern of non-coincidence within the moment" (p. 129). History and chronology are thus for de Man "correlatives" of a structure that is ahistorical, not in the sense that it is eternal or that it transcends the historical, but in the sense that historical categories are fundamentally inapplicable in describing its necessity and form. Chronology can figure the rhetorical nature of language. But the noncoincidence of language with any meaning and the impossibility of reducing language to the status of an object with definable boundaries are both inherent "in" language; the radical contradiction introduced into language by its rhetorical, figural nature is a contradiction *of* language and not of anything else— certainly not of history.

The privilege de Man gives to (literary) language is perhaps clearest in a passage in which de Man briefly sketches a program for the radical transformation of literary history and of history in general. In "Literary History and Literary Modernity," de Man suggests that it may be possible to write a (literary) history that is not purely empirical and thus not naive in its use and implicit conception of language:

> Could we conceive of a literary history that would not truncate literature by putting us misleadingly *into* or *out-*

244

side it, that would be able to maintain the literary aporia throughout, account at the same time for the truth and the falsehood of the knowledge literature conveys about itself, distinguish rigorously between metaphorical and historical language, and account for literary modernity as well as for its historicity? Clearly, such a conception would imply a revision of the notion of history and, beyond that, of the notion of time on which our idea of history is based. . . . The need to revise the foundations of literary history may seem like a desperately vast undertaking; the task appears even more disquieting if we contend that literary history could in fact be paradigmatic for history in general. . . . The task may well be less sizable, however, than it seems at first. All the directives we have formulated as guidelines for a literary history are more or less taken for granted when we are engaged in the much more humble task of reading and understanding a literary text. To become good literary historians, we must remember that what we usually call literary history has little or nothing to do with literature and that what we call literary interpretation—provided only it is good interpretation— is in fact literary history. If we extend this notion beyond literature, it merely confirms that the bases for historical knowledge are not empirical facts but written texts, even if these texts masquerade in the guise of wars or revolution.[6]

De Man thus outlines a new history, no longer dependent on the false self-evidence of categories of truth and falsehood and no longer claiming to dominate literature and language from the outside.

If history were to be redefined along these lines, de Man implies, it would be legitimate to speak of the "historicity" of literature in general and of literary modernity in particular. At the same time, de Man clearly states that the practical basis of such a history would be written or literary texts, and its epis-

[6] "Literary History and Literary Modernity," *Blindness and Insight*, p. 165.

temological basis, the "knowledge literature conveys about itself." The historicity de Man speaks of here thus remains a historicity of language and of the literary text, that is, one defined by the relatively homogeneous sphere of literary language. According to this programmatic statement, it could be said that language has a historicity and that history is dependent on language, but the revelation of such an interdependence would not create an aporia. De Man is not arguing that once history is redefined, there would be no starting point, no way of analyzing history without first analyzing language, and no way of analyzing language without first analyzing history. The interdependence of history and language would not lead to a stalemate, or if it did, the stalemate could be broken by "the much more humble task of reading and understanding a literary text." Reading, "provided it is good," can serve as the starting point for a reworking of history. The historicity of literature and language remains accessible in and through the interpretation of *literary* texts and *literary* language as de Man defines them. History could deal with literature and language only if it were radically transformed, while literature and language are held to be essentially and constitutively adequate to the task of "knowing" their historicity. Or, to put it another way, in the dialogue between literature and history, literature must and does always have the last word.

De Man insists, then, that language cannot be closed off and made into an object with definable limits or boundaries as it has been by structuralist linguists and literary critics. According to him, language is radically self-contradictory; it embraces such discontinuous terms as rhetoric and grammar, direct statement and allegory, revolution and text. But having insisted on the openness of language, de Man ultimately closes language off by interpreting historicity as deriving from the self-contradictory character of language and in this way excluding the possibility that the contradiction "in" language might be so radical that it could no longer be said to derive wholly "from" language. The historicity of language is secondary and not fundamental for de Man because he defines language as "the steady fluctuation of an entity away from and toward its own mode of being, [a] movement [that] occurs in fact as a synchronic juxtaposition" (*Allegories*, p. 163). De Man consistently posits language as an *entity*, arguing, for example, that "language itself" stands under scrutiny in Rousseau's work. However ironical, however self-contradictory and self-negating, de Man's concept of language is the a priori of interpretation and theory in all of his work.

It is necessary, then, to distinguish de Man's work from the formalist and structuralist criticism whose internal contradictions he has criticized. But in the light of this closing off of language, one must inevitably ask if the remarks de Man makes about the intrinsic interpretation of literature do not in some way apply to his own rhetorical interpretation: "The intrinsic interpretation of literature claims to be anti- or a-historical, but often presupposes a notion of history of which the critic is not himself aware" ("Literary History and Literary Modernity," p. 163). Indeed, de Man's theory of language does presuppose a notion of history in which language—in the form of metaphor—engenders itself. For de Man, metaphor is the origin of language in the sense that language is itself essentially metaphorical or rhetorical. De Man consistently argues that the "history" narrating the metaphorical origin of language is merely a figuration of a fundamentally synchronic situation, but he first reduces the complexity of history in order subsequently to negate and transcend it in his model of language. It is only because history has *an* origin for de Man that it can be reduced and gone beyond in and by language and literature. De Man's theory of history is thus essential to his views on language, no matter how negative or deluded the historical moment is for him.

DE MAN'S THEORY of language and its fundamentally literary character is very much in evidence in his reading of Rousseau, and indeed, it could not be otherwise, since, for de Man, Rousseau's work amounts to an "indictment" and a scrutiny of "language itself." According to de Man, the theory of the

fundamentally literary or rhetorical nature of language is in
fact Rousseau's own theory. Thus de Man holds that Rousseau's text is literary in an exemplary sense, for it signifies and
accounts for its own existence as literary language. De Man's
view that Rousseau's text contains a theory of or accounts for
its own rhetorical mode hinges on two points:

> Accounting for the rhetoricity of its own mode [Rous-
> seau's] text also postulates the necessity of its own mis-
> reading. . . . It tells the story, the allegory of its misun-
> derstanding. . . . It can only tell this story as a fiction,
> knowing that the fiction will be taken for fact and the
> fact for fiction; such is the necessarily ambivalent nature
> of literary language. Rousseau's own language, however,
> is not blind to this ambivalence: proof of this lies in *the
> entire organization of his discourse and more explicitly in what
> it says about representation and metaphor as the cornerstone
> of a theory of rhetoric.* ("The Rhetoric of Blindness," p.
> 136, my emphasis)

Though Rousseau's text of necessity generates its own misreading, according to de Man, a "good" reading is still possible thanks to the "entire organization of his discourse" and
to "what it says about representation and metaphor." One
could argue that in de Man's reading the "entire organization"
of Rousseau's discourse in fact hinges on "what it says about
representation and metaphor." Though Rousseau at times states
that denomination is the origin of language and at other times
that metaphor is the origin of language, de Man argues that
the second statement should be, indeed is, privileged over the
first, that it conveys Rousseau's true insight and authorizes us
to regard the first statement as deluded. De Man does not
argue this point, he asserts it. Here, at the outset of his analysis, de Man's reading of Rousseau and his theory of language
reinforce each other in a highly problematic way. Because of
the contradictory nature of Rousseau's statements concerning
the origin of language, we can only be sure Rousseau is telling
us that metaphor is indeed the origin of language if we already

hold that it is and if, as a result, we privilege those passages in which Rousseau declares that metaphor is the origin of language over those passages in which he qualifies or even contradicts this declaration.

Rousseau's affirmation that language is "originally" figural or metaphorical is his central insight, according to de Man, but it is also a misleading statement, for it is phrased in a historical code not ultimately appropriate where language is concerned: "The origin here 'precedes' the present for purely structural and not chronological reasons. Chronology is the structural correlative of the necessarily figural nature of literary language" ("The Rhetoric of Blindness," p. 132). The critic must thus restore to these statements their fundamentally synchronic significance. He can do this if he recognizes two things: one, that according to Rousseau's theory of metaphor, metaphor and language in general have no referent. Thus in concluding his reading of the sixteenth chapter of the *Essai sur l'origine des langues* de Man writes: "The musical sign can refer to silence. . . . Painting refers to the absence of all light and color, and . . . language refers to the absence of meaning" ("The Rhetoric of Blindness," p. 131). And two, the reader must understand that an entity that exists "independently of any specific meaning or intent [as both language and passion do, according to de Man] can never be traced back to a cause or an origin" (p. 132). Thus according to de Man, Rousseau's conception of metaphor of necessity implies a critique of the notion that language is in essence referential and of the correlative notion that language has an origin. When read from the perspective of Rousseau's theory of metaphor, de Man argues, passages in which a term such as "origin" appears can be given their true, synchronic significance. The structural, ahistorical character Rousseau's text ascribes to language thus becomes clear.

But while Rousseau's affirmation in the *Essai* that language is "originally" figural is central in de Man's interpretation, the status of that affirmation remains unclear, both because it is contradicted by other statements made by Rousseau and be-

cause the status of metaphor is itself a problem to be eluci-
dated. These issues come to the fore in de Man's critique of
Derrida's *Of Grammatology*. The focus of de Man's dispute
with Derrida's interpretation of Rousseau is the third chapter
of the *Essai*, in which Rousseau deals with the problem of the
origin of metaphor. At stake in the interpretation of this chapter is the significance of Rousseau's statement that "the first
language must have been figured." As we have seen, de Man
reads this as a declaration of the nonreferential nature of language. According to Derrida's reading of the chapter in question, however, Rousseau does not see metaphor as having no
referent; instead, Derrida argues, Rousseau's theory of metaphor is "classical" in that he considers that though the metaphor does not correspond to the object it names, it does originally correspond to the emotional state of the speaker who
utters it. Derrida argues that for Rousseau, metaphor derives
from representation, and that its figural sense is thus derived
from (the notion of) a primary sense.[7] De Man's objection to
Derrida's interpretation of this passage is curious and highly
significant. He disputes it not because he considers that Derrida has misread Rousseau, at least in the usual sense, but
because Rousseau himself was "wrong" at this point and because, de Man clearly implies, Derrida should have recognized
as much and read the passage accordingly. According to de
Man, metaphor, which has no referent, could only have been
engendered by passion, which also has no referent,[8] and not
by fear or need, which de Man holds refers immediately to

[7] "To repeat the first springing forth of metaphor, Rousseau does not begin
with either good sense or rhetoric. He does not permit himself the use of
literal meaning. . . . But in spite of his intention and all appearance to the
contrary, he also *begins* as we shall see, *with literal meaning.* . . . In a word,
he restores to the *expression of emotions* a literalness whose loss he accepts,
from the very origin, in the *designation of* objects" (*Of Grammatology*, translated by Gayatri Spivak [Baltimore: Johns Hopkins University Press, 1974],
p. 275).

[8] "All passion is to some degree *passion inutile*, made gratuitous by the non-
existence of an object or a cause" ("The Rhetoric of Blindness," p. 134).

concrete things.[9] Thus he concludes: "The third chapter of the *Essai*, the section on metaphor, *should have been centered on pity*, or its extension: love (or hate)" ("The Rhetoric of Blindness," p. 135, my emphasis). Moreover, de Man refers back to this rectification of Rousseau later on, in a footnote to his assertion that Rousseau's text "has no blind spots": "The choice of the wrong example to illustrate metaphor (fear instead of pity) is a mistake not a blind spot" (p. 139). A passage using diachronic terms to describe the fundamentally figural and synchronic nature of language "misleads" or "dramatizes," according to de Man, but can nonetheless be correctly interpreted by the critic who knows what Rousseau purportedly knows: that language is in essence metaphorical and that metaphor is in essence nonreferential. A passage declaring that metaphor represents or refers to something else can only be correctly interpreted by being totally rewritten or denied, so that the "correct" example, pity, is used instead of the "incorrect" example, fear.

Such rewriting of the text is always difficult to justify and becomes even more questionable in the light of the criticisms de Man himself levels at the entire tradition of Rousseau criticism: that it consistently negates "ambivalence" in Rousseau's text, "blotting out the disturbing parts of the work" in order to do away "at all costs with these ambivalences" ("The Rhetoric of Blindness," p. 111). My concern here is not to defend the purity or integrity of Rousseau's text, but rather to ask what de Man's extremely active and deliberate intervention in the text is designed to accomplish, what interpretive system it protects. In the broadest terms, it is designed to defend two essential points: the first is the exteriority of metaphor to what de Man, borrowing explicitly from Derrida, calls "logocentrism" or "Western philosophy"; the second is the simplicity

[9] Thus de Man quotes Rousseau; " 'The first speech was not caused by hunger or thirst, but by love, hatred, pity and anger,' " and adds: "Fear is on the side of hunger and thirst and could never, by itself, lead to the supplementary figuration of language; it is much too practical to be called a passion" ("The Rhetoric of Blindness," p. 135).

of the origin, that is to say, a reductive (and hence reducible) concept of history.

De Man takes the exteriority of metaphor to "logocentrism" to be axiomatic. For him, a language that is fundamentally metaphorical is one that does not refer to any illusory presence or plenitude, but rather to an absence—of meaning of intention, or, what is the same thing, of an object ("The Rhetoric of Blindness," p 131). De Man argues that any theory of language whose first premise is that language is metaphorical by definition "escapes from the logocentric fallacy" which "favors oral language or voice over written language (*écriture*) in terms of presence: . . . the unmediated presence of the self to its own voice" ("The Rhetoric of Blindness," p. 114). De Man thus criticizes Derrida for not acknowledging that Rousseau "means what he says" when he makes metaphor the "origin" of language (even though de Man himself is perfectly willing to argue that Rousseau does not mean what he says when he uses a term like "origin"). But de Man's criticism of Derrida on this point obscures an even more critical point of contention between them, albeit one de Man does not acknowledge: the status of metaphor. De Man consistently argues as if Derrida essentially agrees with him on the question of the exteriority of metaphor to "metaphysics." In fact, both in Derrida's reading of the third chapter of the *Essai* and elsewhere in his work, it is clear that this is not the case.

Central to de Man's interpretation of Rousseau is his assertion that any theory of language that holds that language originates in metaphor and that metaphor is in essence a pure signifier "does not belong to the logocentric 'period.' " This statement is flatly contradicted by "White Mythology," which, with "Le Retrait de la métaphore," constitutes the most detailed treatment of the problem of metaphor in Derrida's work to date.[10] It *confirms* the argument of the section of *Of Gram-*

[10] "White Mythology," *Margins of Philosophy*, translated by Alan Bass (Chicago: University of Chicago Press, 1982). "Le Retrait de la métaphore," *Poésie*, vol. 7 (1978).

matology on the origin of metaphor in Rousseau by showing the role of rhetoric as the more or less naive instrument of a philosophy that furnishes it with all of its fundamental concepts. "White Mythology" also analyzes the conception of metaphor as a pure signifier that puts into question the existence of any prior signified.[11] This conception of metaphor, according to Derrida, is also a philosopheme, and to treat it as if it were not is to assume naively that rhetoric comes before philosophy, when, in fact, all of its organizing concepts—literature, language, the signifier—are furnished by philosophy.[12]

It could be asked if "White Mythology," published after *Of Grammatology*, represents a modification of Derrida's earlier position. In fact, the theses of these two texts are entirely con-

[11] De Man considers that Rousseau's theory of music is an alternative version of his theory of language and asserts that for Rousseau, "music can never rest for a moment in the stability of its own existence. . . . This movement . . . is determined by the nature of the sign as *signifiant*" ("The Rhetoric of Blindness," p. 129). Thus the rhetoricity of language, which de Man similarly describes as noncoincidence of language with itself, would also derive from the nature of the linguistic sign as *signifiant*.

[12] "The concept of metaphor, along with all the predicates that permit its ordered extension and comprehension, is a philosopheme" ("White Mythology," p. 228). "Neither a *rhetoric* of philosophy nor a *metaphilosophy* appear to be pertinent here. . . . Each time that a rhetoric defines metaphor, not only is *a* philosophy implied, but also a conceptual network in which philosophy *itself* has been constituted" (p. 230). In "Structure, Sign, and Play in the Discourse of the Human Sciences" *Writing and Difference* translated by Alan Bass (Chicago: University of Chicago Press, 1978), Derrida comments on the concept of a pure signifier, produced by the radical negation of any concept of meaning or reference. Such a concept of the signifier, Derrida argues, is *also* metaphysical: "The metaphysics of presence is shaken with the help of the concept of *sign*. But . . . as soon as one seeks to demonstrate in this way that there is no transcendental or privileged signified and that the domain or play of signification henceforth has no limit, one must reject even the concept and word 'sign' itself—which is precisely what cannot be done. For the signification 'sign' has always been understood and determined, in its meaning, as sign-of. . . . *If one erases the radical difference between signifier and signified, it is the word 'signifier' itself which must be abandoned as a metaphysical concept*" (p. 281, my emphasis).

sistent. One would have to argue that Derrida does not mean what he says to take any other position. In a long and detailed passage in *Of Grammatology* (pp. 271-272), Derrida states that Rousseau belongs to the logocentric tradition precisely *because* he considers metaphor to be the basis of literary language. The passage is of particular interest in that it describes a literary modernity that strives to assert its autonomy from the classical tradition, a position that de Man claims Rousseau in fact occupies. The literary modernity Derrida describes (using Kafka as his example) must attempt to define itself *against* the poetical and against metaphor. De Man implies that such a step is not necessary since metaphor does not "in fact" represent any original sense: his definition of metaphor is absolute. Derrida's definition of it is *historical*, and it is precisely for this reason that his use of the term is complex. Thus Derrida states both that modern literature has had to attempt to free itself of its subservience to metaphor *and* that, from the point of view of this tradition, the status of metaphor and the status of literature are fundamentally similar inasmuch as the tradition in question has judged both to be "reducible" to voice and to presence. The classical theory of metaphor is certainly not entirely homogeneous, and Derrida argues that there are aspects of Rousseau's analysis of metaphor that threaten the primacy of voice and of presence (*Of Grammatology*, p. 275). But the history of the concept of metaphor cannot simply be set aside in the name of a "nonblinded," "insightful" conception of it. There is no use of the term metaphor that does not in some sense belong to that tradition.

There is a similar contrast between Derrida's and de Man's use of the term "literature." For de Man, the specificity of literature is unconditional and axiomatic. For Derrida, it is "without doubt not simply sure." Just as a "modern" concept of metaphor cannot be purely and simply distinguished from a classical concept of metaphor, so there is no concept of literary modernity that exists independently of a classical literary tradition. All statements about literature are of necessity historical statements, and *for this reason* there is no simple or singular definition of literature. The critique of logocentrism does not constitute a fortiori a defense of literature: *under certain circumstances and in certain contexts a critique of metaphor and of literature may be its most urgent task.*

De Man's rewriting of the chapter on the origin of metaphor and language is thus designed to protect the status of metaphor both within Rousseau's text and within the broader philosophical and literary context.[13] It is also designed to posit a reductive theory of history that is the corollary of any theory of literature—including de Man's—defining literature as closed or self-reflexive.[14] Indeed, de Man's interpretation of the sta-

---

[13] In *Allegories of Reading* de Man's analysis of the passage on the origin of metaphor differs strikingly from his interpretation of it in "The Rhetoric of Blindness": "Yet Rousseau stresses fright, and Derrida is certainly right in stating that the act of denomination that follows—calling the man a giant, a process that Rousseau describes as a figural use of language—displaces the referential meaning from an outward, visible property to an 'inward' feeling" (p. 150). De Man no longer considers it a "mistake" for Rousseau to have chosen fear as an illustration of the figural origin of language. Instead, this choice "complicates and enriches the pattern to a considerable degree" (p. 150). However, these changes in the technical aspect of de Man's argument lead to the same conclusion and still, with more flexibility, defend the same position. They serve to protect the status of metaphor as the origin of language, and they require privileging an implicitly actual or real concept of metaphor as "pure signifier" over a "feigned" concept of metaphor ("feigned" by metaphor itself), according to which it would be dependent in some way on a concept of denomination, reference, and so forth: "Metaphor is error because it believes or feigns to believe in its own referential meaning" (p. 151). "Rousseau conceives of denomination as a hidden, blinded figure" (p. 153).

[14] In two articles, "Deconstruction as Criticism," *Glyph*, vol. 6 (1979) and " 'Setzung' and 'Übersetzung': Notes on Paul de Man," *Diacritics*, vol. 11, no. 4 (Winter 1981), Rodolphe Gasché divides de Man's work into two phases. In the first, which includes the essays in *Blindness and Insight*, he sees de Man as the proponent of a theory of the self-reflexivity of literature. In the second, which begins with the earliest of the essays in *Allegories of Reading*, Gasché holds that de Man's theory of literature has become an "undoing" of self-reflexivity, in which literature simultaneously posits and conceals what it posits. What this very persuasive and rigorous interpretation overlooks is a deeper continuity between these two phases of de Man's work and, specifically, the way both treat the problem of historicity. In *Allegories of Reading* (p. 82), one finds the same devaluation of history and of Derrida's use of "historical" language as in the earlier essay. In both works, this devaluation

tus of history (both in Rousseau's text and in general) is intimately linked to his conception of metaphor, for according to de Man, metaphor is the "origin" of language. De Man ultimately argues that historical terms such as "origin," "diachrony," and the like are fundamentally inappropriate in describing the synchronic situation of language. But this ultimate position does not prevent him from dwelling at length on the question of the origin. Though de Man condemns the concept of the origin as "deluded," his critique of that concept is highly selective. In a Hegelian manner, a concept of the origin, though negated, is at the same time retained and raised to a higher level in his defense of literature.

That de Man's concept of metaphor and of literature depends on a reductive theory of history and a concept of the origin is evident in the steps he takes to defend the *unity* of the origin in Rousseau's work. Derrida's "failure" to correct Rousseau when the latter makes fear or an inward, emotional state the origin or referent of metaphor is criticized by de Man because it contradicts de Man's own definition of metaphor as nonreferential, but also, because if some form of *need* is the origin of language, then chapter 3 of the *Essai* would be in contradiction with chapter 2, where Rousseau asserts that "the first invention of speech is the result not of need, but of passion." De Man argues that Derrida's reading of the third chapter of the *Essai* privileges Rousseau's "mistake" over his fundamental insight: it makes it seem that Rousseau takes need to be the origin of language when he is actually arguing that passion is. This, however, is not what Derrida argues. Instead, Derrida makes an argument to which de Man does not respond: that in Rousseau's *Essai*, need and passion are *both* origins of language, and that the affirmation that passion is

---

is an essential condition of the privilege of literature, and this privilege itself, I would argue, implies a rhetorical rigor, consistency, and self-reflexivity of literary language, even when the term "self-reflexivity" is missing from de Man's vocabulary. For a full discussion of Gasché's interpretation of de Man, see my "Philosophy *before* Literature: Deconstruction, Historicity, and the Work of Paul de Man," *Diacritics*, vol. 13, no. 4 (Winter 1983).

the origin of language does not preclude need from *also* functioning as the (an) origin of language, as *"another origin"* (*Of Grammatology*, p. 224).

De Man insists throughout "The Rhetoric of Blindness" that Rousseau (except for a rare "mistake") consistently posits a *single* origin for metaphor and ultimately for language. That origin, in de Man's view, is a void or an absence, but it is nonetheless a single, unified point. Passion is the simple origin of language. Nothingness is the single "referent" or "meaning" of language and metaphor. De Man reproaches Derrida for arguing that Rousseau derives figural language from need, from a presence or a plenitude, whereas, according to de Man, figural language is nonreferential, for Rousseau, for Derrida, and for himself. Derrida's analysis of the double origin of language does not, however, state that Rousseau is blind to the actual "origin" of language in absence or in a void. Rather it argues that the theory of language as originating in passion and the theory of language as originating in need point to an origin that is irreducibly double, and that, as such, predetermines any opposition that could be made between presence and absence, between passion and need. This Derrida calls "the law of the supplement." It is not a law dictating that figural language has no referent other than nothingness but rather that figural language and language-in-general have their origin in a nature that is never identical to itself—not even in the form of an absence: "All value is determined according to its proximity to an absolute nature. But as this concept is that of a bipolar structure, proximity is a distancing" (*Of Grammatology*, p. 233).

In contrast to Derrida's, de Man's aim is precisely to resolve the contradiction posed by this bipolar origin or nature by positing a void as the origin of figural language. He goes on to argue that when Rousseau writes of the "origin" of language, it is not because Rousseau (or Rousseau's text) is asserting that the nature of language is historical. Instead, de Man argues that it is the nature of rhetorically consistent or literary language to mislead, to give the impression that there exists a nostalgia for or a belief in the origin when in fact what we have is an (allegorical) statement that the origin simply does not exist except as a void. But de Man can interpret Rousseau's statements about the origin of language as "misleading" only *after* he has reduced the complexity of those statements: only after he has determined that for Rousseau, the "origin" of language is metaphor, *not* denomination; passion, *not* need.

It is because Derrida does not share de Man's reductive concept of the origin and of history that he does not privilege Rousseau—or any other writer—the way de Man does. For Derrida, all discourse, that of Rousseau included, belongs to a metaphysical tradition that constitutes the historical heritage of all language: "Rousseau is not alone in being caught in the graphic of supplementarity. All meaning and therefore all discourse is caught there" (*Of Grammatology*, p. 246). To privilege Rousseau as de Man does is to negate what Derrida calls the historicity of Rousseau's discourse—its place "within" a metaphysical tradition in which all discourse, including that of Rousseau, is implicated. The relationship of Rousseau's work to this tradition, Derrida argues, is so complex that the question of Rousseau's "exteriority" to it—de Man's question of whether or not his text has any "blind spots"—has no sense other than that which the metaphysical tradition itself gives it.

The historicity of which Derrida writes here is of a peculiar type: it is the sign that all discourse, all language, is implicated in an "ensemble" that can no longer appropriately be designated by the term "history." If it cannot, it is clearly because for Derrida this historicity is itself negated when the "ensemble" in question is reduced to the status of *a history*. For within that same metaphysical ensemble, history is conceived as a simple linear structure having a single, undivided origin. Once reduced to *a history*, the metaphysical tradition becomes the object of a historical discourse that claims to exist outside and independently of that tradition, but, as Derrida argues, this is never the case. History, like all discourse, is metaphysical.

Derrida judges, then, that the metaphysical tradition cannot be reduced to a history, but this is so precisely because for Derrida the historicity of all discourse is irreducible.

Whatever the differences between them, the historicity of language and historicity in general are no more easily overcome in the work of Rousseau than in the work of Derrida. In de Man's interpretation of Rousseau, language is autonomous and self-consistent; rhetorical language, de Man tells us, is the most rigorous language of all. It is because he considers Rousseau's texts to be an ultimate statement of the metaphorical or rhetorical character of language that de Man can assert that "Rousseau's text has no blind spots." But language and Rousseau's text can only be thus closed off and viewed as accounting rigorously for themselves if the complex historicity Rousseau attributes to language is first reduced to a simple history, and the "origin" of language to a simple origin. I would argue, however, that a historicity such as Rousseau describes, one in which the origin is not simple, cannot be labeled as simply "misleading" in order to be subsequently negated and transcended from the standpoint of some supreme insight into the fundamentally synchronic structure of language. It is because of the complexity of the origin described by Rousseau that (the) historicity (of language) is irreducible.

ROUSSEAU'S most extensive thematic treatment of the concept of the origin is to be found in his *Second Discourse*, the discourse on the origin of inequality. The same complexity Derrida finds in Rousseau's description of the origin of language can also be seen in Rousseau's description of the state of nature. The analysis of the complexity of the origin in Rousseau's work is a first step toward understanding his conception of historicity. If a simple origin cannot be found or even posited in theoretical fashion, then the concept of history becomes problematic, and its linearity, direction, and meaning, uncertain—history in this manner is not reduced but complicated. The element that most clearly introduces complexity into Rousseau's description of the state of nature is his

259

concept of pity. In the *Second Discourse*, pity is not yet *the* mode of historical experience as it will be in *Emile*, but there is an important, albeit indirect, connection between pity and historicity. Rousseau's discussion of pity implies that the tension between the natural and the artificial that Rousseau sees running throughout history is already present at the origin, in the form of pity, and in this sense, the origin is already historical.[15]

Throughout the *Second Discourse* Rousseau takes pains to avoid the pitfall he criticizes in other theorists of the state of nature who, he argues, have only projected backward traits that are characteristic of historical man. Rousseau thus makes a rule for himself: no social or historical event or type of behavior can be referred to in order to understand man's behavior in his natural state. But he seems to make a striking exception to this rule in the case of pity. For of all the principles Rousseau says exist in the state of nature, pity is the most difficult to distinguish from its historical counterpart. It is the one natural faculty still accessible *in its natural form* to the eye of the modern observer who lives in society: "Such is the pure impulse of nature, prior to all reflection; such is the force of natural pity, which the most depraved morals have difficulty destroying, since every day in our theaters one sees the misery of the unfortunate moving and bringing tears to the eyes of people who, if they were in the place of the tyrant, would aggravate the torments of their enemies."[16] By choosing this example to illustrate his argument about pity, Rousseau does

---

[15] Jean Starobinski is an influential critic who has taken the position that tension and contradiction are absent from the state of nature as Rousseau describes it. The state of nature, Starobinski asserts, is "a theoretical postulate, but one that takes on an almost palpable concreteness, by virtue of a language that knows how to give the imaginary all the characteristics of a presence" ("Introduction," *Discours sur l'origine de l'inégalité, Oeuvres complètes*, vol. 3 [Paris: Editions Gallimard, 1966], p. lviii). Earlier he characterizes the state of nature as a "closed plenitude" (p. lvii).

[16] Jean-Jacques Rousseau, *Discours sur l'origine de l'inégalité parmi les hommes*, in *Du contrat social* (Paris: Editions Garnier Frères, 1962), p. 59. All references to the *Second Discourse* are to this edition.

exactly what he reproaches Hobbes and others for doing. He claims to discern traces or remnants of natural behavior in social man, but he may just as well be projecting social behavior backward into the state of nature. The important point here, however, is not only to note this contradiction, but to understand the logic that makes it necessary. Indeed, what is pity *naturally, originally*, and *in essence* that it can be "reproduced" in its natural form in what is, according to the *Lettre à d'Alembert*, an institution that flourishes in the final stages of the decadence of a people, at the point farthest removed from the original state of nature?

An answer to this question is perhaps evident in the second example used by Rousseau to argue the innateness of pity. In contrast to the first, theatrical example of pity cited above, the second—borrowed from Mandeville—is clearly intended to represent nature itself. Nonetheless, it is at the same time structured like a theatrical representation:

> One sees with pleasure the author of the fable of the *Bees*, when forced to recognize man as a compassionate, sensitive being, leave behind, in illustrating his point, his cold, subtle style, in order to convey to us the pathetic image of a man, shut in, who perceives, outside, a ferocious beast tearing a child from the breast of its mother, with his murderous teeth breaking the feeble limbs, and with his claws tearing apart the child's palpitating entrails. What a terrible agitation must be experienced by the witness to an event in which he has no personal stake! What anguish he must suffer at this sight, from not being able to come to the aid of the mother, swooning and unconscious, or the dying infant! (*Discours*, pp. 58-59)

Before analyzing the theatrical structure of this second example, it is important to understand why, despite its artificial character, it nonetheless accurately represents a *natural* principle in Rousseau's view. The perpetrator of the evil here is not human, but an animal. This is in keeping with Rousseau's view that men in their natural state are exempt from violence.

According to Rousseau, men naturally fear each other without that fear ever provoking them to attack each other. In the state of nature, then, violence cannot come from man. A second point is that in this episode the violence is not directed simply at an individual, but at a child before its mother's eyes. The relationship between mother and child is the one human relationship Rousseau qualifies as natural. If it is of shorter duration than the same relationship within civil society, it is nonetheless the only natural relationship of any duration whatsoever. Though in the natural state the mother's care of the child never exceeds the child's need to be cared for, still it causes her, at least temporarily, to identify with her infant. Her feeling for her child is the archetype of pity, just as the infant's helplessness is the archetype of all human vulnerability.[17] The mother's natural emotion is thus the model for the feelings the witness to the action in question will himself experience. From all of these interrelated standpoints, it seems nature itself speaks to the witness of this scene.

In addition to these natural elements, Mandeville and Rousseau's dramatization of nature and of the natural emotion of pity contains other elements more difficult to qualify in the same way. The perpetrator of the violence in this example is nonhuman. Though Rousseau does not, understandably, make it explicit, it would appear that the animal aggressor is necessary in order to guard against the possibility that the scene, which is designed to affirm the influence of nature, does not instead "pervert" that influence: the nonhuman villain is necessary to prevent the spectator from identifying with the perpetrator of the violence and not just with the victims.[18] But

[17] "If man were born big and strong, his size and his strength would be . . . a disadvantage, preventing others from thinking of assisting him; and, abandoned to himself, he would die of misery before knowing his own needs" (*Emile* [Paris: Editions Garnier Frères, 1964], p. 6).

[18] It is an open question whether identification can ever be controlled in any ultimate way—whether or not the spectator of a given scene can be caused to identify only selectively with certain actors or with a single actor in it. Indeed, Rousseau's criticism of fables and of the theater suggests that it can-

though the animal solves one problem, it creates another. For the scene to evoke pity, the violence of the animal must be seen as alien to man and the animal itself, as inhuman. And yet the comparison between the human and the nonhuman, between man and the other animals, while it clearly begins in the state of nature, according to Rousseau, also leads directly away from it.[19]

More important, however, is the question of the distance that Rousseau, following Mandeville, imposes between the spectator and the three actors who are the objects of his attention. The spectator is "shut in" ("enfermé"), the actors are "outside," and the spectator suffers "from not being able to come to the aid of the mother, swooning and unconscious, or the dying infant!" But what would be the *natural* restraint that would prevent natural man from coming to the aid of the swooning mother and the expiring child? Clearly the distance, the inhibition that keeps the spectator "shut in" is a

not: the (fictional) example always invites identification with both or all the actors in a given *scène*. This is an important basis of Rousseau's condemnation of the theater in the *Lettre à d'Alembert*. The audience, he argues, is always secretly disappointed that the villain does not triumph or, what amounts to the same thing, that the least noble instincts of a hero struggling to dominate his own passions do not prevail: "Titus remains Roman in vain; he is the only one who does; all the spectators have married Bérénice" (*Lettre à d'Alembert*, in *Du contrat social* [Paris: Editions Garnier Frères, 1962], p. 165). The fables of La Fontaine are criticized on similar grounds in *Emile*: "Pay attention to children learning their tales, and you will see that if they are able to apply the story, they do so almost always in a way that goes against the intentions of the author, and that rather than trying to avoid the fault one seeks to correct or to preserve them from, they tend to admire the vice by which one takes advantage of the faults of others" (p. 114).

[19] "This reiterated comparison of diverse creatures with himself and with each other must naturally have engendered in the mind of man perceptions of certain relationships. . . . The new insights that resulted from this development augmented his superiority over the other animals by apprizing him of it. . . . Thus the first glance he cast at himself produced his first feelings of pride; thus, knowing only barely yet how to distinguish differences in status, and seeing himself as occupying the highest by virtue of his species, he prepared himself well in advance to claim that position for himself by virtue of his person" (*Discours*, pp. 67-68).

condition of (natural) pity, and yet, clearly too, for such an inhibition to exist, nature must also already be "lost." The action witnessed by the spectator is in fact a *scène*.[20] In the example just cited, the distance that separates the spectator from the event he witnesses has a positive value—it is the sign of the *disinterested* nature of pity. Even in those situations in which we have no direct connection with the events we witness, we immediately identify with the victim, Rousseau argues. But in the *Lettre à d'Alembert*, this same distance has a negative value: "In disputes in which we are more than spectators, we always take the side of justice. . . . I hear it said that tragedy leads to pity through terror. . . . But what is this pity? A passing, useless emotion, . . . a sterile pity that feeds on a few tears and has never prompted the slightest humane act" (p. 140). Thus the distance that separates the spectator from the *scène* is evaluated differently by Rousseau in different contexts. But whether it is treated positively or negatively, that distance is both what makes pity possible and what makes it theatrical. Whether the *scène* be an empirical stage, or a society in which all members play roles, or a *scène* of the peculiar type Rousseau uses to illustrate the naturalness of pity, there is no other pity than that which is aroused in the context of an inherently theatrical situation.

[20] The French word *scène* can be translated into English as both "scene" and "stage." Neither of the English alternatives is wholly satisfactory in the context of Rousseau's discussion of pity, however. "Stage" is too concrete, since it suggests an actual structure of some kind—footlights, a curtain, and so on—whereas Rousseau's example does not. On the other hand, the English word "scene" is not concrete and specific enough. For though it may be defined as "stage," this meaning is rare. Normally it designates a dramatic action either from a play or from life. But Rousseau's example encompasses not just an action, but a specific condition for the perception of the action (an artificial distance from the action) that does indeed exist in an empirical theater, but not necessarily in "life." The theatrical situation in question in Rousseau's discussion of pity thus has both some of the concreteness of a stage and at the same time some of the indeterminacy of a general notion of "dramatic action," and I have chosen to use the French *scène* because it more clearly corresponds at one and the same time to both of these aspects of Rousseau's example than either "stage" or "scene."

There is a tension within Rousseau's description of nature between the artificial, social character of the examples he uses to describe (natural) pity and the asocial or ahistorical character he claims is proper to the state of nature. Similarly, there is a tension within Rousseau's description of pity itself between those elements that are consistent with his description of nature and those elements that imply artifice, a *scène*, and theatricality. The problem faced by the interpreter of Rousseau is that of understanding the meaning of this tension or contradiction, and, more precisely, the significance and status of the *scène* implied by Rousseau's description of pity. Although de Man does not discuss its status at great length, he does evoke the theatricality of pity in "The Rhetoric of Blindness" and refers again to pity in a chapter of *Allegories of Reading* entitled "Metaphor" in which he analyzes the *Second Discourse*. In these brief references, de Man clearly indicates that he considers the *scène* of pity to be a figure of the literary or the rhetorical—that is, of "language itself"—and hence of the "delusiveness" of all concepts of nature and of the origin: "But pity, the arch passion in Rousseau is itself, as Derrida has very well perceived, inherently a fictional process that transposes an actual situation [?] into a world of appearance, of drama and literary language: all pity is in essence theatrical" ("The Rhetoric of Blindness," p. 132).[21] The *scène* would obey the logic of metaphor in de Man's interpretation of the *Essai sur l'origine des langues*. It would be both the origin of inequality and history, in the sense that metaphor is the origin of language for de Man, and the negation of the concept of origin—

---

[21] In *Allegories of Reading* de Man writes: "The concept of pity has been definitively treated by Jacques Derrida. We can therefore begin [the analysis of the *Second Discourse*] with the concept of freedom" (p. 139). But, the claim that he agrees with Derrida, or here, that there is nothing to be added to what Derrida says about pity, in fact refers back to an *interpretation* of Derrida that argues that the deconstruction of metaphysics is a more or less explicit defense of the privilege of literature. The mere fact that de Man here "acknowledges" Derrida's "definitive" treatment of pity clearly indicates what *his own* interpretation of that concept is.

the sign that Rousseau considers both nature and origin to be "delusive" concepts. Like literature or metaphor, then, the *scène* would signify in and of itself the "deconstruction" or demystification of the concepts of origin, nature, presence, and the like. As such, the *scène*, like literature and language, would be *non*natural and *non*original.

The indeterminacy of the *scène* described by Rousseau, however, is so radical that it functions not only as the negation of nature and the origin but also *as nature* and *as origin*. This is apparent in what could be called Rousseau's other discourse on the origin of inequality, the *Lettre à d'Alembert*, in which Rousseau discusses the *scène* in its most concrete form. In this essay, he argues that inequality is normally introduced into human society by the establishment of a theater, and portrays himself as defending the Genevan republic against the corruption that would inevitably result if d'Alembert's suggestion that a theater be established there were carried out. His claim that in its present state, without a theater, Geneva represents a more primitive form of society is based on the argument that of all contemporary European societies, the Genevan republic is closest to the original form of society: Greek democracy. Greek democracy functions as the origin of history in the *Lettre à d'Alembert*, for it reproduces in a cultural and historical setting the equality and freedom of the state of nature. Greek democracy does not know the social distinctions—the privileges of a few and the deprivation of the many—that characterize those societies in which the theater flourishes, and in his criticism of d'Alembert, Rousseau argues that the theater is normally both the sign and the cause of a historical decline that takes societies away from their democratic origin. But Rousseau is in a sense obliged to acknowledge that the theater is *also* original. For though he considers Sparta, a democracy that had no theater, to be the normal origin of history, at the same time he recognizes that the origin of history is double: Athens has both democracy and theater. In Athens, the theater is not a sign of corruption, but rather of the vigor of democratic institutions: "Since tragedy had something of a sacred character at its origin, at first the actors were

considered more as priests than as mere actors. . . . Since all
the subjects of the plays were drawn from the ancient history
of the nation so revered by the Greeks, they saw these same
actors less as players of fables than as learned citizens who
represented, before the eyes of their fellow citizens, the history
of their country" (*Lettre à d'Alembert*, p. 185). Though it would
be profane and antirepublican in Geneva, the *scène* is sacred
and republican in Athens. Though the establishment of a theater in Geneva would lead that republic away from its Spartan
model or origin, the theater, in its Athenian form, is also original.

Rousseau's description of the theater and of theatricality
thus accumulates a series of propositions that taken together
constitute a paradox: (1) the *scène*—the theatricality—implied
by his description of pity is a nonnatural element of the state
of nature; that is; it is a structure within nature in which the
negation of the natural origin by history and society is already
programmed; and (2) theatricality is also original. Athenian
democracy with its theater is another origin of history. Theatricality is thus present at the origin as the negation of the
origin, but it is also part of the structure of the origin. Thus,
like the natural or the original itself, theatricality is radically
heterogeneous, at once natural and nonnatural, original and
nonoriginal.

As paradoxical as this definition of theatricality may seem,
it alone can account for the contradictory value attached to
theatricality throughout Rousseau's work. The contradiction
cannot be reduced, moreover, by arguing that different "types"
of theatricality are the object of praise on the one hand and
blame on the other. Such an interpretation is directly contradicted by the fact that it is always the "virtues"of theatricality
that are its "defects"; that is to say it is always what is most
"primitive" in theatricality that is also the most decadent. This
is most striking if one compares two passages, one from the
Lettre à d'Alembert, the other from the *Second Discourse*. In the
former, already cited in part, Rousseau is arguing that the
theater is not natural, but the sign of the nonnatural. Accordingly, pity, the theatrical emotion, is not here interpreted as

the sign of man's proximity to his natural state or of the re-cuperability of a natural state, but rather as a sign of man's abjectness and of an unbridgeable distance between social and natural man:

> I hear it said that tragedy leads to pity through terror. But what is this pity? A passing, useless emotion that lasts no longer than the illusion that produced it; a remnant of natural feeling soon stifled by passion, a sterile pity, that feeds on a few tears and has never produced the slightest humane act. *Thus the bloodthirsty Sulla was made to cry by the story of evils he had not wrought himself; thus the tyrant of Pheres hid himself at the theater, out of fear of being seen to moan with Andromache and Priam, whereas he would listen without emotion to the cries of so many unfor-tunates who were slaughtered every day by his orders.* (*Lettre à d'Alembert*, p. 140, my emphasis)

In the *Second Discourse*, in a passage also previously cited in part, Rousseau argues the contrary—that pity, rather than being theatrical and perverse, is natural and that in pitying, man harkens to the voice of nature itself. Much of this passage is identical to the one from the *Lettre à d'Alembert*, and yet the sense of it differs dramatically:

> Such is the pure impulse of nature, prior to all reflection; such is the force of natural pity, which the most depraved morals have difficulty destroying, since every day in our theaters one sees the misery of the unfortunate moving and bringing tears to the eyes of people who, if they were in the place of the tyrant, would aggravate the torments of their enemies; *like the bloodthirsty Sulla, so sensitive to evils that he did not cause, or to one Alexander of Pheres, who dared not attend a performance of any tragedy, out of fear of being seen to moan with Andromache and Priam, whereas he would listen without emotion to the cries of so many citizens who were slaughtered every day by his orders.* (p. 59, my emphasis)

The same examples, the same characters (Sulla and Alexander), even the same phrases can be used to illustrate both the irresistible power of *natural* pity over men *and* the sterility and perversity of pity, because pity itself represents both the natural foundation of morality and the last stage of depravity. This contradiction is necessitated by the "original" nature of pity and of the theatrical *scène*: both are fundamentally natural and nonnatural at the same time.

The paradox of the theater is apparent in perhaps its most condensed form in the simple juxtaposition of these two passages, but it is certainly not limited to them, because, in Rousseau's work, theatricality itself is not merely confined to the theater. Man's historical and social existence is theatrical in a crucial sense, as even this brief evocation in the concluding passages of the *Second Discourse* reveals: "everything having been reduced to appearances, everything becomes factitious and feigned. . . . We have only a deceptive, frivolous, exterior honor without virtue, rationality without wisdom, and pleasure without happiness" (p. 92). These lines already prepare the way for the *Lettre à d'Alembert*, for they describe the degradation of social man in precisely the terms Rousseau uses there to describe the degradation inherent in acting: "Wherein lies the talent of the actor? In the art of counterfeit, of taking on another character besides his own, of appearing different from what he is, of becoming passionate in cold blood, of saying something other than what he thinks, as naturally as if he really thought it" (p. 186). In each case, it is the same discrepancy between appearance and reality that is condemned.

Rousseau's evaluation of the theatricality that prevades social and historical life is as paradoxical as his evaluation of the institution of the theater in the *Lettre à d'Alembert*. On the one hand Rousseau normally deplores the alienation created by social role playing and testifies to the depth of his own uneasiness with the roles his social existence has imposed on him. Thus he characterizes six years passed in the salons of Paris as the "state of being in the world the most contrary to my nature . . one of those brief moments in my life in which I became another and ceased to be myself . . . but rather than lasting six days, six weeks, it lasted close to six years."[22] Or, as he comments elsewhere in a similar vein: "I would love society as others do, if I were not sure of appearing not only to poor advantage, but completely other than I am" (*Confessions*, p. 129). But though Rousseau normally condemns role playing as contrary to nature (human nature and his own), in certain circumstances the playing of a role permits Rousseau to behave spontaneously and naturally. Book IV of the *Confessions* contains one incident that illustrates this point particularly well: Rousseau's liaison with Mme de Larnage. From Rousseau's point of view, this relationship was especially memorable in that it permitted him, for once, to behave authentically in relation to another: "She had given me the confidence whose lack has almost always prevented me from *being myself. At that moment, I was myself*" (p. 291, my emphasis). And yet, ironically, during his entire acquaintance with Mme de Larnage, Rousseau passes himself off as an English Jacobite named Dudding. His disguise or role is clearly crucial to Rousseau's spontaneity in this episode, for when he contemplates the possibility of being unmasked, he quickly abandons all thought of attempting to repeat his fine experience: "In the adventurer's role that I would be taking up again, I might be less lucky than the first time; it wouldn't take more . . . than a single person who had been in England, who knew the English or who knew their language, to unmask me" (p. 299). Theatricality in the *Confessions* thus obeys the same law as in the *Lettre à d'Alembert*, a law with its exception built into it thanks to the contradictory nature of the theater. Just as the theater is both a perverting influence on democracy in the case of Sparta and one of the principal props of democracy in the case of Athens, so the social mask is both a perversion and a privileged vehicle for the revelation of the self.

The paradox in Rousseau's logic is the same whether he is

---

[22] *Les Confessions* (Paris: Editions Garnier Frères, 1964), p. 495.

discussing the theater per se or the theatricality of the social world, and this sameness is as important to Rousseau's discussion of theatricality as is his paradoxical evaluation of it. The formal similarity between the two spheres is, of course, a literary commonplace, but Rousseau's description of their relationship indicates something more radical than mere similarity. Indeed, though Rousseau distinguishes between the "metaphorical" theatricality of social and historical processes and the "concrete" theatricality of the stage, what he describes in his *Confessions* is a contamination of these spheres by each other, a contamination in which theatricality becomes a condition of historical experience rather than a quality of it. The tendency of theatricality to exceed any frame or delimitation is the direct corollary of the paradoxical (natural and unnatural) status of the theater. The difficulty of simply locating and defining theatricality *within* history or within an analysis of historical situations points back to the "original" theatricality that is revealed in the *Second Discourse* to be synonymous with *the very possibility* of history.

Emile, perhaps more directly than any other of Rousseau's works, thematizes the relationship between theatricality and history, for the character Jean-Jacques uses the study of historical texts to create a relationship between Emile and history comparable to that between the spectator and a stage. The relation Rousseau establishes between the student of history and the theatergoer is no mere analogy, however, when considered from the perspective of a generalized and unlocalizable theatricality that is neither purely of the world nor purely of the stage, but of both at once. Historiography does not merely repeat or represent historical and social processes, it also "repeats" their theatricality.[23] As a result, historiography, like the

---

[23] In "Typographie," *Mimesis: des articulations* (Paris: Flammarion, 1975), Philippe Lacoue-Labarthe discusses the possibility and the implications of a generalized theatricality or representation, a "concept" that he argues is outlined in Freud's notion of "primary identification" and in Nietzsche's writings on tragedy. According to such a generalized notion of representation, "the *re* of *repetition* would determine—and prevail over—all notions of presentation

theater, will be treated by Rousseau as both a problem and a solution, both good and bad, natural and unnatural.

Emile's introduction to history corresponds to a new set of problems that confront his educator as his pupil enters puberty. Though Emile has not been totally isolated as a child, Rousseau nonetheless ends Book II by asserting that, up until now, Emile has had no social relations (p. 244) but that his awakening sexuality now makes them indispensable and inevitable. As Rousseau asserts repeatedly, pity, not reason, is the basis of morality. Thus he argues that the teacher must awaken his pupil's pity for men in order to ensure that these new social relations do not undermine the predisposition to adopt moral principles that Jean-Jacques has instilled in his pupil by isolating him from society. In Rousseau's view, it is because history spontaneously creates a theatrical relationship between the student and the humanity he considers from a distance that it is the most efficacious instrument for arousing pity in the adolescent:[24]

> In order to make the human heart accessible to him without running the risk of spoiling his, I would like to show men to him from a distance, show them to him in other

(of 'objective' display, of derived or secondary exteriorization, of spectacle for a subject, etc.)." He goes on to ask: "Would not mimesis, . . . this primary, constitutive mimesis, necessitate the construction of the hypothesis of an 'other *scène*'—still a *scène* assuredly, but not yet a 'spectacular' one, separated from any hall, from any space perhaps, in any case inaccessible to any perception whatsoever, where, each time, without the conscious knowledge of the supposed subject, the prescribed scenario of desire would play itself out? A 'scene' of which the stage itself, whether of life or of the theater, however it were disposed . . . would never be . . . but an exterior lining or understudy (p. 242).

[24] And, one could add, for maintaining his isolation. The theme of isolation is constantly evoked in Rousseau's reflections on the theater, and like the theater itself, it is evaluated now positively, now negatively. In *Emile*, Rousseau positively evaluates the power of history to create a theatrical relationship that isolates Emile from other men. In the *Lettre à d'Alembert*, the reverse is true: "It is believed that we congregate in the theater, when it is there that we are isolated from each other" (p. 134).

times or in other places, and in such a way that he could
see the *scène* without ever being able to act on it. This is
the time for history; . . . through history, he will see men
as a simple spectator, without interest and without passion, as their judge, not as their accomplice nor as their
accuser. (p. 282)

Negative and unnatural, at least in their normal social form,
in the *Lettre à d'Alembert*, pity and theatricality are positive
and natural in *Emile*. Whereas in the *Lettre à d'Alembert*,
Rousseau denounces pity and the theater on the basis of specific charcteristics, in *Emile, those same characteristics* cause
Rousseau to view the arousal of Emile's pity and his exposure
to the *scène* of history as essential to his moral education.

There are, Rousseau admits further on in his text, dangers
inherent in the theatricality of history, but his initial paragraph anticipates them and reveals why, at this point, it is
because of is theatricality that history is also the best remedy
for those very dangers. A distance between the spectator and
the *scène* is a constituent element of pity, and in the case of
history, the temporal and spatial distance separating Emile from
the historical subject seems to ensure that no illusion of proximity will jeopardize Emile's detachment. Whereas an invisible
hand must somehow confine the spectator who sees an animal
tearing an infant from its mother's arms, the hard "realities"
of time and space perform the same function in the case of
history. As a student of history, Emile can identify with men
enough to feel pity for them, but not so much that he simply
becomes one of them, adopting their values and social hypocrisy.

The distance separating the student of history from the historical stage awakens his pity, and it also prevents pity from
becoming perverse. If pity is at times valued and at times condemned by Rousseau, one of the reasons is that the distinction between pitying someone and remaining indifferent to
his suffering often seems so slight. All pity is potentially perverse, because it assumes a distance between the pitying sub-

ject and the sufferer and because that distance causes the subject to take pleasure from the suffering of others: "Pity is sweet because in putting oneself in the place of the sufferer, one nonetheless experiences the pleasure of not suffering like him" (*Emile*, pp. 259-260). When described in this language, pity is all but indistinguishable from the attitude that Rousseau condemns as characteristic of philosophy, reason, and self-interest: " 'Perish, if you will; I am safe' " (*Discours*, p. 60). Pity in the face of actual suffering always borders on this perverse attitude. But pity for the suffering of an Augustus or an Alexander retains its moral character.

History is like theater not only in that it implies a stage and a distance between the spectator and the action, but also in that it is comprised of both a "represented" and a "representing" element.[25] Rousseau deliberately separates them in his *Lettre à d'Alembert* and argues that the representing element or the "apparatus of representation" is even more morally dangerous than the represented element. The actions depicted on the theatrical stage are more often than not bad examples, according to Rousseau, but, he argues, just as in ancient Greece a virtuous woman was dishonored by public praise, so even virtue can be perverted by the process of representation itself. In introducing Emile to history, Jean-Jacques exposes his pupil not only to the actions of historical characters but to historiography—the representation of historical action. If the representing element of history does not, at least initially, seem as dangerous as the representing element of the theater, it is because the educator, Jean-Jacques, has such a capital role in determining exactly how history will be represented to his pupil. Jean-Jacques does not actually write the histories that Emile reads, but he does determine which historians are read. By controlling the type of historical representation to which Emile is exposed, his mentor can presumably transform what is a

[25] In *Le Respect des femmes* (Paris: Editions Galilée, 1982), Sarah Kofman argues that the *Lettre à d'Alembert* as a whole is organized around this concept of the representing element or representation "in itself" and the connection Rousseau establishes between it and femininity.

negative element in the case of the theater into a positive element in the study of history.

According to Rousseau's description, all the virtues of history derive from its theatrical character. But as he concentrates his attention on historiography or historical representation itself, it becomes clear that the defects of history also derive from that character. Or rather, the virtues of history are also defects, just as the virtues of the theater are. Rousseau criticizes the theater for presenting its audience with essentially vicious or morally weak characters, and then argues that the theater corrupts even when its heroes and heroines are indeed models of virtue. Or, to condense the argument even further and thereby reveal its paradox, the theater does not offer models of virtue, and it corrupts when it offers models of virtue. This same contradictory logic is also apparent when Rousseau considers history in a more critical light: history has faults, but/ and it is equally defective when those faults are corrected. For example, one of the principal virtues of history lies in its capacity to show Emile what lurks behind the façade of words with which men hide their true character. "To know men it is necessary to see them act. In society one hears them talk; they display their discourses and hide their actions: but in history they [the actions] are unveiled, and one judges them [men] according to facts" (p. 282). But the concrete nature of history, which can permit the student to penetrate appearances and discover the underlying reality, can also be its downfall: "Of what importance to me are facts in themselves, when the reason for them remains unknown to me? And what lessons can I draw from an event of whose true cause I am ignorant?" (p. 283). "History in general is defective in that it only keeps track of perceptible, conscpicuous facts that one can ascertain by names, places, and dates; but the slow, progressive causes of these facts, which cannot be similarly determined, always remain unknown" (p. 285). Using the same curious logic with which he condemns the theater in the *Lettre à d'Alembert*, Rousseau argues that history is valuable because it is factual, that history is defective because it is factual, and that history is not, in any case, factual: "Moreover, the facts described in history are far from being an exact image of the same facts such as they happened: they change form in the head of the historian, they mold themselves after his interests, they take on the color of his prejudices. Who knows how to put the reader exactly on the *scène* in order to see an event as it occurred?" (p. 283).

A similar pattern emerges when Rousseau advances to the level of the philosophical history that this double disqualification of "factual" history necessitates. As we have seen, history is worthless if it does not raise what are essentially philosophical issues such as casuality and ethics, but "the worst historians for a young man are those who make judgments. The facts! The facts! And let him judge for himself" (p. 282). Moreover, Rousseau is particularly critical of the philosophical historians of his own day: "The philosophical spirit has turned the reflections of several writers of this century in that direction; but I doubt that the truth gains from their work. The rage for systems having got hold of all of them, none seeks to see things as they are, but as they are compatible with his system" (p. 285). History, then, is defective when it gives us anything over and above the facts, and defective when it gives us only the facts.

The contradictory logic of Rousseau's criticism of history is not the only thing about it that recalls his condemnation of the theater, however. Ultimately, Rousseau considers the pity inspired by the study of history to be as problematic and even as dangerous as the pity experienced by the theatergoer. History, like the theater, invites a form of identification that inheres in pity, but that perverts it at the same time: "I see by the manner in which young people are expected to read history that they are transformed, so to speak, into all the characters they see. . . . But as for Emile, if it comes to pass even once . . . that he prefers to be an other than himself, were that other Socrates, were he Cato, all is lost" (p. 290). Whereas "purely factual" history provides no lesson and no understanding, history that "goes beyond" those facts presents all the risks of fiction in its more or less successful striving for truth. That risk is that the subject will be alienated from himself— that Emile will cease to be Emile and become merely an actor on the historical stage.

Theatrical conventions are apparent not only in Rousseau's discussion of Emile's study of history however. As Rousseau describes it, Emile's "lived history" is also governed by such conventions—it is written and directed by his mentor, Jean-Jacques. The events of Emile's childhood are thus events in a special sense: their meaning as events is predetermined with respect to a *telos*—that of man, or of the man Emile is to become—just as the events of a play are all foreshadowings of a given denouement. Emile's education is altogether exceptional—and Rousseau suggests that the practical impossibility of putting this educational program to work is one of the factors that caused him to present it in a fictional or theoretical form. But in staging Emile's existence, Rousseau is not merely taking advantage of the freedom given to him by fiction and refused to him by "history" and "reality." As we have seen, all historical and social life as Rousseau describes it involves a discrepancy between appearance and reality identical in form to that characteristic of an empirical theater. Emile's mentor's attempt to control his pupil's experience by exploiting this discrepancy is thus grounded in what Rousseau describes as the nature of history itself.

The theatricality of Emile's education is blatant—so much so that Rousseau ridicules a particularly inept critic, a M. Formey, who believes that Rousseau is being literal when he shows gardeners, maids, and circus workers giving Emile sermons Jean-Jacques himself would not presume to give him:

"This player of shell games, he says, who prides himself on besting a child and gravely preaches to his instructor is a character right out of the world of the Emiles." The witty Mr. Formey was unable to surmise that this little *scène* was arranged, and that the juggler was instructed as to the role he was to play; for this, of course, I did not expressly say. But how many times, on the other hand, have I declared that I was not writing for people to whom everything must be told! (p. 193)

The naive remark of M. Formey prompts Rousseau to underline an essential point, albeit one normally left tacit between Rousseau and his readers. Indeed, were Rousseau obliged to note Jean-Jacques's every intervention prior to narrating the situation in which he was intervening, his declarations would have completely overshadowed the narration of Emile's story. For there is nothing in Emile's education that is not prearranged in this sense. The setting for Emile's education is just that, a setting or decor, if not constructed by Jean-Jacques, nonetheless very carefully chosen. All of the encounters and events taking place in this setting are already to a great extent predetermined by it and thus by Jean-Jacques. In the episode in which he has Emile cultivate a plot of land, only to learn that it is the property of someone else and that, as a result, he is in danger of losing the fruits of his labor, Rousseau points to the setting as a constitutive element of the action. Only in the country would Emile's "natural" capacity to imitate have led him to want to garden. According to Rousseau the lesson of this episode—that property has a natural basis in the rights of the first to occupy a given piece of land—is thus in large measure implicit in the environment. The human environment of Emile's education is also a decor, for, according to Rousseau, in a small village, the governor of a (wealthy) child can manipulate the inhabitants fairly freely (pp. 85-86). The theatricality of specific examples Rousseau gives to illustrate his educational theory is even more blatant, for they are frequently in dialogue form. One of the three or four written dialogues that occur in the text of *Emile*, in which Jean-Jacques, Emile, and Robert, the gardener, are the protagonists, is perhaps most instructive in this respect, for in addition to being presented in dialogue, it also clearly demands the type of prior arrangement or script that Rousseau, in his attack on Formey, acknowledges exists for every incident in Emile's existence.

The compromise that is ultimately struck between Robert and Emile could very likely have been disadvantageous to Robert had he not received some kind of compensation or promise of compensation in advance from Emile's mentor, and this need for prior arrangement underscores the theatricality of this, and, indeed, all the episodes in *Emile*.

Emile's mentor thus exploits a discrepancy between "reality" and "appearance" just as does the director of any play, but whereas in the *Lettre à d'Alembert* the existence of this discrepancy is a cause and a symptom of decadence, in *Emile* it is the condition of moral progress. Once again, it is *the same characteristics* of the theatrical *scène* criticized by Rousseau in the *Lettre à d'Alembert* that are positively evaluated in *Emile*. Emile, for example, lives the events of his childhood and youth without questioning the conditions that make them possible. He accepts the naturalness or reality of the events he witnesses, and manifests a complementary lack of curiosity as to what Jean-Jacques's function in his life is. Though Jean-Jacques, the adult, nearly always accompanies him and appears to have no more knowledge than he does, to learn as he learns, to express surprise when he does, and though Emile will have noticed that his questions always seem to lead somewhere, still Emile will never ask what his purpose is.[26] Emile, then, will be naive and literal; his attention will be given to the "represented" and not to the "representing" element of his existence. And yet, in the *Lettre à d'Alembert*, when the illusion of the theater is so strong that the spectator confounds events on the stage with events in life, then the theater becomes truly dangerous. The young theatergoer is lost when the passions aroused by the ideal image of womanhood incarnated in a Constance or a Cénie are projected onto the "women without honor" of real life (*Lettre à d'Alembert*, p. 160).

[26] Or at least, he will only ask once, not at the age of five or six, but much later, when he learns that men earn their living by being engaged in an occupation. When Jean-Jacques replies that he can only answer Emile's question once Emile has answered it for himself, Emile will be content with this enigmatic response and never again ask the question.

If Rousseau's educational technique seemingly imparts to Emile the naiveté of the theatergoer, Jean-Jacques himself seems to incarnate the cynicism—the professional cynicism—of the actor or director. Whereas, in the *Lettre à d'Alembert* Rousseau insists that there should be no discrepancy between appearance and reality, and that it is precisely the contrast between the stage virtue of the actors and their behind-the-scenes vices that constitutes the ultimate form of depravity, in *Emile* the situation is quite the opposite:

> In a village, the tutor will be much more the master of the objects he will want to present to the child; his reputation, his discourse, his example will have an authority that they would not have in a city; because of his being helpful to everyone, each person will hasten to oblige him, to be esteemed by him, to show himself to the disciple such as the teacher would want him to be in fact; and if he does not give up vice, he will abstain from scandal; that is all we need to realize our goal. (pp. 85-86)

Like a good director, Rousseau is concerned here only with the actors' performance and not their private lives. Once again, then, Rousseau interprets as a condition of moral progress what he also condemns as a sign of decadence. The theatricality that signifies the estrangement of the actor from nature also signifies Emile and Jean-Jacques's proximity to it.

Throughout Rousseau's work history is thus conceptualized as a *scène*. The determination of Rousseau's view of history hinges on the radically paradoxical status of this *scène* and the related terms of theatricality and pity. All three are both natural and unnatural, both signs that the origin is lost and signs that it can be recovered, even that is has already been recovered. If history is conceptualized as a *scène* in Rousseau's work, it is because it has the same complexity, the same paradoxical nature. Indeed, as Rousseau describes it, history has two irreconcilable meanings: it is both degradation and progress, and thus its movements cannot be described by any continuous line, or even by several, disparate series. For no line or series can both lead away from a point and continue to return to it at the same time, and no single point can be the origin of such a double, contradictory movement. If one defines history as a linear movement from an origin to an end, then Rousseau's texts are not in any way historical; his evocation of history is entirely negative. But in the terms of Rousseau's work, to define history in this way is to reduce its complexity. And it is only once the complexity of history has been thus reduced that one can argue that Rousseau's work implicitly rejects history itself when it undercuts teleology or eschatology. If Rousseau cannot be said to be writing a (genetic) history insofar as the movement he describes is double and contradictory, nonetheless, the contradictory nature of this movement is precisely what makes it irreducible to synchrony. The "return" to the origin is an irreducible moment of Rousseau's work, and the description of the origin cannot be dismissed as the "mere dramatization" of a fundamentally synchronic situation; for what is described in the origin is differentiation and complexity—what I have called theatricality—at the source.

The (theatrical) origin is neither present nor absent, neither natural nor nonnatural, and thus it continually asserts itself as difference and complexity within any structure it organizes—just as in the Paris that is held up by Rousseau as the end point of history, the theater orients the spectator in the direction of the natural origin, even though in Geneva its establishment would bring disorientation and corruption, a moving way from the origin. Theatricality cannot be identified with any single term or any specific series of terms; it is no more aesthetic or literary than philosophical, historical, ethical, or political. In certain contexts, a given conception of literature may have a crucial role to play in undermining the dogmatism that posits history as linear and homogeneous, as governed by rules of logic or reason, or as susceptible of being analyzed within an interpretive framework that assumes the possibility of unambiguous meaning. But it is equally possible for language, or literature, or even a simple notion of theatricality, to play the dogmatic role, and indeed, not literature nor history nor any of the other terms ever simply plays one role or the other. Language (which concept?) is not the simple origin of history, just as history (which history?) is not the simple origin of language. Rather, it is the contradictory implication of linguistic and historical origins and ends with each other that Rousseau's texts (his "historical" and "fictional" texts) force us to confront in the fundamental theatricality they inevitably return to at their most literary and historical moments.

The conception of language and literature that informs de Man's interpretation of Rousseau does then represent a critical response to both traditional and modern theories that posit language and literature as definable objects with discrete boundaries. Such theories of literature in particular, de Man argues, have caused critics to view Rousseau's work as split into two distinct parts. "The apparent duality of Rousseau's complete writings, a whole that consists in part of political theory, in part of literature (fiction and autobiography), has inevitably led to a division of labor among the interpreters, thus bringing to light latent incompatibilities between political scientists, cultural historians, and literary critics" (*Allegories*, p. 135). De Man's interpretation of the status of language in the *Second Discourse* as well as in the *Essai sur l'origine des langues* implicitly proposes a resolution of this persistent dualism, a resolution in which a single structure—that of language as de Man argues Rousseau conceives it—organizes all of Rousseau's work. Political theory, literature, history, and the theory of language can no longer be considered distinct fields, de Man argues, once it is understood that history and politics, though they may assume an extralinguistic referent for language, are in fact also governed by its fundamentally metaphorical nature. "The *Social Contract*," writes de Man, "persists in performing what it has shown to be impossible to do"; that is, it persists in positing a referent for the political text, when in fact it, like all texts, is grammatical—it can only function in the absence of a referent or a determinable meaning (*Allegories*, p. 275).

De Man's reading of Rousseau seeks to resolve a dualism that has, according to de Man, characterized all previous interpretations of Rousseau. But his reading also clearly points beyond the field of Rousseau scholarship to a definitive theorization of the relationship between history and fiction (or history and literature). De Man argues that a determinable meaning cannot be attached to the political or historical text any more than to the literary text, because language determines all illusions of meaning and because the nature of language is fundamentally literary or rhetorical. The only boundary between literature and history, then, would be the false one drawn by a history (or a literary criticism) that is blind to its own rhetoricity. He thus asks those who read with him to assume the burden of an unrelenting vigilance and resistance to attempts to close off language and suspend its critical power, whether those attempts take the form of structuralism, formalism, or linguistics. From this standpoint, his position represents a critique, but also a refinement and radicalization of all of these. It is a critique of the formalisms of White or Genette inasmuch as de Man argues that the boundary between language and literature, between figurative and literal language upon which all literary formalisms rest, is "delusive." It is a critique of the structuralism of Barthes or Todorov insofar as de Man refuses to locate the linguist or literary critic "outside" of language and thereby denies his privilege as the arbiter of the distinctions between different types or levels of discourse.

Equally important, de Man's rhetorical criticism is a critique of traditional historicism, a critique not to be ignored. We cannot simply return to history as the putative ultimate ground or context for all "events," linguistic or other, because, as de Man argues, history is dependent on language. Whether "lived" or "written," history too is a complex code or text. In this sense, there is no ultimate, neutral space beyond language, and hence beyond fiction, in which history can ground itself. One could say that de Man's concept of literature is most open at this point, and yet it is also here that literature closes itself off, for it is highly questionable to identify nature and history as "masquerades" and language and the text as the entities they disguise, as de Man in fact does. De Man's critique of (genetic) history yields a complex notion of literature irreducible to the status of a mere object for either literary history or structural analysis. But he stops short of revising the notion of history in the way he has revised and complicated the notion of literary language, and it is because the historical remains unproblematic for de Man that he can ultimately subordinate it to the literary. In contrast, Rousseau's analysis of the theatricality of history indicates that the opacity and complexity of language, along with the power to fictionalize, that is, to suspend and complicate reference and meaning, are not just characteristic of literature or fiction but also inherent in nature, society, and history. In this way, Rousseau's presentation of theatricality constitutes a radical complication not only of literature, but of history as well. For when history is not reduced to linearity and conceived in terms of a unique origin and end, then it has no clearly definable inside or outside, and must be considered as "original," as inescapable as language itself.

CONCLUSION

History/Fiction and Contemporary Theory

IN ARGUING that the fundamental preoccupation of the French Enlightenment is the problematic relationship between history and fiction, I have sought to understand the Enlightenment "on its own terms" but also to establish a dialogue between the Enlightenment and contemporary critical theory. Perhaps the most urgent question contemporary theory contributes to this dialogue is that of the specificity of the literary text. Indeed, many currents of modern critical theory give a special, privileged status to literature and the literary text, though in each case that specificity may be defended in somewhat different terms. For example, we have seen how Gérard Genette's ironic formalism has the effect of privileging lyric poetry as the quintessentially literary genre, in opposition to the theater, which he holds to be the most mimetic, and hence the least literary of the three genres. Linguistic critics too, while challenging the special status given to literature by traditional literary critics, nonetheless ultimately privilege it in a different way. For many of them, literature (or the poetic) is a specific form of language in which, to use Roman Jakobson's terms, "the focus is on the message for its own sake";[1] it is language whose object is language itself. The linguistic analysis of literature thus differentiates self-reflexive, poetic language from cognitive, contextual, or emotive language and makes the poetic into the quintessence of the linguistic on the basis of its self-reflexivity. As we have also seen in a critic of

[1] Roman Jakobson, "Linguistics and Poetics," *The Structuralists from Marx to Lévi-Strauss*, edited by Richard and Fernande De George (New York: Anchor Books, 1972), p. 93.

structuralism such as Paul de Man, whose definition of the literary text is an explicit critique of the view that literary language can be objectified or systematized as it is by linguistic critics, literature is privileged for what de Man claims is its structural "awareness" that language cannot be treated as a mere object. For better or for worse, a structuralist and post-structuralist concern with the specificity of language or the text seems to lead to a privileging of literature.

One of the significant effects of this emphasis on the specificity and privilege of literary language has been to shed new light on familiar texts, to open them up to various readings and interpretations not possible before. In the process, a "modernist" canon has been created in which previously neglected authors have taken the place of those who were extensively treated by traditional criticism or in which previously canonized authors figure in a new light. Though volumes of criticism have already been written on Diderot and Rousseau, for example, the interest in the specificity of literature has, if anything, enhanced their stature by establishing it on a new footing. *Jacques le Fataliste*, in particular, now appears as an exemplar of modern concerns in the way it uses formal devices to undercut certainties about the functioning of narration and language. Rousseau's entire corpus has been reevaluated from the standpoint of his *Essai sur l'origine des langues*, in which he explicitly treats problems of language and poetics central to modern critical theory. In its emphasis on the self-reflexivity of the literary text, this textual, poetic, or rhetorical interpretation of canonical authors implicitly or explicitly rejects both thematicism and historicism, that is, both the notion that the literary text is a (mere) example of ideas or concepts and the postulate that it is an expression of its historical period. And yet interpretations growing out of a concern for literary specificity are themselves often, though not always, dependent to a significant extent on thematicism, if not historicism, insofar as the text is viewed as being inherently more complex, more literary, more "modern," if it explicitly (thematically) treats the question of language, or if formal or literary complexity and irony are acted out, that is exemplified, as in a text like *Jacques le Fataliste*.

By drawing attention to the way in which language and metaphor determine all discourse independently of any referent, the intentions of an author, or the constraints of any historical or social context, the emphasis on the specificity of literature has resulted in a putting into question of naive distinctions between literature and what are sometimes called referential forms of discourse such as history, philosophy, and science. But this emphasis has also had the paradoxical effect of recreating a new form of the canon and thus a new tradition, because the question of the specificity of literature has so often been argued in terms of a relatively limited number of privileged texts. Voltaire and Montesquieu have a place beside Diderot and Rousseau in the present study, then, not because it seeks to restore the traditional canon of eighteenth-century philosophical and literary texts, but rather in order to show that the texts that figure most prominently in the traditional history of ideas, the ones that have even been abandoned to thematicism and historicism by modern theory, in their own way challenge themeticism and historicism and the sets of opposing concepts upon which they are based: reason and madness, form and substance, history and fiction.

Ultimately, however, it is not only at the level of our modernist or even "poststructuralist" canon that we have tended to redraw the boundary between history and fiction, but also at the level of our underlying conception of literature as a uniquely privileged mode of discourse or language. In his *Essai sur les connaissances humaines*, Condillac complains that memory and imagination have previously been defined in such a confusing fashion that what is said to describe memory could be applied equally well to imagination and vice versa. One could similarly "complain" that many theorists who have attempted to give a positive answer to the question of literary specificity have assigned to the literary text such attributes as contradiction, paradox, self-reflexivity, a predominance of the formal over the substantial, without having convincingly argued that those attributes are any more specific to literature or to a notion of textuality derived from literature than to any other form of language or discourse (whether political, historical, scientific, logical, etc.), or, ultimately, to any so-called nonlinguistic element (whether "reality," "the world," or "nature"). We have no reason to presuppose that these other discourses or elements are not themselves paradoxical, duplicitous, self-reflexive, or formal in nature or structure, and, as my readings of the works of Voltaire, Montesquieu, Diderot, and Rousseau argue, we are equally, if not more entitled to suppose the reverse. The question of the specificity of literature is critical, then, not insofar as it gives positive characteristics to literature, but rather insofar as it reveals a literarity or textuality that cannot be confined to literature. Respect for the literary does not necessarily imply an idealization and delimitation of literature per se; it can rather, as it does here, lead to a generalization of the literary, a recognition that it contaminates the scientific, the historical, the logical, the philosophical, and is in turn contaminated by them.

A common concern of the writers who figure in this study is the way history is undermined by its "other" (fiction), which, in the form of the irrational, the ideal, the unperceived or unconscious, is already within it. This view of fiction as a subversive, critical element within history corresponds in many ways to a modern view of literature as a particularly critical form of language irreducible to a sense, an intention, or a referent. But a concern with history in this radically contradictory form is also what, in all of these writers, most clearly challenges the privilege so often given to literature today. For literature cannot simply dominate, incorporate, or exclude a history whose common border with literature cannot be fixed with any certainty.

It should be stressed that to challenge the certainties that have resulted from an emphasis on or even exclusive preoccupation with literary specificity is not to oppose an eighteenth-century philosophy of history to a modern notion of literature. Insofar as both positions imply closure and homogeneity, both are challenged by the works read here and by the form of historical-textual criticism elaborated through their analysis. For all these works, the critical force of history expresses itself in the question of the origin, whether it be the origin of reason, culture, monarchy, perception, narrative, or the figural. And, *as a question*, the search for the origin, like the attempt to define literary specificity, has great strategic value. That search makes problematic what is given as self-evident and eternal. It reverses the process by which concepts, language, and institutions "naturalize" themselves and thereby tend to become monolithic and immobile. It represents a force already at work in systems and structures, differentiating them from themselves and undermining them from within. Clearly such a critical concept of history cannot even begin to emerge without history being the subject of a vigorous debate and even a radical critique of the type existing in the Enlightenment and reinaugurated in our own day by structuralism. But this critical notion of history also runs the risk of becoming obscured as the reaction to structuralism and poststructuralism sets in and history is claimed once again to be a source of certainties, a single, overriding context for all possible relationships.

I have sought, then, to underscore the radical, critical force of the question of history in each of the figures treated here, but the force of history is also inseparable from its recuperative effects, those produced when it is determined in terms of a simple origin, when it is made to conform to the very rules of logic and reason that, in its radical, critical form, it challenges. A critical concern with history does not mean simply differentiating between a "good" critical history and a "bad" historicist history that creates orders and systems, but rather analyzing how these two "aspects" of history are in fact inseparable. It is because history provides both radical questions and naive certainties that it should never be treated as a master discipline, but neither should it ever be reduced to rhetoric or fiction, even though the challenge each of these poses to the integrity of history should now, as it was in the Enlightenment, be taken seriously. Like literature, history, in its most critical sense, is constituted as a set or series of complicated relations of opposition and inclusion: its boundaries can neither be fixed nor erased without seriously reducing its complexity and critical force.

The structure that characterizes the relationship between history and literature or history and fiction is not, however, confined to them: the relations between philosophy and history, science and literature, and literature and philosophy can also be interpreted as so many open boundaries. Interdisciplinary studies are certainly not new, but one could argue that recent debates among theorists have tended toward a new type of interdisciplinarity in which the different fields no longer figure only as substantial entities with their own coherence and clear-cut limitations or as parts of a larger, unified field of knowledge. In the type of interdisciplinary approach that this study encourages, the relationship between fields would be seen as a condition of their existence rather than the reverse; the way each conceptualizes and figures the other field or fields would be taken as the key to understanding it. This approach, whether applied to the general problem of knowledge or to individual texts, would be difficult to classify or label. It would be neither literary theory nor textual criticism, neither philosophy of history nor simple history. It would not even be "theory," insofar as that might claim to organize or give coherence to a given set of documents, texts, or objects without considering the problem of the status of its object: that is, the fact that no object of theory ever exists in itself but only becomes an object once it has been delimited by theory.

Whatever the abuses, whatever the dogmatism and naiveté with which theory has been defended in recent years, the interest in it nonetheless represents a significant and positive development in all the fields that have been touched and to some extent transformed by a concern for their theoretical foundations. Theory itself is not new, but a new emphasis on theory has made possible the exposure of, and to a certain extent even the liberation from the unstated hypotheses and ideologies informing the critical practices of a number of disciplines. But theory itself is limited: like any number of characters in *Jacques le Fataliste*, its servant is also its master. Theory can be, and in some sense always is, the object of its object, and this means that the literary, philosophical, and historical texts treated as examples of a theoretical position have as much to say about theory as it has to say about them. The problem of the theorist is how to respect the relative specificity of the texts he studies, but the particular difficulty of doing so is apparent in the fact that though there is a broad agreement on the necessity and desirability of such respect, there is very little agreement as to what a text is, let alone the status of individual texts. In many instances, however, it seems clear that a professed respect for the text has a paradoxical effect. In the *Lettre à d'Alembert*, Rousseau tells us that the ancient Greeks had infinite respect for women and accordingly made them supreme in the domestic sphere, while at the same time protecting—or prohibiting—them from taking part in public life. We have finally come to see this kind of "respect" as suspicious, and yet our respect for texts frequently has an analogous result. The text is idealized, made supreme in its own sphere, but banished from all others, including the theoretical. And this delimitation and domestication of the text, while they may reflect an idealization and valorization of it, are also perfectly compatible with a tacit condemnation and contempt for the text as the "object" of theory.

It is not by accident that the theater is a problem that recurs in this study as a whole. It first appears in the second chapter, as part of an analysis of Voltaire's recognition that even the rational monarch, Peter the Great, must stage his triumphs and power. It comes up again in Chapter Five, as a frame for perception in the work of Diderot and Condillac. And it figures, still again, in the final chapter on Rousseau. If the theater is evoked at key moments of my analysis, it is no doubt because it seemed to be the best means of articulating the continual transgression of the boundary between the literary and the historical, the fictional and the real, whether in the

Enlightenment or in the contemporary theoretical texts examined. As I have used it, "the theater," or rather the theatrical, is neither simply a metaphor nor a concept. It points to a textuality that is not simply of the text; that is, it underscores the fact that textuality is not of necessity and in essence a positive or empirical concept. The theater signifies the irruption of what is posited as the nontextual in the textual, while, at the same time, it reveals the fictive, theatrical characteristics of the historical event. Though the notion of theatricality is central to the argument of this study, it should be stressed that the term clearly has potential abuses: the most obvious being a conflation of history and fiction in which the political and the historical are neutralized. Such a general theory of fiction as theatricality questions everything except its own concept of fiction; it ignores the way in which that concept, even as it claims to obliterate the distinction between history and fiction, depends itself on an unquestioned and naive view of history to which it opposes itself in order to assert its own singularity and preeminence. Theatricality in this study, on the contrary, functions to challenge not only attempts to fix the boundary between fiction and history, but also efforts to erase it.

The tasks of understanding the Enlightenment in its own terms and of addressing some of the most urgent questions facing theory and criticism today are not, then, mutually exclusive; rather, they imply each other. This does not mean that the question of the specificity of the Enlightenment no longer has any meaning; quite the contrary. Like the boundary between history and fiction, the boundary between the Enlightenment and our contemporary period cannot be erased. But, at the same time, that boundary never functions unproblematically, and this means that it should no longer be possible to write an intellectual history of the period that points to a resolution and transcendence of its tensions and contradictions or to look at it with the serenity such a synthetic and totalizing perspective implies. In a sense, there never was an Enlightenment if by that we mean a unified totality, that is, a clearly bounded, albeit complex event that occurred two centuries ago. But it is precisely because of its lack of unity, because of the fundamental complexity of this "event" or "period" that something that could still be called the Enlightenment lives on in history. Doubtless the debates of the Enlightenment are those of a particular time and place, but that we should recognize ourselves in those debates is inevitable, even as we learn from them to recognize the contradictory historicity of our "own" languages.

INDEX

aesthetics, 24, 77, 83, 91, 167, 190, 234, 281
Alembert, Jean le Rond d', 166
allegory, 242n, 246
Althusser, Louis, 130-135 138-139, 142-143, 149, 151-152, 154, 157-159
analytical thought, 5
Anglo-American philosophy of history, 8, 57, 201-202
Annales school, 20
anthropology, 5, 96, 98, 101-102, 106-107, 116, 122, 127
aristocracy (form of government), 137n, 155-156
Aristotle, 20, 65, 70-72, 137n, 143-146

Bakhtin, M. M., 224n
Barthes, Roland, 7, 23, 99-104, 114-116, 121, 126, 203-205, 207, 236, 283
Belaval, Yvon, 191n
Benveniste, Emile, 206-207, 236
Berkeley, George, 164, 165n
Bernac, Henri, 58n
Booth, Wayne, 222, 226
boundary, 3-5, 7-8, 10, 14, 16, 22, 27-28, 55, 95, 127, 163, 180, 207, 212-213, 223, 233, 246, 282-283, 287, 290-292
bourgeoisie, 46

canon (literary), 286-287
Carroll, David, 61n
Cassirer, Ernst, 11-12, 16, 166-167
causality, 227, 229-232
Charles XII, 51-52, 75, 80, 90-91

China, 39-41, 43-44, 54, 80, 85
Colbert, Jean-Baptiste, 46, 49
Collingwood, R. G., 20, 202-203
Condillac, Etienne Bonnot de, 24, 163, 165-182, 188-190, 193-194, 196-199, 287, 291; *Essai sur l'origine des connaissances humaines*, 165-181, 199, 287; *Logique*, 179, 180, 182; *Traité des sensations*, 168, 170n, 178, 179n, 180
consciousness, 168-169, 171-173, 175-176, 196
context (problem of), 19, 134-135, 137, 143-144, 146, 149, 158n, 201, 221, 223-224, 229, 233, 255, 281, 283, 287, 289
continuity, 32, 36, 46, 61n, 148
Cournot, Antoine-Augustin, 204
culture, 6, 37-39, 41, 43, 84-85, 87-90, 95, 102, 106-108, 114-117, 119, 121-122, 126-128, 135, 143, 289

Danto, Arthur, 201, 203-204, 207, 230-231
deconstruction, 265n, 266
de Man, Paul, 25-26, 234-259, 265, 282-284, 286
democracy, 137n, 155-156, 266, 270
Derrida, Jacques, 26-27, 30-31, 38n, 99n, 140n, 169n, 188n, 224n, 242-244, 250-256, 258-259, 265n
despotism, 110-111, 121-122, 124, 126, 137n, 138n, 144-148, 152, 154-157
destiny, 77, 86-89, 216-217, 226

Library of Congress Cataloging in Publication Data

Gearhart, Suzanne, 1947-
    The open boundary of history and fiction.
    Includes bibliographic references and index.
        1. French literature—18th century—History and
criticism. 2. Historiography. 3. Fiction. 4. France—
Intellectual life—18th century. 5. Enlightenment.
I. Title.
PQ265.G4 1984   840'.9'005   84-2162
ISBN 0-691-06608-6 (alk. paper)